# Information Resources in the Arts
## A Directory

# Information Resources in the Arts

## A Directory

Compiled by Lloyd W. Shipley
National Referral Center

Library of Congress      Washington      1986

**Library of Congress Cataloging-in-Publication Data**

Shipley, Lloyd W.
  Information resources in the arts.
  Supt. of Docs. no.: LC 1.2:In2.

  Includes indexes.
  1. Arts commissions—United States—Directories.
  2. Arts—United States—Directories.   I. National
Referral Center (U.S.)   II. Title.
NX110.S48 1986 700'.25'73      85-600227
ISBN 0-8444-0512-4

For sale by the Superintendent of Documents, U.S. Government Printing Office,
Washington, D.C. 20402

# Contents

# Foreword

The performing arts in the United States have been a vital part of our culture since colonial times. Whether in the concert hall, the country church, or the community theater, the arts in all their forms and all their styles have flourished, adding richness and diversity to American life. Over the last century, a network of associations and organizations has grown up to serve the arts and the audiences that enjoy them; these organizations provide a tremendous variety of services that enable artist and audience to communicate more effectively with each other. As with so many fields of endeavor, it has become clear that effective communication in the arts depends upon the free flow of ideas. In order to achieve this goal, the National Referral Center, in cooperation with the Performing Arts Library and various arts groups, has identified a number of information-sharing organizations specializing in various aspects of one or another of the performing arts. These organizations, in turn, have indicated a willingness to share information about themselves and, where appropriate, about the constituencies they serve.

In order to make this information available and useful to a wider audience in the arts community, we have prepared a directory of these organizations that will enable its user to identify easily an organization or organizations by most common areas of interest and to compare and contrast groups with varying interests by using the indexes.

This directory is composed of a series of sections into which all the arts organizations are grouped. These sections best represent the main areas of interest or activity of each organization and, more importantly, the headings that users are most likely to check. Accompanying these main sections are three indexes that group all of the organizations geographically, alphabetically, and by areas of interest chosen by the arts groups themselves as best expressing the scope of their activities. The user should note that some of these areas may overlap.

This directory is something of an experiment. At this stage we are trying to identify groups that should be listed in future editions as well as to improve the listings of those groups that are already listed. Our intention is to make the world of the performing arts accessible to persons outside the arts. It is our hope that they will help us to improve future editions by pointing out shortcomings in the present one.

We hope that this directory will lead to an improved arts information network, whereby libraries, performing groups, education and service organizations, and funding bodies will be better able to fulfill their respective mandates and enhance the quality of performing arts in this country.

Peter J. Fay
*Head Librarian*
*Performing Arts Library*

# Preface

The National Referral Center (NRC) in the Library of Congress is a free referral service which directs those who have questions concerning any subject to organizations that can provide the answer.

NRC uses a subject-indexed, computerized file of 14,000 organizations, called information resources by the center. The NRC file, which is maintained by professional analysts and editors, is used primarily by the center's referral specialists. It also is accessible to readers at the Library of Congress through computer terminals located in various reading rooms and nationwide to subscribers to the DOE/RECON computer network operated by the Department of Energy and the MEDLARS network operated by the National Library of Medicine (file name DIRLINE).

The concept of an information resource is broadly defined to include any organization, institution, group, or individual with specialized information in a particular field and a willingness to share it with others. The criterion for registering an organization is not its size but its ability and willingness to provide information to others on a reasonable basis.

This is a preliminary and experimental edition of a directory for which we perceive a real need in the area of the arts. It is at best a generous sampling of the arts resources in the NRC data base. We have worked closely with the Library of Congress Performing Arts Library at the Kennedy Center, attempting to include numerous examples of our many arts resources, both performing and nonperforming. We realize this preliminary edition is neither complete nor comprehensive.

We shall appreciate suggestions for improving the content of the next edition, which is intended to appear within the next two years. We hope this directory will generate sufficient interest within the various arts communities to bring about an increase in the number of arts information resources registered with the NRC. For a registration form or further information, please contact: Resources Analysis Section, National Referral Center, Library of Congress, Washington, D.C. 20540. Telephone: (202) 287-5680.

We are indebted to a number of persons for valuable assistance in compiling this directory: Peter J. Fay, Performing Arts Library, deserves special appreciation for his foreword, as well as his patient and enthusiastic support and advice; Robert Glenn Wright, Professor of English, Michigan State University, and a former staff member of the National Referral Center, for initial organization of the directory entries; Norman G. Lamb, National Referral Center, for copy procurement; Vivian F. Coon, National Referral Center, for typing and proofreading; and Benjamin F. Hull, National Referral Center, for his editorial assistance and indexing.

Lloyd W. Shipley
*Head, Resources Analysis Section*
*National Referral Center*

# Federal, State, and Local Government Agencies

**1**

## Alabama State Council on the Arts and Humanities

323 Adams Ave.
Montgomery, AL 36130
Tel.: (205) 261-4076          PUB69-17944

Partially funded by the National Endowment for the Arts, the Council attempts to create more interest in the arts, funds local organizations active in bringing performing and visual arts before the public, and assists organizations and individuals in obtaining funding.

**Areas of Interest:** Arts in Alabama.

**Holdings:** Collections in the above area.

**Publications:** *Ala-Arts* (annual); *Ala-Arts News* (bimonthly newsletter); journal articles, state-of-the-art reviews, directories, data compilations, guidelines, brochures, annual statements.

**Information Services:** Answers inquiries; provides advisory, reference, and literature-searching services; conducts seminars and workshops; distributes publications; makes referrals to other sources of information; permits on-site use of collections. Services are free and available to anyone.

**Approval Date:** 11/84

**Latest Information Date:** 1/86

**Index Terms:** Alabama; Art commissions; Federal aid to the arts; State encouragement of the arts; Performing arts; Visual arts; Financial support.

**2**

## Alaska Department of Education
## Alaska State Council on the Arts (ASCA)

619 Warehouse Ave., Suite 220
Anchorage, AK 99501
Tel.: (907) 279-1558          PUB69-19835

Funded by both the Alaska State Legislature and the National Endowment for the Arts, ASCA provides grants and services to arts organizations and artists in Alaska and supports such programs as Arts in Education, Performing Arts Touring, Traditional Alaskan Native Art, and Percent for Art in Public Buildings. It manages eight grant programs providing funds to both individual artists and nonprofit arts groups.

**Areas of Interest:** Dance, music, theater, visual arts, crafts, media arts, opera/musical theater, folk arts, literature, and multidiscipline arts projects.

**Holdings:** The Alaska Contemporary Art Bank is a collection of 500 works of art by living Alaskan artists. The works are available for loan to state offices throughout Alaska and to the offices of Alaska's Congressional delegation in Washington, DC.

**Publications:** *Bulletin* (monthly); *Guide to Programs and Services* (annual); program brochures, catalogs, reports, minutes. Publications are available to sight-impaired persons through tape recordings.

**Information Services:** Answers inquiries; provides advisory, consulting, and reference services; conducts seminars and workshops; organizes conferences; distributes publications and collected data. Services are available to the public. Grants are restricted to Alaskan nonprofit organizations and qualified Alaskan individuals active in the arts.

**Contact:** Ms. Christine D'Arcy, Executive Director

**Approval Date:** 3/85

**Latest Information Date:** 3/85

**Index Terms:** Arts; Performing arts; Dance; Music; Operas; Music theater; Folk art; Literature (fine arts); Visual arts; Handicrafts; Art management; Cultural programs; Museums (institutions); Federal aid to the arts; Grants; Technical assistance; Lecturers; Alaska; Art education; International arts activities; Handicapped arts services.

**3**

## Arizona Commission on the Arts

417 West Roosevelt St.
Phoenix, AZ 85003
Tel.: (602) 255-5882          PUB69-18201

The Commission offers funding for arts projects of nonprofit Arizona arts organizations; arts programs serving small communities; fellowships in visual arts, creative writing, and music; traveling exhibition service; artists-in-education project; art in public places; and technical assistance.

**Areas of Interest:** Arts in Arizona; performing arts (music, dance, theater); visual arts; education and expansion arts (multimedia, multicultural constituents); grant writing; legal problems in the arts; health hazards; arts legislation; community development.

**Holdings:** Resource center for artists and arts administration in the business area of the arts; traveling exhibition service.

**Publications:** *Bi-Cultural Information Quarterly*; monthly bulletin; reports, bibliographies, guide to programs, artists' guide.

**Information Services:** Answers inquiries; provides advisory and consulting services; conducts seminars and workshops; distributes publications; makes referrals to other sources of information. Services are available to arts organizations, artists, and the general public.

**Approval Date:** 2/84

**Latest Information Date:** 1/86

**Index Terms:** Arizona; Arts; Art management; Visual arts; Creative writing; Music; Technical assistance; Grants; Fellowships; Cultural exchange; Artists as teachers; Health hazards; Legislation; Dance; Touring exhibitions; Performing arts; Theater; Community development.

## 4

**Arkansas Arts Council**

225 East Markham, Suite 200
Little Rock, AR 72201
Tel.: (501) 371-2539                    PUB69-17971

A division of the Arkansas Department of Natural and Cultural Heritage supported in part by agencies of the U.S. government, the Council channels grants to state cultural organizations, programs, and projects.

**Areas of Interest:** Artists in schools; artists' residencies; workshops; grants; corporate support of the arts; museums; arts and crafts; dance; music; painting; performing arts; visual arts; fund raising; public funds available for arts; special projects.

**Holdings:** Films; computerized data base of mailing lists, artists, grants, etc.

**Publications:** *Arts Council News* (quarterly); *Folklife* (quarterly newsletter); monthly arts calendar.

**Information Services:** Answers inquiries; provides advisory, technical assistance, reference, and direct loan services; conducts seminars and workshops; evaluates data; distributes publications; makes referrals to other sources of information. Technical assistance services are limited to Arkansas arts organizations; other services are available to anyone.

**Contact:** Mr. Bill Puppione

**Approval Date:** 2/85

**Latest Information Date:** 2/85

**Index Terms:** Arkansas; Cultural organizations; State encouragement of the arts; Federal aid to the arts; Financial support; Technical assistance; Art patronage; Grants; Museums (institutions); Crafts; Dance; Music; Painting; Performing arts; Visual arts; Fund raising; Art education.

## 5

**Arkansas Department of Parks and Tourism**
**Ozark Folk Center**

P.O. Box 500
Mountain View, AR 72560
Tel.: (501) 269-3851                    PUB69-20391

The Center is an outdoor museum devoted to depicting traditional Ozark culture.

**Areas of Interest:** Traditional crafts and music of the Ozarks, 1800–1940.

**Holdings:** 3,000 books, 1,000 items of sheet music, 1,000 records, 300 tapes of field recordings.

**Information Services:** Answers inquiries; provides advisory, reference and reproduction services; evaluates data; conducts seminars and workshops; makes interlibrary loans; makes referrals to other sources of information; permits on-site use of collections. Services are free, except for reproduction services, and available to those with serious scholarly interests.

**Approval Date:** 7/84

**Latest Information Date:** 1/86

**Index Terms:** Arts resources; Open air museums; Handicrafts; Music; Ozarks.

## 6

**Bowling Green-Warren County Arts Commission**

416 East Main St.
Bowling Green, KY 42101
Tel.: (502) 782-2787                    PUB69-20203

Funded in part by state and local governments, the Commission sponsors professional touring groups, gallery exhibits, a school and community outreach program, classic film screenings, special projects for the handicapped, disadvantaged youth, and senior citizens, and Focus on Kentucky (a celebration of state professional artists). Membership in Arts Alliance, Inc., the volunteer support arm, currently numbers 458 and is open to anyone.

**Areas of Interest:** Arts for rural populations, including dance, music, theater, opera and music theater, indigenous and folk arts, literature, visual arts, and crafts; arts education; art appreciation for children; fund raising.

**Publications:** *Marquee* (monthly newsletter and calendar).

**Information Services:** Answers inquiries; provides advisory, inservice teacher training, reference, literature-searching, and reproduction services and information on R&D in progress; conducts classes and workshops; distributes publication; provides speakers; makes referrals to other sources of information. Services are available to nonprofit organizations and are provided free, except for reproduction services. The Commission's facilities are accessible to the handicapped.

**Contact:** Gerri Combs, Executive Director

**Approval Date:** 1/84

**Latest Information Date:** 1/86

**Index Terms:** Arts resources; Rural population; Art commissions; Dance; Music; Theater; Operas; Music theater; Literature (fine arts); Visual arts; Handicrafts; Fund raising; Outreach programs; Community art projects; Teacher training; Artists as teachers; Handicapped arts services; Folk art.

---

### 7

**California Arts Council**

1901 Broadway, Suite A
Sacramento, CA 95818
Tel.: (916) 445-1530          PUB69-20246

Funded by the California legislature, the Council makes grants to artists and arts organizations in California through such programs as Artists in Residence and Organizational Grants.

**Areas of Interest:** Dance; music; theater; media arts; literature; performance art; visual arts; architecture; arts education.

**Holdings:** Computerized application and evaluation data on all Council grantees in organizational and artists in residence programs by fiscal year, 1979/80 to the present; staff reference library.

**Publications:** *State of the Arts* (bimonthly); *Program Guidelines* (annual, by fiscal year).

**Information Services:** Answers inquiries or refers inquirers to other sources of information. Services are free to California residents. The Council maintains teletypewriter (TTY) facilities for the hearing-impaired and is accessible to the handicapped.

**Contact:** Mr. Bob Reid, Acting Director

**Approval Date:** 1/84

**Latest Information Date:** 1/86

**Index Terms:** Arts resources; California; Dance; Music; Theater; Curriculum design; Handicapped arts services; Art and state; Comprehensive arts education; Literature (fine arts); Performance art; Visual arts; Architecture.

---

### 8

**Canadian Consulate General
Cultural Affairs**

1251 Avenue of the Americas
New York, NY 10020
Tel.: (212) 586-2400          PUB69-20243

The Cultural Affairs office provides information on and financial and practical assistance for presentations of the arts and culture of Canada within the New York City metropolitan area.

**Areas of Interest:** Arts of Canada, including dance, music, theater, opera and music theater, indigenous and folk arts, literature, performance art, visual arts, architecture, crafts, and design arts; museum programs; multidisciplinary programs.

**Holdings:** This office has access to the Library of the Consulate General.

**Publications:** *ARTNEWS* (nine issues a year, listing Canadian cultural events in the New York City area); exhibition brochures.

**Information Services:** Answers inquiries; provides advisory services; distributes publications; makes referrals to other sources of information. Advisory services are limited to selected groups and events; publications are limited to selected contacts. All services are free. Requests for addresses, statistics, and other specific information should be addressed to the Library of the Consulate General; requests for more general information and for referrals should be addressed to the Cultural Affairs office. A major project of the Cultural Affairs office is the operation of 49th Parallel/49e Parallele, a showcase gallery for contemporary Canadian visual art, located at 420 West Broadway, New York, NY 10012, tel.: (212) 925-8349.

**Contact:** Mr. Robert Handforth, Cultural Officer

**Approval Date:** 2/84

**Latest Information Date:** 1/86

**Index Terms:** Arts resources; Canada; Dance; Music; Theater; Operas; Music theater; Folk art; Literature (fine arts); Performance art; Visual arts; Architecture; Handicrafts; Design; Museum programs; Cultural relations; International arts activities.

**9**

## Chicago Office of Fine Arts

78 East Washington St.
Chicago, IL 60602
Tel.: (312) 744-6630                    PUB69-20232

The Office was organized to survey and assess the needs of the arts, identify and evaluate legislation, policies, and programs affecting the arts, and to create an environment in Chicago in which the arts can flourish. It provides city and private funds to arts organizations and artists, services in the form of technical assistance and resources, and presents numerous U.S. and foreign exhibits and performances throughout the year. The Office is interested in more foreign involvement.

**Areas of Interest:** Dance; music; theater; media arts; opera and music theater; indigenous and folk arts; literature; performance art; visual arts; comprehensive arts education; arts management; fund raising; multidisciplinary programs.

**Holdings:** Collections relevant to the above areas.

**Publications:** *Art Post* (quarterly newsletter); annual report; books, directories, videotapes, posters. A list of publications appears in the annual report.

**Information Services:** Answers inquiries; provides advisory and reference services and information on research and development in progress; evaluates and analyzes data; conducts seminars and workshops; distributes publications and data compilations; provides speakers; makes referrals to other sources of information; permits on-site use of collections. Except for certain publications sold at cost, services are generally free and available to arts organizations or artists working within the Chicago area and to researchers from any area. Office facilities are accessible to the handicapped.

**Contact:** Mr. Richard Kohnen, Coordinator

**Approval Date:** 1/84

**Latest Information Date:** 1/86

**Index Terms:** Arts resources; Dance; Music; Theater; Operas; Music theater; Folk art; Literature (fine arts); Performance art; Visual arts; Comprehensive art education; Art management; Fund raising; Needs assessment; Technical assistance; International arts activities; Handicapped arts services.

**10**

## Colorado Council on the Arts and Humanities

770 Pennsylvania St.
Denver, CO 80203
Tel.: (303) 866-2617                    PUB69-19957

Sponsored by the National Endowment for the Arts, the Council provides grants and technical assistance for artists and arts organizations in Colorado. Activities include placement of professional artists in school settings through an Arts-in-Education program.

**Areas of Interest:** Dance; music; theater; media arts; opera and music theater; indigenous and folk arts; literature; performance art; visual arts; crafts; design arts; museum programs; teacher training; curriculum design; arts management; fund raising; multidisciplinary studies.

**Holdings:** Small resource library of arts administration publications.

**Information Services:** Answers inquiries; provides advisory and technical assistance services; conducts seminars and workshops; provides speakers; makes referrals to other sources of information; permits on-site use of collection.

**Contact:** Ms. Andrea Edwards, Staff Assistant

**Approval Date:** 1/84

**Latest Information Date:** 1/86

**Index Terms:** Dance; Music; Theater; Media arts; Operas; Music theater; Folk art; Design; Museum programs; Literature (fine arts); Visual arts; Handicrafts; Teacher training; Curriculum design; Art management; Fund raising; Grants; Technical assistance; Artists-in-residence; Arts resources.

**11**

## Connecticut Commission on the Arts

340 Capitol Ave.
Hartford, CT 06106
Tel.: (203) 566-4770                    PUB69-17968

The Commission encourages the arts in Connecticut through participation in and promotion, development, acceptance, and appreciation of artistic and cultural activities.

**Areas of Interest:** The arts as they relate to the cultural activities of Connecticut; arts administration.

**Holdings:** Reference library of about six hundred books; computerized listings of arts organizations in Connecticut.

**Publications:** *State of the Arts* (newsletter; six issues a year); program guide (annual); *Artists in the Classroom; The Impact of Artistic & Cultural Activities on Connecticut's Economy* (1981); *The Arts and the New England Economy* (1981).

**Information Services:** Answers inquiries; provides advisory services; conducts seminars and workshops; evaluates data; distributes publications; makes referrals to other sources of information; permits on-site use of collections. A charge is made for some publications. All services are available to anyone.

**Approval Date:** 5/84

**Latest Information Date:** 1/86

**Index Terms:** Connecticut; Cultural activities; Cultural administration; Cultural programs; Art management; Art appreciation; State encouragement of the arts.

## 12

**Delaware Department of State
Division of Historical and Cultural Affairs
Delaware State Arts Council**

820 North French St.
Wilmington, DE 19801
Tel.: (302) 571-3540         PUB69-18083

Partially funded by the National Endowment for the Arts, the Council supports, promotes, and develops the arts in Delaware and insures that each citizen has access to quality arts programs. Grants for arts programs are made to qualified groups incorporated in Delaware and to Delaware citizens.

**Areas of Interest:** Music; theater; dance; opera; visual arts; crafts; literature; community-based arts.

**Publications:** *Delaware Artline* (bimonthly); poetry anthologies, directories, program guides, artists-in-schools publications.

**Information Services:** Answers inquiries; provides advisory, consulting, and reference services; conducts seminars and workshops; evaluates and analyzes data; distributes publications; makes referrals to other sources of information. Services are free and available to arts organizations, artists, and Delaware residents.

**Approval Date:** 2/84

**Latest Information Date:** 1/86

**Index Terms:** Delaware; Music; Theater; Dance; Operas; Community art projects; Mass communication; Visual arts; Crafts; Literature (fine arts).

## 13

**District of Columbia Commission on the Arts and Humanities (DCCAH)**

420 Seventh St. NW., 2d Floor
Washington, DC 20004
Tel.: (202) 724-5613         PUB69-19971

Funded by the National Endowment for the Arts and the Government of the District of Columbia, DCCAH is the designated state arts agency for the District of Columbia and, as such, apportions grants-in-aid to individual artists and nonprofit arts organizations in the District and annually supports three major initiatives: (1) ARTS, D.C. (a CETA arts employment agency), (2) the Mayor's Art Awards (an arts recognition ceremony), and (3) the National Symphony Orchestra Youth Fellowship Program (providing music training to District area youth).

**Areas of Interest:** Dance; music; theater; media arts; opera and music theater; literature; performing arts; visual arts; crafts; design arts; special education; multidisciplinary studies. Special programs include an Artists-in-Education project, placing professional artists in residence at educational institutions, and a Special Constituencies project, providing arts training, exposure, and accessibility to persons physically or mentally handicapped, the elderly, the institutionalized, and the incarcerated.

**Publications:** Annual guidelines for each of its grant award programs.

**Information Services:** Answers inquiries; provides advisory services and letters of support to worthy individuals and arts organizations to aid them with fund-raising projects and other activities; conducts seminars and workshops; provides speakers; makes referrals to other sources of information. Services are free and available to District of Columbia resident artists and arts organizations.

**Contact:** Pamela Holt, Grants Officer

**Approval Date:** 4/84

**Latest Information Date:** 1/86

**Index Terms:** Dance; Music; Theater; Media arts; Operas; Music theater; Literature (fine arts); Special education; Performing arts; Visual arts; Handicrafts; Design; Artists-in-residence; Grants-in-aid; Handicapped arts services; Art education; Arts resources.

## East Bay Center for the Performing Arts

339 11th St.
Richmond, CA 94801
Tel.: (415) 234-5624                    PUB69-19929

A nonprofit community arts center and an agency of the United Way of the Bay Area, the Center provides arts instruction and performance opportunities to all persons, regardless of income, background, age, disability, or ethnic origin. Special activities include an after-school program of dance, music, and theater instruction in Bay Area public schools; demonstrations and lectures in public schools; a theater company for senior citizens performing original works dealing with issues of aging; neighborhood arts festivals; programs affording instruction and performance opportunities for the disabled; and arts instruction in institutional settings.

**Areas of Interest:** Arts in the community, including dance, music, theater, media arts, opera and music theater, indigenous and folk arts, literature, and visual arts; the arts as an agent for social change and social reconciliation; dance therapy; music therapy; special education; teacher training; curriculum design; arts management; fund raising; multidisciplinary studies.

**Holdings:** Library.

**Information Services:** Answers inquiries; provides advisory and consulting services and speakers; makes referrals to other sources of information. Except for consultations and provision of speakers, services are free. All are available to anyone with a serious interest in building a community arts program. All facilities of the Center are accessible to the handicapped.

**Contact:** Mr. Willie D. D. Morris and Mr. Jordan Simmons, Codirectors

**Approval Date:** 2/84

**Latest Information Date:** 1/86

**Index Terms:** Community art projects; Dance; Music; Theater; Teacher training; Media arts; Curriculum design; Folk arts; Literature (fine arts); Historic preservation; Special education; Musicotherapy; Visual arts; Dance therapy; Art management; Fund raising; Community involvement; Social change; Handicapped arts services; Lecturers; Arts resources.

## Fairfax County Department of Recreation and Community Services
## Performing and Fine Arts Division

11212 Waples Mill Rd.
Fairfax, VA 22030
Tel.: (703) 691-2671                    PUB69-17907

The Division provides citizens of Fairfax County with opportunities for artistic expression, cultural recreation, and audience enjoyment through sponsorship of performing arts productions and exhibitions and shows in fine arts.

**Areas of Interest:** Dance; children's theater; youth drama; musical presentations; art shows; crafts and photography exhibitions.

**Information Services:** Answers inquiries; provides advisory and reference services; conducts seminars and workshops; evaluates and analyzes data; lends choral shells, risers, and other performance equipment; makes referrals to other sources of information. Loans of equipment are sor..etimes subject to a rental fee; other services are free. All are available to anyone.

**Approval Date:** 2/84

**Latest Information Date:** 1/86

**Index Terms:** Performing arts; Fine arts; Dance; Community recreation programs; Drama; Music; Handicrafts; Photography; Exhibitions.

## Florida Department of State
## Division of Cultural Affairs

State Capitol
Tallahassee, FL 32301
Tel.: (904) 488-1083                    PUB69-20217

Partially funded by the National Endowment for the Arts, the Division of Cultural Affairs provides services encouraging the development of arts directly or indirectly benefiting all Florida citizens and visitors. These services are provided through the administration of grants, by serving as the general arts information liaison between local, state, and federal arts agencies and local arts organizations, and through special programs, including an Artists-in-Education and technical assistance programs. Activities include sponsorship of U.S. artists in performance and exhibition abroad and foreign artists in the United States and the conduct of cooperative projects with foreign groups. In keeping with its interest in more foreign involvement, the Division is planning future international projects.

**Areas of Interest:** Dance; music; theater; media arts; opera and music theater; indigenous and folk arts; literature; performance art; visual arts; architecture; crafts; design arts; comprehensive arts education; special education; museum programs; arts management; fund raising; multidisciplinary programs.

**Publications:** *Grant and Touring Guidelines* (annual); *Florida Cultural Directory* (biennial); journal articles, bibliographies, program guides, reprints.

**Information Services:** Answers inquiries; provides reference and literature-searching services; evaluates and analyzes data; conduct seminars and workshops; distributes publications; makes referrals to other sources of information. Services are free and available to anyone. The Division's facilities are accessible to the handicapped and include TTY equipment.

**Contact:** Chris Doolin, Director

**Approval Date:** 2/84

**Latest Information Date:** 1/86

**Index Terms:** Arts resources; Florida; Cultural events; Cultural programs; Dance; Music; Theater; Operas; Music theater; Folk art; Literature (fine arts); Special education; Performance art; Visual arts; Architecture; Comprehensive art education; Handicrafts; Museum programs; Art management; Grants; Cultural exchange; International arts activities; Handicapped arts services; Artists as teachers; Technical assistance.

---

**17**

---

### Georgia Department of Education
### Arts and Humanities Unit

1958 Twin Towers East
205 Butler
Atlanta, GA 30334
  Tel.: (404) 656-7520          PUB69-20348

The Unit provides educational programs in the arts and humanities for K–12 instructional levels, arts education teacher training programs, and arts in education curriculum documents, including the disciplines of music, visual arts, dance, and drama. Special programs include the Georgia Governor's Honors Program, a six-week residency program for gifted secondary students in English, music, dance, drama, visual arts, communications, foreign languages, mathematics, social studies, and science.

**Areas of Interest:** Comprehensive arts education programs; music; visual arts; curriculum design; teacher training.

**Publications:** *Arts and Humanities State Plan; Visual Arts Education Guidelines, K–12; Music for Elementary Schools; Music for Middle Schools.*

**Information Services:** Answers inquiries; provides advisory, consulting, reference, literature-searching, and current-awareness services and information on research in progress; evaluates and analyzes data; conducts seminars and workshops; provides speakers; distributes publications; makes referrals to other sources of information. Services are generally available for a fee to anyone. The Unit's facilities are accessible to the handicapped.

**Contact:** Dr. Frank Crockett, Coordinator

**Approval Date:** 4/84

**Latest Information Date:** 1/86

**Index Terms:** Arts resources; Comprehensive art education; Music; Curriculum design; Visual arts; Teacher training; Handicapped arts services.

---

**18**

---

### Hawaii Department of Accounting and General Services
### State Foundation on Culture and the Arts

335 Merchant St., Room 202
Honolulu, HI 96813
  Tel.: (808) 548-4145          PUB69-20205

Funded by the National Endowment for the Arts and the State, the Foundation is the official arts agency for Hawaii. It provides funding for local arts organizations, the Art-in-Public-Places program, and the Hawaii Department of Education's Artists-in-Schools program. Other activities include the sponsorship of touring professional arts companies and artists in Hawaii.

**Areas of Interest:** The arts in Hawaii; arts funding in Hawaii; arts management; arts in public places.

**Holdings:** Over 2,800 relocatable works of art and 225 commissioned works of art located at various public sites.

**Publications:** *Program Guidelines for Project Funding* and *Hawaii Cultural Resource Directory* (both annual).

**Information Services:** Answers inquiries; provides advisory services; evaluates and analyzes data; conducts seminars and workshops; makes referrals to other sources of information. Information services are free and available to anyone.

**Contact:** Sarah M. Richards, Executive Director

**Approval Date:** 1/84

**Latest Information Date:** 1/86

**Index Terms:** Arts resources; Hawaii; State encouragement of the arts; Financial support; Grants; Artists as teachers.

---

**19**

### Idaho Commission on the Arts

Statehouse
Boise, ID 83720
Tel.: (208) 334-2119, 334-2170,
  or 334-2171                    PUB69-17939

**Location:** Alexander House, 304 West State St.

The Commission conserves, develops, and improves the state's artistic resources; makes arts of highest quality accessible to Idaho citizens; provides economic opportunities for artists; and enhances the awareness of the arts as a basic human need.

**Areas of Interest:** Grants and other assistance available to organizations and individuals in dance, theater, prose, poetry, film, music, architecture, visual arts and crafts, and folk arts, or any whose purpose is to promote the arts.

**Holdings:** Data, books, studies, pamphlets, and other materials on the administrative, management, production, and legal aspects of the arts; computerized data base for grants management, mailing lists, and arts resources.

**Publications:** State-of-the-art reviews, R&D summaries, directories, data compilations, reprints.

**Information Services:** Answers inquiries; provides advisory, reference, and current-awareness services; provides information on R&D in progress; conducts seminars and workshops; distributes publications; makes referrals to other sources of information; permits on-site use of collections. Services are available to anyone. Seminars and workshops require payment of a fee; other services are free.

**Approval Date:** 5/84

**Latest Information Date:** 1/86

**Index Terms:** Idaho; Performing arts; Dance; Motion pictures; Music; Architecture; Literature (fine arts); Visual arts; Crafts; Folk art; Grants.

---

**20**

### Illinois Arts Council
### Public Information Office

100 West Randolph St., Suite 10-500
Chicago, IL 60601
  Tel.: (312) 793-6750                    PUB69-18441

The Council provides grants, programs, and services to individual artists, community arts councils, and nonprofit arts organizations.

**Areas of Interest:** Arts services; community arts development; creative artists in Illinois; dance; film and video arts; literature; music; public media; theater arts; visual arts, including photography.

**Publications:** Program information, brochures, abstracts, indexes, directories, guidelines.

**Information Services:** Answers inquiries; provides advisory and reference services; evaluates data; conducts seminars and workshops; distributes publications; makes referrals to other sources of information. Services are free and available to anyone.

**Approval Date:** 4/85

**Latest Information Date:** 4/85

**Index Terms:** Performing arts; Art commissions; Artists; Creativity; Dance; Motion pictures; Visual arts; Literature (fine arts); Music; Theater; Photography; Grants; Cultural programs; Illinois.

---

**21**

### Indiana Arts Commission

32 East Washington St., 6th Floor
Indianapolis, IN 46204
  Tel.: (317) 232-1268                    PUB69-17979

Sponsored in part by the National Endowment for the Arts, the Commission (the state arts agency) encourages the participation in and presentation of arts and cultural resources of Indiana.

**Areas of Interest:** Crafts; dance; design arts; education; expansion arts; folk arts; literature; media arts, including film, radio, and television; music; museums; visual and performing arts; exhibitions; artists; community arts; arts councils.

**Holdings:** Various National Endowment for the Arts guidelines.

**Publications:** Quarterly newsletter, reports, directories, handbooks.

**Information Services:** Answers inquiries; provides advisory, consulting and reference services; conducts seminars and workshops; evaluates data; distributes publications and data compilations; makes referrals to other sources of information; permits on-site use of collection. Services are free and available to anyone.

**Approval Date:** 2/84

**Latest Information Date:** 1/86

**Index Terms:** Indiana; Art commissions; State encouragement of the arts; Crafts; Dance; Design; Education; Folk art; Literature (fine arts); Motion pictures; Radio arts; Television arts; Music; Museums (institutions); Visual arts; Performing arts; Arts; Exhibitions; Community art projects; Artists.

---

**22**

---

### Institute of Puerto Rican Culture
### General Library of Puerto Rico

500 Ave. Ponce de Leon
San Juan, PR 00906
Tel.: (809) 724-2680          PUB69-20237

The Library supports and complements the purpose of the Institute of Puerto Rican Culture in the promotion, enrichment, and preservation of local cultural values. It maintains international exchange programs and serves as a distribution center for the Institute's publications.

**Areas of Interest:** History, literature, folklore, dance, music, theater, opera and music theater, indigenous and folk arts, and performance art of Puerto Rico; historic preservation; multidisciplinary studies.

**Holdings:** About seventy thousand volumes.

**Publications:** Bibliographies, indexes.

**Information Services:** Answers inquiries; provides advisory, reference, literature-searching, indexing, and reproduction services; analyzes data; conducts seminars and workshops; makes interlibrary loans; distributes publications; makes referrals to other sources of information; permits on-site use of collection. Except for reproductions, services are free and all are available to anyone. The Library is accessible to the handicapped.

**Contact:** Sra. Esther Lugo Hill, Director

**Approval Date:** 1/84

**Latest Information Date:** 1/84

**Index Terms:** Arts resources; Puerto Rico; History; Literature (fine arts); Folklore; Dance; Music; Thea-

ter; Operas; Music theater; Folk art; Performance art; Historic preservation; Cultural heritage; International arts activities; Handicapped arts services.

---

**23**

---

### Iowa Arts Council

State Capitol Complex
Des Moines, IA 50319
Tel.: (515) 281-4451          PUB69-17941

**Location:** 1223 East Court

The official state agency for receiving and disbursing state and federal funds in the arts, the Council develops arts resources in Iowa and seeks to break down geographic, economic, and social barriers and stereotypes limiting access to and enjoyment of the arts.

**Areas of Interest:** Arts in Iowa; poetry; short fiction; dancing; theater; drawing; painting; sculpture; photography; cinema; video; architecture; folk arts; marionette and puppet arts; mime; music; arts programs for the elderly, the institutionalized, adjudicated youth, and the handicapped; artists-in-residence programs for schools and state and county parks; touring programs of exhibits and performers; community sponsorship of individual artists; provision of works of art in state buildings; grants.

**Holdings:** Sixteen touring exhibits; Artist/Slide Registry; computerized mailing lists; computerized visual arts facilities directory; computerized grant data.

**Publications:** *Iowa Arts News* (bimonthly); *Annual Calendar of Summer Art Fairs; Community Arts* (newsletter); *"In Box"* (an artists' opportunities newsletter; monthly); biennial reports, program reports, bibliographies, data compilations, reprints, handbooks, a catalog of films and slides available on loan, Iowa artists' postcards.

**Information Services:** Answers inquiries; provides advisory, consulting, and reference services; lends films and slides; conducts seminars and workshops; distributes publications; makes referrals to other sources of information. Services are available to anyone and most are provided free.

**Approval Date:** 2/84

**Latest Information Date:** 1/86

**Index Terms:** Iowa; Art commissions; State encouragement of the arts; Cultural programs; Poetry; Literature (fine arts); Dance; Performing arts; Painting; Sculpture; Photography; Cinematography; Visual arts; Folk art; Mimes; Puppeteers; Music; Architecture; Financial support; Art and state.

## 24

### Kentucky Arts Council

Berry Hill
Frankfort, KY 40601
Tel.: (502) 564-8076          PUB69-17973

Established to develop and promote support for the arts and artists in Kentucky, the Council focuses on strengthening arts-producing and arts-sponsoring organizations and on helping them reach out and increase public involvement in the arts through grants and staff assistance.

**Areas of Interest:** Support and development for the arts and artists in Kentucky; arts management; access to, understanding of, and participation in the arts for Kentuckians.

**Publications:** *Kentucky Arts Council Report;* directories, newsletters.

**Information Services:** Answers inquiries; provides advisory, consulting, and reference services; conducts seminars and workshops; distributes publications and data compilations; makes referrals to other sources of information. Services are free and available to anyone. Computerized mailing list labels are available at a modest charge.

**Approval Date:** 2/84

**Latest Information Date:** 1/86

**Index Terms:** Kentucky; Art commissions; State encouragement of the arts; Art and state; Cultural organizations; Fund raising; Art management; Art patronage; Community involvement; Grants.

**Areas of Interest:** Dance; music; theater; media arts; opera and music theater; indigenous and folk arts; literature; landscape design; performing arts; visual arts; architecture; crafts; design arts; arts management; fund raising; comprehensive arts education; museum programs; multidisciplinary studies; grants administration; community arts development.

**Publications:** *ArtSpectrum* (quarterly magazine); *Program Guidelines for State Arts Grants* (annual) and a resources directory for the handicapped (both additionally available in large print, braille, and cassette editions); a triennial report; materials on community arts development and Louisiana folklife; *Arts-in-Education* brochure.

**Information Services:** Answers inquiries; provides advisory, consulting, and reference services; conducts seminars and workshops; lends films and art works; provides speakers; distributes publications; makes referrals to other sources of information. Services are available to all nonprofit arts organizations, arts sponsors, universities, public schools, and individual artists; some are available to the public. Facilities are accessible to the handicapped.

**Contact:** Ms. Linda Rigell, Arts Information Coordinator

**Approval Date:** 1/84

**Latest Information Date:** 1/86

**Index Terms:** State encouragement of the arts; Dance; Music; Theater; Media arts; Operas; Music theater; Folk art; Literature (fine arts); Landscaping; Performing arts; Visual arts; Architecture; Comprehensive art education; Handicrafts; Design; Museum programs; Art management; Fund raising; Technical assistance; Handicapped arts services; Arts resources.

## 25

### Louisiana Department of Culture, Recreation and Tourism
### Office of Cultural Development
### Division of the Arts

P.O. Box 44247
Baton Rouge, LA 70804
Tel.: (504) 925-3930          PUB69-19945

**Location:** 666 North Foster Dr.

Sponsored by the National Endowment for the Arts, the Division makes grants and provides technical assistance to artists and arts organizations in Louisiana and supports such programs as arts in education and arts for special audiences, including the aging and the disabled.

## 26

### Louisiana Department of Culture, Recreation and Tourism
### Office of the State Library
### Louisiana State Library

P.O. Box 131
Baton Rouge, LA 70821
Tel.: (504) 342-4923          PUB69-2850

**Location:** 760 Riverside North

**Areas of Interest:** All aspects of the social, biological, and physical sciences and engineering appropriate to the support of a state library system; Louisiana history, politics, folklore, and folksongs.

**Holdings:** The Readers' Services collection consists

of about 318,325 books, 92,926 talking books and 15,640 works in braille, 1,204 current subscriptions to periodicals and newspapers, 2,482 films, 2,692 records, and 13 video cassettes. The Louisiana collection contains about 48,790 cataloged items, 100,000 uncataloged documents, 800 maps, 9,400 photos and prints, 10,147 reels of microfilm, and 185 drawers of Louisiana vertical file materials. There are numerous files on the Long family, including the Huey P. Long scrapbooks, and a complete set of the Acts of Louisiana Legislature, Territorial and State. The Louisiana section is a complete historical depository for state documents. The Library is the cooperating regional library for Louisiana of the Library of Congress's National Library Service for the Blind and Physically Handicapped.

**Publications:** Reports, bibliographies, newsletters.

**Information Services:** Answers inquiries; provides consulting, reference, and literature-searching services; provides duplication services free to some users and at cost to others; makes referrals; makes inter-library loans to state residents; makes direct loans to state officials and employees; permits on-site use of collections.

**Approval Date:** 8/84

**Latest Information Date:** 1/86

**Index Terms:** Science and technology; Louisiana; History; Law (jurisprudence); Folklore; Folk music; Government.

## 27

### Maine State Commission on the Arts and the Humanities

State House Station No. 25
Augusta, ME 04333
Tel.: (207) 289-2724     PUB69-17943

Supported by the National Endowment for the Arts and the Maine legislature, the Commission is designated as the official agency of the state to receive and disburse funds made available by the federal government for programs related to support of the arts.

**Areas of Interest:** Arts resources and cultural events in Maine.

**Publications:** *Art Services Bulletin* (monthly newsletter); *Cultural Events Calendar* (monthly); *Maine Touring Artists Program* (annual catalog of performing and visual artists available for work); *Guide to Grants and Services* (annual); *Maine Arts Resources*; brochures.

**Information Services:** Answers inquiries; conducts seminars and workshops; distributes publications; makes referrals to other sources of information. Services are free and available to anyone.

**Approval Date:** 2/84

**Latest Information Date:** 1/86

**Index Terms:** Maine; Art commissions; State encouragement of the arts; Financial support; Cultural events; Cultural programs; Federal aid to the arts.

## 28

### Massachusetts Council on the Arts and Humanities Research Department

80 Boylston St., 10th Floor
Boston, MA 02116
Tel.: (617) 727-3668     PUB69-18112

Funded primarily by the Commonwealth of Massachusetts and partially by the National Endowment for the Arts, the Council stimulates and encourages the study, practice, and appreciation of the arts and humanities in the public interest through identification of and provision of financial and technical assistance to high quality arts and humanities programs in Massachusetts.

**Areas of Interest:** Community cultural resources; organizational support; contemporary arts.

**Holdings:** Small resource library on arts and humanities research, management, program development and administration, fund-raising, model and pilot programs, and other agencies' cultural programs.

**Publications:** Reports, bulletins, directories.

**Information Services:** Answers inquiries; provides advisory and reference services; conducts seminars and workshops; distributes publications; makes referrals to other sources of information; permits on-site use of collections. Some publications require postage; other services are free. All are available to anyone.

**Approval Date:** 1/86

**Latest Information Date:** 1/86

**Index Terms:** Massachusetts; Cultural resource management; Art management; Dance; Literature (fine arts); Music; Creative art; Theater; Humanities; Visual arts; Performing arts; Art education; Fund raising; Cultural programs.

## 29

### Michigan Council for the Arts (MCA)

1200 Sixth Ave.
Detroit, MI 48226
    Tel.: (313) 256-3735 (General office)
        (313) 256-3732 (Information services)
        (800) 572-1160 (Artists' hotline;
        toll-free in Michigan)      PUB69-18089

Administratively a unit of the Michigan Department of Management and Budget's Bureau of Special Boards and Commissions, MCA supports the arts and artists in Michigan through technical assistance, consultation, field services, and distribution of funds granted by the Michigan legislature and the National Endowment for the Arts.

**Areas of Interest:** Arts and artists in Michigan, including providing funding for nonprofit arts projects and works by Michigan creative artists, visual arts facilities and services, and survey data on Michigan artists; arts administration, including funding sources, proposal development, accounting and legal aspects, promotion, and publicity; community-based arts projects; arts institutions; arts-in-education programs; local arts resources; arts legislation.

**Holdings:** Collections in the above areas, including a publications library.

**Publications:** *MCA Newsletter* (quarterly); *Grantsletter*; *Artist Update* (newsletter for artists); reports, journal articles, directories, program guidelines, data compilations, brochures, special publications.

**Information Services:** Answers inquiries; provides advisory, consulting and reference services; conducts seminars and workshops; distributes publications; makes referrals to other sources of information. Services are free and available to residents of Michigan.

**Approval Date:** 2/84

**Latest Information Date:** 1/86

**Index Terms:** Michigan; Arts; Artists; Crafts; Fairs; Art management; Cultural administration; Grants; Advertising; Promoting; Consulting services; Technical assistance; Community art projects; Art education; State encouragement of the arts; Legislation.

## 30

### Minnesota State Arts Board

432 Summit
St. Paul, MN 55102
    Tel.: (612) 297-2603 (out-of-state)    PUB69-17982
        (800) 652-9747 (toll-free in-state)

The Board stimulates and encourages the creation, performance, and appreciation of arts in Minnesota.

**Areas of Interest:** Music; dance; drama; literature; folk art; architecture; painting; sculpture; photography; graphic arts; crafts; costume and fashion design; motion pictures; television; radio; tape; sound recording.

**Holdings:** Computerized data base on individuals and arts organizations requesting funds or funded by the Board (1978–present) and general mailing list, both coded according to national standard (NISP) categories.

**Publications:** *Arts Board News* (quarterly); reports, standards, directories, brochures.

**Information Services:** Answers inquiries; provides advisory, consulting, and reference services; conducts seminars and workshops; distributes publications; makes referrals to other sources of information. Information services are available free to anyone. Financial assistance programs are restricted to tax-exempt, nonprofit organizations engaged in arts activities and individual artists.

**Approval Date:** 2/84

**Latest Information Date:** 1/86

**Index Terms:** Minnesota; Art commissions; State encouragement of the arts; Art appreciation; Music; Dance; Drama; Folk art; Architecture; Painting; Sculpture; Photography; Graphic arts; Crafts; Fashion design; Television arts; Radio arts; Motion pictures; Sound recordings; Literature (fine arts).

## 31

### Missouri Arts Council

Wainwright State Office Complex
111 North 7th St., Suite 105
St. Louis, MO 63101
    Tel.: (314) 444-6845      PUB69-17970

A division of the Missouri Department of Economic Development, the Council receives financial support from the state and the National Endowment for the Arts. The Council stimulates and encourages the growth, development, and appreciation of the arts in Missouri through financial assistance and support services for the state's nonprofit, tax-exempt art organizations and sponsorship of statewide arts programs.

**Areas of Interest:** Dance; theater; music; media; visual arts; literature; community development; touring; artists-in-education.

**Publications:** *Artlogue* (bimonthly); handbooks, standards and guidelines, directories, bibliographies, data compilations.

**Information Services:** Answers inquiries; provides advisory and reference services; conducts seminars and workshops; evaluates data; distributes publications; makes referrals to other sources of information. Services are free and available to anyone.

**Approval Date:** 9/84

**Latest Information Date:** 1/86

**Index Terms:** Arts; Dance; Music; Theater; Visual arts; Literature (fine arts); Educational programs; Art appreciation; State encouragement of the arts; Cultural programs; Cultural organizations; Financial support; Technical assistance; Cultural activities; Touring exhibitions; Missouri.

## 32

### Montana Arts Council

35 South Last Chance Gulch
Helena, MT 59620
Tel.: (406) 444-6430                    PUB69-19963

Funded by the National Endowment for the Arts and the State of Montana, the Council was established to extend resources and services to communities, organizations, and individuals in order to stimulate the quality of arts programming throughout Montana and to effectively and efficiently manage the available human, financial, and material resources in the best interests of the producers and consumers of the arts in the state.

**Areas of Interest:** Dance; music; theater; media arts; opera and music theater; literature; performing arts; visual arts; arts accounting and management, including budgeting, planning organizational and program development, personnel management, problem solving, fund raising, media relations, and legal aspects affecting arts administration. Special projects include identification of local artists and of financial and employment opportunities available to local artists; making of grants and awards; networking; an artists-in-schools and communities program; and the Montana Folklife Project.

**Holdings:** The Montana Folklife Archive; print and audiovisual materials about the arts and arts development. In addition, the Council has placed over 450 books and pamphlets in nineteen Montana libraries covering such topics as community arts administration, arts in education, and folklore collecting and maintains computerized files of over sixteen hundred Montana artists by art form and place of

residence and all grants made by the Council by date, amount, and purpose.

**Publications:** Directory of state, regional, and national arts and cultural organizations; pamphlets; brochures.

**Information Services:** Answers inquiries; provides advisory, consulting, reference, literature-searching, and current-awareness services and information on research in progress; evaluates data; conducts seminars and workshops; provides speakers; distributes publications and data compilations; provides audiovisual materials to elementary and secondary schools; makes referrals to other sources of information. Except for the cost of materials, services are free and are available to nonprofit arts organizations, government agencies at all levels, and individual Montana artists. Facilities include equipment for the screening of films, slide-tape shows, and videotapes and are available by appointment. Provision is made for access to all faccilities by the handicapped.

**Contact:** Mr. David E. Nelson, Executive Director

**Approval Date:** 1/84

**Latest Information Date:** 1/86

**Index Terms:** Montana; State encouragement of the arts; Dance; Music; Theater; Media arts; Operas; Music theater; Folk art; Literature (fine arts); Arts resources; Visual arts; Art management; Fund raising; Program development; Problem solving; Grants; Awards; Artists-in-residence; Community art projects; Handicapped arts services.

## 33

### National Foundation on the Arts and the Humanities
### National Endowment for the Arts

c/o Ms. Joan Shantz, Director of Public Information
1100 Pennsylvania Ave. NW.
Washington, DC 20506
Tel.: (202) 682-5400                    PUB69-7755

The National Endowment for the Arts is an independent agency of the federal government created in 1965 to encourage and assist the nation's cultural resources. It has developed its programs toward the achievement of three basic goals: (1) to promote the broad dissemination of cultural resources of the highest quality across the land; (2) to assist our cultural institutions to provide greater public service and to improve artistic and administrative standards; and (3) to support creativity among our most gifted artists, encourage the preservation of our cultural heritage, and advance the quality of life of our nation. This is accomplished through awarding fellowships to individuals of exceptional talent and matching grants to nonprofit, tax-exempt organizations.

**Areas of Interest:** Dance; design arts; expansion arts; folk arts; international arts; inter-arts (cross-disciplinary); literature; media arts (film/radio/television); museums; music; opera-musical theater; theater; the visual arts. The Endowment also awards grants to state arts agencies and regional groups, fosters collaboration among the members of the public arts support network, and places practicing professional artists in educational settings. A limited number of fellowships for arts managers are available.

**Holdings:** A library/information center of 5,000 volumes, 100 journal subscriptions, and 10 drawers of vertical file materials. Materials collected include research reports, economic impact surveys, and agency documents and publications. Major subject interests are the arts and government, arts administration, cultural history, the economics of the arts, and grantsmanship. The Endowment's Grants Office maintains a data base containing information relating to Endowment grants and applications only.

**Publications:** *The Arts Review* (quarterly magazine); *Annual Report; Guide to the National Endowment for the Arts;* application guidelines for each Endowment program; application deadlines; *Challenge Grant Experience.* The Research Division publishes periodic reports on arts-related subjects, which are available from the Publishing Center for Cultural Resources, 625 Broadway, New York, NY 10012.

**Information Services:** Visitors are welcome to call for an appointment to visit the library and the Public Information Office. Most materials are available on an interlibrary loan basis. All inquiries about Endowment programs and policies as well as requests for Endowment publications should be directed to the Office of Public Information, National Endowment for the Arts, at the address and phone number above.

**Approval Date:** 11/84

**Latest Information Date:** 1/86

**Index Terms:** Federal aid to the arts; Grants; State encouragement of the arts; Art and state; Performing arts; Graphic arts; Folk art; Literature (fine arts); Museums (institutions); Music; Operas; Theater; Cultural administration; Cultural history; Visual arts; Arts resources; Arts management; Fellowships.

## 34

**National Foundation on the Arts and the Humanities**
**National Endowment for the Arts**
**Office for Special Constituencies**

1100 Pennsylvania Ave. NW.
Washington, DC 20506
Tel.: (202) 682-5532
(202) 682-5496 (TTY)        PUB69-19267

The Office conducts an advocacy and technical assistance program to make the arts more accessible to handicapped people, older adults, veterans, and people in hospitals, nursing homes, mental institutions, and prisons. It provides information and technical assistance to artists, arts organizations, and consumers concerning accessible arts programs. Through the Endowment's grant-making programs, the Office supports model projects that demonstrate innovative ways to make the arts accessible. By means of cooperative agreements with other federal agencies, the Office helps educate administrators and professionals about the benefits of arts programming. Applicants who have an arts project involving handicapped persons, institutionalized persons, or senior citizens may request technical assistance from the Office in shaping their projects.

**Areas of Interest:** Accessibility of the arts to handicapped people; barrier-free design; organizations serving handicapped people; advocacy of arts programs for handicapped, older, and institutionalized populations.

**Publications:** *The NEA 504 Regulations; The Arts and 504* (available in mid-1985); resource materials.

**Information Services:** Answers inquiries; provides advisory and reference services; distributes publications; makes referrals to other sources of information. Services are free and available to anyone.

**Contact:** Ms. Wendy Lim

**Approval Date:** 2/85

**Latest Information Date:** 2/85

**Index Terms:** State encouragement of the arts; Handicapped persons; Rehabilitation; Art education; Information services.

## 35

**Nebraska Arts Council**

1313 Farnam-on-the-Mall
Omaha, NE 68102-1873
Tel.: (402) 554-2122        PUB69-18202

Funded in part by the National Endowment for the Arts, the Council seeks to stimulate and encourage the study and presentation of the arts in Nebraska, and public interest and participation therein.

**Areas of Interest:** Design arts; dance; arts education; expansion arts; folk arts; literature; film, radio, and television arts; museums; music; opera and musical theater; theater arts; visual arts; arts administration.

**Holdings:** About five hundred titles in arts administration.

**Publications:** Guidelines related to grants and programs.

**Information Services:** Answers inquiries; provides advisory, consulting, and reference services; conducts seminars and workshops; evaluates and analyzes data; distributes publications; makes referrals to other sources of information; permits on-site use of collections. Services are free and available to anyone.

**Contact:** Ms. Cheryl Wilhelm

**Approval Date:** 2/85

**Latest Information Date:** 2/85

**Index Terms:** Nebraska; Arts; Design; Dance; Art education; Folk art; Literature (fine arts); Cinematography; Radio arts; Television arts; Museums (institutions); Music; Operas; Performing arts; Visual arts; Art management.

---

## 36

### Nevada State Council on the Arts (NSCA)

329 Flint St.
Reno, NV 89501
Tel.: (702) 789-0225     PUB69-19970

Funded by the National Endowment for the Arts, the State of Nevada, and private contributors, NSCA provides information services, technical assistance, and grants to nonprofit, tax-exempt Nevada arts organizations and Nevada artists and administers an Artists-in-Residence program, placing professional artists in residence at schools, school districts, and other educational settings.

**Areas of Interest:** Dance; music; theater; media arts; opera and music theater; indigenous and folk arts; literature; performing arts; visual arts; architecture; crafts; design arts; comprehensive art education; arts management; multidisciplinary studies; museum programs; funding sources for artists and arts organizations; arts employment opportunities; arts marketing; grantsmanship; networking; touring; sponsor development.

**Holdings:** About two hundred books and journals. NSCA maintains an arts registry, providing a marketplace for Nevada's artists and a cost-effective resource for Nevada's presenters and sponsors.

**Publications:** Quarterly newsletter; annual grants guidelines; descriptive brochure.

**Information Services:** Answers inquiries; provides advisory, consulting, and reference services; evaluates data; conducts seminars and workshops; provides speakers; lends materials from its collections; distributes publications and transcriptions of its arts registry; makes referrals to other sources of information. Services are free and available to anyone.

**Contact:** Mr. William Fox, Executive Director

**Approval Date:** 1/84

**Latest Information Date:** 1/86

**Index Terms:** State encouragement of the arts; Dance; Theater; Music; Media arts; Operas; Music theater; Folk art; Literature (fine arts); Performing arts; Visual arts; Architecture; Comprehensive art education; Handicrafts; Design; Museum programs; Art management; Fund raising; Grants; Artists-in-residence; Arts; Employment opportunities; Art marketing; Touring programs; Nevada; Arts resources.

---

## 37

### New Hampshire State Council on the Arts

40 North Main St.
Concord, NH 03301
Tel.: (603) 271-2789     PUB69-19972

Sponsored by the state governor and legislature and the National Endowment for the Arts, the Council provides four programs; grants to arts organizations and individual artists in New Hampshire, touring arts assistance, Artists-in-the-Schools, and Percent for Art.

**Areas of Interest:** Dance; music; theater; media arts; opera and music theater; indigenous and folk arts; literature; landscape design; performing arts; visual arts; architecture; crafts; design arts; arts management; teacher training; special education; museum programs; multidisciplinary studies.

**Information Services:** Answers inquiries; provides advisory services; evaluates data; conducts seminars and workshops; provides speakers. Services are provided to artists and arts organizations in New Hampshire; information is available to visitors. The Commission maintains a teletypewriter (TTY) for the convenience of the hearing-impaired.

**Contact:** Mr. Robert J. Hankins, Executive Director

**Approval Date:** 1/84

**Latest Information Date:** 1/86

**Index Terms:** State encouragement of the arts; State arts agencies; Dance; Music; Theater; Media arts; Operas; Music theater; Folk art; Literature (fine arts); Special education; Landscaping; Performing arts; Visual arts; Architecture; Handicrafts; Design; Museum programs; Art management; Artists-in-residence; Touring programs; Grants; Technical assistance; Handicapped arts services; Arts resources.

## 38

### New Jersey State Council on the Arts

109 West State St., CN 306
Trenton, NJ 08625
Tel.: (609) 292-6130                    PUB69-20234

The Council makes grants and provides technical assistance to artists and arts organizations in New Jersey and supports such programs as arts in education, arts festivals, and crafts markets. In addition, the Council serves as an information and referral agency addressing the needs of handicapped persons in the state. It receives an annual appropriation from the state legislature and supplemental financial support from the National Endowment for the Arts.

**Areas of Interest:** Dance; music; theater; media arts; opera and music theater; indigenous and folk arts; literature; performance art; visual arts; architecture; crafts; design arts; arts management; fund raising; comprehensive arts education; teacher training; multidisciplinary studies.

**Holdings:** Arts Management Collection of publications available to the New Jersey arts community through the Council office and twenty seven other New Jersey public libraries; Arts Inclusion Slide Registry; Crafts Slide Registry; Performing Artists Registry. The registries contain tapes, files, and slides on New Jersey visual and performing artists.

**Publications:** *Arts New Jersey* (quarterly newsletter); monthly bulletin; reports.

**Information Services:** Answers inquiries; provides advisory, reference, and literature-searching services; conducts seminars and workshops; provides speakers; sponsors major conferences; distributes publications; makes referrals to other sources of information. Except for some seminars and workshops, services are free and all are available to anyone.

**Contact:** Mr. Jeffrey A. Kesper, Executive Director

**Approval Date:** 1/84

**Latest Information Date:** 1/86

**Index Terms:** Arts resources; Dance; Music; Theater, Teacher training; Operas; Music theater; Folk art; Literature (fine arts); Performance art; Visual arts; Architecture; Comprehensive art education; Handicrafts; Art management; Grants; Technical assistance; New Jersey.

## 39

### New Jersey State Teen Arts Program

841 Georges Rd.
North Brunswick, NJ 08902
Tel.: (201) 745-3898                    PUB69-20215

Sponsored by New Jersey state and local government agencies and private organizations, the Program seeks to identify, promote, and encourage the talents of teenagers, to strengthen arts curricula in New Jersey schools, and to develop community audiences.

**Areas of Interest:** Teenagers and the arts, including dance, music, theater, media arts, opera and music theater, indigenous and folk arts, literature, performance art, visual arts, crafts, and design arts; comprehensive arts education; special education; museum programs; arts, art festival, art extension, art outreach, and art education planning and management; fund raising; multidisciplinary studies.

**Holdings:** Information on artists and arts organizations.

**Publications:** Annual calendar illustrated with student art work; journal articles, program standards, critical reviews, directories, data compilations, project reports.

**Information Services:** Answers inquiries; provides advisory, reference, and current-awareness services; evaluates and analyzes data; conducts seminars and workshops; lends materials; distributes publications and audiovisual materials; provides speakers; makes referrals to other sources of information; permits on-site use of collections. Services are available to anyone; some are provided free and others at cost. A number of Program activity sites are accessible to the handicapped.

**Contact:** Debi Rubel, Program Director

**Approval Date:** 1/84

**Latest Information Date:** 1/86

**Index Terms:** Arts resources; Arts and teenagers; Dance; Music; Theater; Curriculum design; Operas; Music theater; Folk art; Literature (fine arts); Special education; Performance art; Visual arts; Comprehensive art education; Handicrafts; Museum programs; Art management; Fund raising; Outreach programs; Festivals.

## 40

### New York State Council on the Arts

80 Centre St.
New York, NY 10013
Tel.: (212) 587-4967            PUB69-17983

The Council encourages participation in and appreciation of New York's cultural resources and disburses state funds to nonprofit organizations within New York.

**Areas of Interest:** Arts funding; arts management; state programs developing public access to the visual and performing arts, architecture, design, historic sites, literature, museums, media, and arts activities within the Black, Asian, European, Hispanic, and Native American communities.

**Publications:** Reports, guidelines.

**Information Services:** Answers inquiries; provides advisory, consulting, and reference services; conducts seminars and workshops; evaluates data; makes referrals to other sources of information. Requests for information from the public are honored; more extensive services are generally available only to nonprofit arts organizations within the state.

**Approval Date:** 7/84

**Latest Information Date:** 1/86

**Index Terms:** New York (State); State encouragement of the arts; Financial support; Art and state; Art management; Visual arts; Performing arts; Architecture; Design; Historic sites; Literature (fine arts); Museums (institutions); Motion pictures; Radio arts; Television arts; Cultural activities; Minority groups.

## 41

### North Carolina Department of Cultural Resources
### North Carolina Arts Council

221 East Lane St.
Raleigh, NC 27611
Tel.: (919) 733-2821            PUB69-19944

Sponsored by the National Endowment for the Arts and the State of North Carolina, the Council provides grants for artists and arts organizations in North Carolina and supports such programs as artists-in-schools, artists-in-residence, touring arts, community

arts projects, and arts producing organizations.

**Areas of Interest:** Dance; music; theater; media arts; opera and music theater; indigenous and folk arts; literature; performance art; visual arts; crafts; design arts; community arts; arts management; fund raising; multidisciplinary studies.

**Holdings:** Records of grants awarded and requested; computerized mailing list of constituent addresses; publications of other state arts agencies. The Council maintains a Consultants Registry to assist groups in finding the most capable resource people.

**Publications:** *State of the Arts* (annual report); bimonthly updates; program handbooks; data compilations. Council publications are recorded on tape at the North Carolina Library for the Blind and Physically Handicapped.

**Information Services:** Answers inquiries; provides advisory and reference services; evaluates data; conducts seminars and workshops; makes direct and interlibrary loans; provides speakers; distributes publications and mailing lists; makes referrals to other sources of information; permits on-site use of collections. Some services are provided free to all users; others involving specialized data, such as mailing lists, are charged at cost. Services are available to anyone, with priority given to North Carolina residents. Facilities are accessible to the handicapped.

**Contact:** Ms. Mary B. Regan, Executive Director

**Approval Date:** 1/84

**Latest Information Date:** 1/86

**Index Terms:** State encouragement of the arts; Dance; Music; Theater; Media arts; Operas; Music theater; Folk art; Literature (fine arts); Performing arts; Arts resources; Handicrafts; Design; Art management; Community art projects; Artists-in-residence; Handicapped arts services; Fund raising; Lecturers; Cultural resources management.

## 42

### North Dakota Council on the Arts

Black Bldg., Suite 606
Fargo, ND 58102
Tel.: (701) 237-8962            PUB69-19907

The Council is the official arts agency for the State of North Dakota.

**Areas of Interest:** Dance; music; theater; media arts; opera and music theater; indigenous and folk arts; literature; landscape design; performance art; architecture; visual arts; crafts; design arts; arts management; fund raising; multidisciplinary studies.

**Holdings:** A folk arts collection was begun by the Council and is now housed in the North Dakota Heritage Center, Bismarck.

**Publications:** Newsletter, biennial report, books, journal articles, project reports, grant application guidelines, reprints.

**Information Services:** Answers inquiries; provides advisory, consulting, and reference services; conducts seminars and workshops; distributes publications; makes referrals to other sources of information. Services are free and available to artists and arts organizations in North Dakota. Facilities are accessible to the handicapped.

**Contact:** Ms. Donna Evenson, Executive Director

**Approval Date:** 10/85

**Latest Information Date:** 10/85

**Index Terms:** North Dakota; Arts resources; Dance; Music; Theater; Media arts; Operas; Music theater; Folk art; Literature (fine arts); Landscape architecture; Performing arts; Visual arts; Handicrafts; Design; Art management; Fund raising; Cultural heritage; Handicapped art services.

---

## 43

### Pennsylvania Council on the Arts

P.O. Box 1323
Harrisburg, PA 17105-1323
Tel.: (717) 787-6883          PUB69-17980

**Location:** Finance Bldg., Room 216

An agency of state government funded by the legislature, the Council encourages and develops the arts in Pennsylvania through technical assistance, special projects, and grants-in-aid to qualified arts organizations and individual creative artists.

**Areas of Interest:** All art forms in the performing, visual, and literary arts.

**Holdings:** Lists of grants recipients for the past three years, amounts of monies received, and descriptions of funded projects. Council mailing list and grants management system are computerized according to the NISP (National Information Systems Project) standards.

**Publications:** Quarterly newsletter, directories, booklets, brochures, *Guide to Programs*.

**Information Services:** Answers inquiries; provides advisory, consulting, and reference services; conducts seminars and workshops; evaluates data; distributes publications and data compilations; makes referrals to other sources of information. Services are free, except for certain seminar materials, and available to nonprofit groups and creative artists.

**Approval Date:** 2/84

**Latest Information Date:** 1/86

**Index Terms:** Pennsylvania; State encouragement of the arts; Technical assistance; Grants-in-aid; Performing arts; Visual arts.

---

## 44

### Rhode Island State Council on the Arts (RISCA)

312 Wickenden St.
Providence, RI 02903
Tel.: (401) 277-3880          PUB69-18199

Funded in part by several federal, state, and local government agencies, RISCA administers Rhode Island's programs, grants, and funding aimed at developing the arts resources of the state.

**Areas of Interest:** Performing, visual, literary, and environmental arts in Rhode Island; arts management.

**Holdings:** Literature relating to arts issues; mailing list of artists, arts organizations, and agencies and individuals interested in the arts; computerized data base of grants and programs; considerable background information on establishing arts programs for the handicapped, elderly, and institutionalized.

**Publications:** *RISCA Report* (monthly); other reports, documents, reprints.

**Information Services:** Answers inquiries; provides advisory, consulting, and reference services; conducts seminars and workshops; evaluates and analyzes data; distributes publications and data compilations; makes referrals to other sources of information. Nominal fees are charged for attendance at some workshops; other services are free. All are available to groups who provide arts opportunities or activities as a primary or secondary service.

**Approval Date:** 2/84

**Latest Information Date:** 1/86

**Index Terms:** Rhode Island; Performing arts; Visual arts; Art management; Art appreciation; State encouragement of the arts; Grants; Cultural programs.

## 45

**Santa Barbara Museum of Art**

1130 State St.
Santa Barbara, CA 93101
Tel.: (805) 963-4364          PUB69-20200

The Museum has an open membership of about 2,500 persons.

**Areas of Interest:** Visual arts; architecture; film arts; crafts; museum programs; comprehensive arts education.

**Holdings:** About seven thousand paintings, sculptures, and graphic and ethnic arts objects (particular strengths are Greek and Roman antiquities, eighteenth- to twentieth-century American paintings, European and American drawings and prints, Oriental art, African art, and dolls); about thirty thousand library items; about thirty thousand slides.

**Publications:** *Gallery Notes*; monthly calendar; exhibition and education catalogs (about ten a year); annual report; curricula.

**Information Services:** Answers inquiries; provides advisory, reference and reproduction services; conducts seminars and workshops; makes direct and interlibrary loans; distributes publications and audiovisual educational materials; provides speakers; makes referrals to other sources of information; permits on-site use of collections. Except for reproductions, services are free and all are available to anyone. Facilities include a separately funded Education Department with classroom space. Museum facilities are accessible to the handicapped and special tours of the collections are provided to them.

**Contact:** Ron Crozier, Librarian

**Approval Date:** 10/84

**Latest Information Date:** 1/86

**Index Terms:** Museums (institutions); Arts resources; Visual arts; Architecture; Cinematography; Handicrafts; Comprehensive art education; Performance art; Paintings; Graphic arts; Antiquities; International arts activities.

## 46

**South Carolina Arts Commission**

1800 Gervais St.
Columbia, SC 29201
Tel.: (803) 758-3442          PUB69-20231

Partially funded by the National Endowment for the Arts, the Commission makes grants and provides technical assistance to artists and arts organizations in South Carolina and supports such programs as artists in education, touring arts, rural arts, artist development, and media arts production. Its facilities are accessible to the handicapped.

**Areas of Interest:** Dance; music; theater; media arts; literature; visual arts; crafts.

**Holdings:** The Commission is jointly responsible with the South Carolina Museum Commission for the State Art Collection, currently consisting of over two hundred pieces.

**Publications:** *Artifacts* (bimonthly newsletter); *Independent Spirit* (quarterly); *Eye on the Arts* (bimonthly); *Guide to Grants and Fellowships* (annual); poetry anthologies.

**Information Services:** Answers inquiries; provides advisory and consulting services; evaluates data; conducts seminars and workshops; lends films and filmmaking equipment; distributes publications; makes referrals to other sources of information. Film and video editing equipment and studio space are rented to filmmakers. Information and technical assistance are given free. Some programs are directed at specific audiences; others are available to the public.

**Contact:** Ms. Scott Sanders, Executive Director

**Approval Date:** 2/84

**Latest Information Date:** 1/86

**Index Terms:** Arts resources; South Carolina; Art commissions; Cultural heritage; Artists as teachers; Touring programs; Dance; Music; Theater; Literature (fine arts); Visual arts; Handicrafts; Motion pictures; Education programs; Community art projects; Performing arts; Architecture; Handicapped arts services.

## 47

**South Dakota Department of Education and Cultural Affairs**
**Office of Fine Arts**

108 West 11th St.
Sioux Falls, SD 57102
Tel.: (605) 339-6646          PUB69-19909

The Office of Fine Arts is also known as the South Dakota Arts Council (SDAC). As the state arts agency for South Dakota, it serves as an advisory board.

**Areas of Interest:** Dance; music; theater; literature; visual arts; crafts; arts management; multidisciplinary studies.

**Information Services:** Answers inquiries; provides advisory and reference services; evaluates and analyzes data; conducts seminars and workshops. Services are free and available to artists and arts organizations in South Dakota.

**Contact:** Ms. Charlotte Carver, Executive Director

**Approval Date:** 4/85

**Latest Information Date:** 4/85

**Index Terms:** South Dakota; Dance; Music; Theater; Literature (fine arts); Visual arts; Handicrafts; Art management; Fine arts; Cultural activities; Arts resources.

## 48

### Tennessee Arts Commission

320 Sixth Ave. N., Suite 100
Nashville, TN 37219
Tel.: (615) 741-1701          PUB69-19894

The Commission provides grants and technical assistance for artists and arts organizations in Tennessee and encourages education in the arts and public interest in the cultural heritage of the state.

**Areas of Interest:** Dance; music; theater; opera and music theater; indigenous and folk arts; performance art; visual arts; architecture; crafts; media arts; design arts; comprehensive arts education; teacher training; museum programs; arts management; fund raising.

**Holdings:** The Commission owns and operates the Tennessee State Museum and a library of films by independent artists.

**Publications:** *The Arts Report;* listings of fairs, festivals, and exhibitions; project reports; program guidelines.

**Information Services:** Answers inquiries; provides advisory, technical assistance, reference, and literature-searching services; provides speakers; conducts seminars and workshops; distributes publications; makes direct and interlibrary loans of materials; makes referrals to other sources of information; permits on-site use of collections. Except for shipping, repair, and replacement costs of materials, services are free and all are available to anyone. The Commission's facilities are accessible to the handicapped.

**Contact:** Bennett Tarleton, Executive Director

**Approval Date:** 8/85

**Latest Information Date:** 8/85

**Index Terms:** Arts resources; Dance; Music; Theater;

Operas; Folk art; Performing arts; Visual arts; Architecture; Handicrafts; Design; Art education; Teacher training; Museums (institutions); Cultural programs; Art management; Fund raising; Grants; Technical assistance; Cultural heritage; Handicapped arts services.

## 49

### Texas Commission on the Arts

Box 13406, Capitol Station
Austin, TX 78711
Tel.: (512) 475-6593
(1-800) 252-9415          PUB69-17975

**Location:** 920 Colorado St.

Partially funded by the National Endowment for the Arts, the Commission offers technical and financial assistance to nonprofit arts organizations, units of government, and educational institutions.

**Areas of Interest:** Performing and visual arts organizations, local arts councils, and individual artists in Texas; arts administration; artists-in-education; touring visual and performing arts.

**Holdings:** Artists' registry; mailing lists and labels.

**Publications:** Biweekly staff news, semiannual report, surveys, program and informational brochures and materials.

**Information Services:** Answers inquiries; provides advisory, consulting, and reference services; conducts seminars and workshops; makes referrals to other sources of information. Except for consultations, services are free and available to anyone.

**Approval Date:** 3/84

**Latest Information Date:** 1/86

**Index Terms:** Texas; Art commissions; State encouragement of the arts; Technical assistance; Financial support; Performing arts; Visual arts; Cultural organizations; Art management; Art education.

## 50

### Utah Arts Council

617 East South Temple
Salt Lake City, UT 84102
Tel.: (801) 533-5895          PUB69-18088

Partially funded by the National Endowment for the Arts and the Western State Arts Foundation, the Council serves as the Utah state agency charged with furthering the arts in all their phases.

**Areas of Interest:** Grants assistance; folk arts; visual arts and museum services; community outreach; arts in rural areas; artists in schools; grants-in-aid to non-profit organizations; film and media development.

**Holdings:** The Utah Art Collection of over six hundred items; computerized mailing list; access to other computerized data bases.

**Publications:** Quarterly newsletter; *Sketchbook of Services;* annual report, teacher resource packages, brochures.

**Information Services:** Answers inquiries; provides advisory services; conducts seminars and workshops; distributes publications; makes referrals to other sources of information; permits on-site use of collection. Services are free and available to anyone.

**Approval Date:** 3/84

**Latest Information Date:** 1/86

**Index Terms:** Utah; Performing arts; Folk art; Visual arts; Museums (institutions); Community art projects; Art education; Grants; Artists as teachers; Festivals.

## 51

### Vermont Council on the Arts (VCA)

136 State St.
Montpelier, VT 05602
Tel.: (802) 828-3291                    PUB69-20235

Sponsored by the National Endowment for the Arts and the State of Vermont, VCA makes grants and provides technical assistance to artists and arts organizations in Vermont and directs an artists-in-education program.

**Areas of Interest:** Dance; music; theater; media arts; opera and music theater; indigenous and folk arts; literature; landscape design; performance art; visual arts; architecture; crafts; design arts; comprehensive arts education; fund raising; museum programs; multidisciplinary studies.

**Publications:** *Artery* (newsletter); handbook; artist register; annual report.

**Information Services:** Answers inquiries; provides advisory, consulting, and reference services; evaluates data; conducts seminars and workshops; provides speakers; sponsors foreign artists and performers; conducts cooperative projects with foreign groups; distributes publications; makes referrals to other sources of information. Except for seminars, workshops, and publications, services are generally free and available to all residents of Vermont and to others.

**Approval Date:** 1/84

**Latest Information Date:** 1/86

**Index Terms:** Arts resources; Vermont; Dance; Music; Theater; Operas; Music theater; Folk art; Literature (fine arts); Landscaping; Performance art; Visual arts; Architecture; Comprehensive art education; Handicrafts; Design; Museum programs; Fund raising; Financial support; Technical assistance; International arts activities.

## 52

### Virginia Commission for the Arts

101 North 14th St., 17th Floor
Richmond, VA 23219
Tel.: (804) 225-3132                    PUB69-17981

The Commission supports and stimulates excellence in the arts and encourages accessibility to the arts for all Virginians.

**Areas of Interest:** Dance, literary arts; media arts; music; theater; visual arts.

**Publications:** *Art News* (bimonthly).

**Information Services:** Answers inquiries; provides advisory and consulting services; evaluates data; distributes publication; makes referrals to other sources of information. Information services are free and available to anyone. Financial assistance programs are restricted to Virginia groups only.

**Approval Date:** 2/84

**Latest Information Date:** 1/86

**Index Terms:** Virginia; State encouragement of the arts; Financial support; Dance; Literature (fine arts); Music; Theater; Visual arts.

## 53

### Washington State Arts Commission (WSAC)

Mail Stop GH-11
Olympia, WA 98504
Tel.: (206) 753-3860                    PUB69-19939

**Location:** 9th and Columbia Bldg.

Funded by the State of Washington and the National Endowment for the arts, WSAC provides grants and technical assistance for artists and arts organizations in Washington and supports such programs as artists in schools, art in public buildings, touring arts, and a cultural enrichment program.

**Areas of Interest:** Dance; music; theater; media arts; opera and music theater; indigenous and folk arts; literature; landscape design; performance art; visual arts; architecture; crafts; design arts; art therapy; dance therapy; music therapy; special education; comprehensive arts education; teacher training; curriculum design; museum programs; arts management; fund raising; multidisciplinary studies.

**Holdings:** Small library of books, reports, and other materials on arts and arts administration; over six hundred works of art in all media. A mailing list and grant records are computer-based.

**Publications:** *Washington Arts* (newsletter); *Guide to Programs*; lists of state arts resources; various statistical and research reports; various agency program and project reports; study guide materials.

**Information Services:** Answers inquiries; provides technical assistance and reference services; evaluates data; conducts seminars and workshops; lends materials; provides speakers; distributes publications and data compilations; makes referrals to other sources of information; permits on-site use of collections. Except for the cost of reproduction, services are free and available to anyone, subject to Washington (State) freedom of information laws and regulations, which generally excludes commercial interests. Accessibility of facilities generally follows NEA guidelines.

**Contact:** Mr. Michael A. Croman, Executive Director

**Approval Date:** 1/84

**Latest Information Date:** 1/86

**Index Terms:** Dance; Music; Theater; Teacher training; Media arts; Curriculum design; Operas; Music theater; Folk art; Literature (fine arts); Special education; Musicotherapy; Landscaping; Performance art; Visual arts; Architecture; Comprehensive art education; Handicrafts; Design; Museum programs; Dance therapy; Art management; Fund raising; National Endowment for the Arts; Grants; Technical assistance; Touring programs; Cultural resources management; Lecturers; Handicapped arts services; Art resources.

---

**54**

## Wisconsin Arts Board

123 West Washington Ave.
Madison, WI 53702
   Tel.: (608) 266-0190       PUB69-19962

An agency of Wisconsin State government, the Board provides grants and technical assistance for artists

and arts organizations in Wisconsin. Activities include the study of artistic and cultural activities within the state, assistance to arts activities, assistance to communities in creating and developing their own arts programs, encouragement and assistance for freedom of artistic expression, and the planning and implementation of a program of contracts with or grants-in-aid to groups and individuals of exceptional talent engaged in or concerned with the arts.

**Areas of Interest:** Dance; music; theater; media arts; opera and music theater; indigenous and folk arts; literature; performance art; visual arts; architecture; crafts; design arts; museum programs; comprehensive arts education; teacher training; curriculum design; arts management; fund raising; multidisciplinary studies.

**Holdings:** Data base access in the above areas on financial support of the arts, resource directories, and mailing lists.

**Publications:** *Bulletin* (quarterly); *Wisconsin Arts and Crafts Fairs* (annual); *Guide to Programs and Services.*

**Information Services:** Answers inquiries; provides advisory and technical assistance services; conducts seminars and workshops and cosponsors a summer arts camp for high school students; provides speakers; distributes publications; makes referrals to other sources of information; permits on-site use of collections. Services are free and available to anyone, with priority for residents of Wisconsin.

**Contact:** Mr. Marvin Weaver, Executive Director

**Approval Date:** 4/84

**Latest Information Date:** 1/86

**Index Terms:** Wisconsin; State encouragement of the arts; Dance; Music; Theater; Media arts; Curriculum design; Operas; Music theater; Folk art; Literature (fine arts); Performing arts; Visual arts; Architecture; Comprehensive art education; Handicrafts; Design; Museum programs; Art management; Fund raising; Handicapped arts services; Artists-in-residence; Arts resources.

---

**55**

## Woonsocket Education Department
## Art Shared by People Investing in Relevant Education (ASPIRE)

c/o Woonsocket High School
777 Cass Ave.
Woonsocket, RI 02895
   Tel.: (401) 762-2200 Ext. 311      PUB69-20338

Funded by the Rhode Island Department of Education, other state agencies, institutions, and private corporations, ASPIRE identifies students in the Woonsocket public schools who are gifted and talented in the visual arts, develops support curricula for grades 4–12, and furnishes the students with special exhibition outlets. It has conducted cooperative projects with foreign groups and is interested in more foreign involvement.

**Areas of Interest:** Visual arts education for gifted children.

**Publications:** *Portfolio Preparation Guide* (manual on assembling a portfolio for art school admission).

**Information Services:** Answers inquiries; provides advisory services; distributes its publication and slide/tape programs; provides speakers. Services are free for Rhode Island residents and are subject to a fee for others.

**Contact:** Dr. Henry B. Cote, Co-Director

**Approval Date:** 2/84

**Latest Information Date:** 1/86

**Index Terms:** Education of the gifted; Visual arts; Arts resources; Art management.

# National and Regional Arts Service Organizations

## Acadiana Arts Council

P.O. Box 53762
Lafayette, LA 70505
Tel.: (318) 233-7060 PUB69-20349

The Council maintains community arts facilities, administers regional arts and education programs, serves as a clearinghouse for information and as a ticket distributor for community arts organizations, and conducts other local art agency activities.

**Areas of Interest:** Arts in Louisiana, including dance, music, theater, and visual arts; comprehensive arts education; fund raising.

**Publications:** *Info* (magazine).

**Information Services:** Answers inquiries; conducts seminars and workshops; distributes publication; makes referrals to other sources of information. Services are available for a fee to anyone.

**Contact:** Mr. Tom Boozer, Executive Director

**Approval Date:** 1/84

**Latest Information Date:** 1/86

**Index Terms:** Arts resources; Louisiana; Dance; Music; Theater; Visual arts; Comprehensive art education; Fund raising.

## Affiliated State Arts Agencies of the Upper Midwest (former)
## Arts Midwest (current)

528 Hennepin Ave., Suite 310
Minneapolis, MN 55403
Tel.: (612) 341-0755 PUB69-18200

Funded by the National Endowment for the Arts and the member state arts agencies of Iowa, Minnesota, North Dakota, South Dakota, and Wisconsin, the Affiliation fosters and promotes the arts in the region to increase the knowledge, appreciation, and instruction in and of the arts in the five-state area.

**Areas of Interest:** Performing and visual arts touring programs and related services; arts data management services.

**Publications:** Program announcements and guides, presenters' directory, mailing list services.

**Information Services:** Answers inquiries; provides advisory and consultant services according to time and staff availability; conducts seminars and workshops; distributes publications; makes referrals to other sources of information. Services are free, unless extensive, and available to residents of the five-state area.

**Approval Date:** 2/84

**Latest Information Date:** 1/86

**Index Terms:** Performing arts; Visual arts; Touring programs; Art management; Public education; Art appreciation; Midwestern United States.

## Alabama Humanities Foundation

P.O. Box A-40
Birmingham-Southern College
Birmingham, AL 35254
Tel.: (205) 324-1314 PUB69-21079

Sponsored by the National Endowment for the Humanities, AHF grants funds to nonprofit organizations active in the promotion of the understanding, appreciation, and use of the humanities, and conducts its own public programs.

**Areas of Interest:** Alabama history, philosophy, languages, literature, linguistics, archaeology, jurisprudence, art history and criticism, ethics, comparative religion, and those aspects of the social sciences employing historical or philosophical approaches; public policy and programs in the humanities.

**Holdings:** Collections in the above areas; computerized data base on past grants awarded and Alabama humanities scholars.

**Publications:** Humanities Forum (annual); program announcements; brochures describing grant programs.

**Information Services:** Answers inquiries; provides advisory and reference services; evaluates data; conducts seminars and workshops; distributes publications; makes referrals to other sources of information; permits on-site use of collections. Services are free and available to nonprofit groups and adults.

**Approval Date:** 3/85

**Latest Information Date:** 1/86

**Index Terms:** Alabama; Humanities; History; Philosophy; Languages; Literature (fine arts); Linguistics; Archaeology; Law (jurisprudence); Art history; Criticism; Ethics; Religion; Social sciences; Public policies; Grants-in-aid; National Endowment for the Humanities.

## 59

**American Society of Artists, Inc. (ASA)**

P.O. Box 1326
Palatine, IL 60078
  Tel.: (312) 751-2500 or 991-4748       PUB69-20554

**Location:** North Michigan Ave., Chicago, IL

**Areas of Interest:** Fine art; arts and crafts; art and craft shows; lecture and demonstration service.

**Holdings:** Names and addresses of about ten thousand American artists and crafts people.

**Publications:** *A.S.A. Artisan* (quarterly newsletter for members); *Art Lovers Art and Craft Fair Bulletin.*

**Information Services:** Answers inquiries; provides reference services; conducts lectures and demonstrations; offers special arts services, including assistance in purchasing art and craft supplies; presents art shows, craft shows, and art and craft shows; distributes publications. Services are primarily for members, but others will be assisted.

**Approval Date:** 7/84

**Latest Information Date:** 1/86

**Index Terms:** Arts resources; Fine arts; Arts and crafts movement; Exhibitions.

## 60

**Art Administrators of New Jersey (AANJ)**

c/o Harry Wilson
Art Department Chairman
Summit High School
Summit, NJ 07971
  Tel.: (201) 273-1494       PUB69-20350

AANJ is an association of between thirty and sixty school art administrators, directors, college art professors, and supervisors. Membership is available to all certified art education supervisory personnel.

**Areas of Interest:** Administration of the arts, including visual arts, architecture, landscape design, media arts, indigenous and folk arts, crafts, and design arts; art therapy; teacher training; curriculum design; museum programs.

**Information Services:** Provides advisory, consulting, reference, current-awareness, and reproduction services and information on research in progress; evaluates and analyzes data; conducts seminars and workshops; provides speakers; distributes data compilations; makes referrals to other sources of information. Services are available at cost to the membership. AANJ's facilities are accessible to the handicapped.

**Contact:** Harry Wilson, Chairman

**Approval Date:** 1/84

**Latest Information Date:** 1/86

**Index Terms:** Arts resources; Art management; Visual arts; Architecture; Landscaping; Media arts; Folk art; Handicrafts; Design; Art therapy; Teacher training; Curriculum design; Museum programs; Handicapped arts services.

## 61

**Artists Foundation, Inc.**

110 Broad St.
Boston, MA 02110
  Tel.: (617) 482-8100       PUB69-20211

A public, nonprofit organization partially funded by grants from federal, state, and local government agencies and private foundations and corporations, the Foundation awards fellowships to practicing Massachusetts artists and administers an artists in residence program for schools and cultural institutions, an artists services program, and a research and publication program. It participates in international conferences, conducts cooperative projects with foreign groups, sponsors performances and exhibits abroad, and, in keeping with its interest in more foreign involvement, is currently planning future international projects.

**Areas of Interest:** Integration of artists' work into school curricula and community environments; conversion of commercial property into living and working spaces for artists and market demand for such conversions; business, legal, and marketing information for artists working in such fields as painting, printmaking, sculpture, photography, poetry, fiction, drama, dance, crafts, music composition, television, and film.

**Publications:** Books, project reports, curricula and teaching materials, directories. A publications list is available.

**Information Services:** Answers inquiries; provides advisory services; evaluates and analyzes data; conducts seminars and workshops; provides speakers; distributes publications; makes referrals to other sources of information. Except for workshops and publications, services are free and all are available to anyone.

**Contact:** Mr. Ron P. Rothman, Executive Director

**Approval Date:** 1/84

**Latest Information Date:** 1/86

**Index Terms:** Arts resources; Artists; Professional development; Artists-in-residence; Artists-as-teachers; Curriculum design; Educational programs; Dance; Music; Teacher training; Literature (fine arts); Performance art; Visual arts; Comprehensive art education; Handicrafts; Sculpture; Photography; Poetry; Drama; Video art; Motion pictures; Lecturers; International arts activities.

## 62

### Arts and Business Council, Inc. (ABC)

130 East 40th St.
New York, NY 10016
Tel.: (212) 683-5555      PUB69-18437

Partially funded by the National Endowment for the Arts, the New York State Council on the Arts, and the Rockefeller Foundation, ABC is an independent, nonprofit organization composed of seventy corporations and an equal number of arts organizations that exists to promote understanding and communication between the arts and business. It creates working situations and programs that provide the arts with needed support from business and gives business access to the public through the arts. Ongoing programs include the Business Volunteers for the Arts, a technical assistance program giving management aid.

**Areas of Interest:** New trends in the arts; role of the arts in corporate public relations and marketing; role of corporations and corporate executives in support of the arts and arts projects; corporate involvement in the community; proposal and program development; arts management; evaluation and administration of nonprofit organizations.

**Publications:** *Winterfare* (annual compilation of arts organizations and their programs); annual report (documents ABC activities in the previous year).

**Information Services:** Answers inquiries; provides advisory, reference, and literature-searching services; conducts seminars and workshops; trains corporate executives to serve as volunteer consultants to arts organizations; distributes publications; makes referrals to other sources of information. Services are available free to all nonprofit, tax-exempt, and incorporated arts organizations.

**Approval Date:** 3/85

**Latest Information Date:** 3/85

**Index Terms:** Corporations; Art patronage; Cultural activities; Community art projects; Art management; Cultural organizations; Arts centers; Financial support; Technical assistance; Performing arts; Festivals; Motion pictures; Nonprofit organizations; Museums (institutions); Visual arts; Volunteer training; Arts.

## 63

### Arts Carousel/Arts with the Handicapped Foundation

Box 342, Station P
Toronto, Ontario, CANADA M5S 2S8    PUB69-21077

**Areas of Interest:** Improvement in the quality of life for individuals with handicaps through visual arts, drama, and creative writing.

**Publications:** Newsletter; resource materials.

**Information Services:** Answers inquiries; conducts seminars and workshops; distributes publications; makes referrals to other sources of information. Fees, if any, are based on the individual's ability to pay. Services are available chiefly to the physically handicapped, but helping agencies and the general public are also served.

**Contact:** Mr. Michael Seary

**Approval Date:** 10/84

**Latest Information Date:** 10/84

**Index Terms:** Arts resources; Art therapy.

## 64

### Arts Center of the Ozarks (ACO)

P.O. Box 725
Springdale, AR 72765
Tel.: (501) 751-5441      PUB69-20566

**Location:** 216 West Grove St.

A nonprofit, community-level arts organization partially funded by the Arkansas Arts Council and the National Endowment for the Arts, ACO provides quality arts education and entertainment for northwest Arkansas communities, offering opportunities for creative expression in theater, music, visual arts and crafts, and dance.

**Areas of Interest:** Theater; music; visual arts and crafts; dance.

**Holdings:** Extensive costume collection; music library; theater library.

**Publications:** *The Callboard* (monthly newsletter); *Calendar of Events* (brochure).

**Information Services:** Answers inquiries; provides advisory services; conducts educational seminars and workshops in the areas above; provides entertainment; lends materials; makes referrals to other sources of information; permits on-site use of collections. Services are available to anyone; some may be provided for a fee.

**Approval Date:** 11/84

**Latest Information Date:** 1/86

**Index Terms:** Arts centers; Arts resources; Theater; Music; Visual arts; Arts and crafts movement; Dance; Artistic expression; Arkansas.

---

### 65

**Association of College, University and Community Arts Administrators (ACUCAA)**

6225 University Ave.
Madison, WI 53705-1099
Tel.: (608) 233-7400                 PUB69-19920

ACUCAA is an organization of 950 members, most of whom present performing arts events in some form or fashion, including university concert series, festivals, community arts agencies, civic centers, historic theaters, and a variety of other groups. Membership is available to organizations abroad.

**Areas of Interest:** Arts administration and financial management, including leadership development, marketing the arts, computer selection and implementation, time management, personnel management, fund raising, presenting the performing arts, marketing the community arts agency, job stress and burnout, improving brochure and graphic design, negotiating and contracting, group sales, and consumer behavior.

**Holdings:** National Data Base includes type of organization, programming activity, audiences served, facility(ies), sources of revenue, staff, computer uses, and more.

**Publications:** Books, directories, bibliographies, journal articles, project reports, reprints. A price list is available.

**Information Services:** Answers inquiries; provides advisory, consulting, and reference services and information on research in progress; conducts seminars and workshops; provides speakers; distributes publications in the United States and abroad; makes referrals to other sources of information. Services may be subject to a fee and are available to anyone.

**Contact:** Mr. R. William Mitchell, Assistant Director

**Approval Date:** 8/85

**Latest Information Date:** 8/85

**Index Terms:** Art management; Financial management; Fund raising; Community art projects; Performing arts; Touring programs; Professional development; Information services; Art resources; Marketing; Lecturers; Promoting; Personnel management; Job stress; Leadership development; Graphic arts; Negotiations; Contracts; Arts centers; Computers.

---

### 66

**Atlanta Art Papers, Inc.**

P.O. Box 77348
Atlanta, GA 30357
Tel.: (404) 885-1273                 PUB69-20241

**Location:** 972 Peachtree St., Suite 214

Atlanta Art Papers, Inc. promotes and presents the art and artists of the city, state, and region, and educates the general public regarding contemporary art issues and activities.

**Areas of Interest:** Contemporary arts in the Southeast, with an emphasis on visual arts, but including architecture, crafts, dance, design arts, film, indigenous and folk arts, music, performance art, and theater; schedules of exhibits, performances, screenings, and exhibitions in the region; employment opportunities, studio space, services, publications, workshops, classes, and symposia available to the Southeastern arts community; legal aspects of the arts; arts management; arts marketing.

**Holdings:** Library of arts magazines and books.

**Publications:** *Art Papers* (bimonthly; also available on recordings for the blind and in microfiche from Bell & Howell Co., Old Mansfield Rd., Wooster, OH 44691); catalogs from selected regional arts institutions.

**Information Services:** Answers inquiries; provides advisory, consulting, and video documentation services; conducts seminars and workshops; distributes publications; provides speakers; makes referrals to other sources of information; permits on-site use of collections. Services are available to artists and nonprofit arts organizations at a reduced fee. Facilities of Atlanta Art Papers, Inc. that are available to artists and nonprofit arts organizations for a fee as time permits include a Lanier EZ-1 microprocessor, Racal Vadic communications modem, office equipment, light table and layout equipment, portable light table, meeting room with meeting table, its mailing list, a bulk rate permit, and portable tape recorders.

**Contact:** Xenia Zed, Editor

**Approval Date:** 1/84

**Latest Information Date:** 1/86

**Index Terms:** Arts resources; Contemporary art; Southeastern United States; Dance; Music; Folk art; Performance art; Visual arts; Architecture; Handicrafts; Design; Museum programs; Art management; Motion pictures; Theater; Cultural exhibitions; Employment opportunities; Artists studios; Workshops; Publications; Education; Legal aspects; Art marketing; Lecturers; Handicapped arts services.

---

**67**

## Box Office Management International (BOMI)

c/o Ms. Patricia Spira, Executive Director
500 East 77th St., Room 1925
New York, NY 10021
Tel.: (212) 570-1099          PUB69-19398

A nonprofit, worldwide professional association of box office managers, financial directors, controllers, and marketing and systems directors in the performing arts and sports. BOMI serves as a resource center addressing the mutual concerns of control and service in the ticket industry. It is dedicated to the advancement of operations, marketing, and research in the field of box office management.

**Areas of Interest:** Manual and computerized ticketing sales, systems, and controls.

**Publications:** *BOMI Newsletter* (bimonthly); brochures.

**Information Services:** Answers inquiries; provides advisory, consulting, and reference services and information on R&D in progress; evaluates and analyzes data; conducts seminars and workshops; distributes publications and data compilations; makes referrals to other sources of information; publicizes job opportunities in the ticketing field. Answers to brief inquiries and referrals are provided free to anyone; other services are available to nonmembers on a fee basis.

**Approval Date:** 2/85

**Latest Information Date:** 2/85

**Index Terms:** Performing arts; Sports; Ticket sales; Computer applications; Employment opportunities; Systems management; Sales management.

---

**68**

## Caldwell Arts Council

601 College Ave. SW.
Lenoir, NC 28645
Tel.: (704) 754-2486          PUB69-21074

Sponsored by state and local government agencies and private sources, the Council supports the arts in Caldwell County. Activities include gallery exhibits; a fall festival of the arts, folk arts, and performing arts; summer classes for children; an Artists-in-the-Schools program; and classes and workshops for adults and children in arts, crafts, and music. International activities include the sponsorship of foreign artists in local exhibitions and performances.

**Areas of Interest:** Dance; music; theater; opera and music theater; indigenous and folk arts; performing arts; visual arts; architecture; crafts; special education; teacher training; historic preservation; arts management; fund raising.

**Holdings:** The Lelia Judson Tuttle Collection of fine arts and artifacts of pre-Maoist China includes handmade clothing, jewelry, fans, paintings on silk and pottery, photographs, scrolls, tapestries, carvings, figurines, vases, dishes, boxes, bottles, dolls, and other articles in rare woods, brass, ivory, and porcelain.

**Publications:** *Area Arts Calendar* (monthly); *The Folk Art File* (2d ed., 1983; a resource book of area artists, folk artists, and crafts people); invitations to gallery exhibits and receptions (monthly).

**Information Services:** Answers inquiries; provides advisory, reference, and reproduction services, conducts workshops; lends materials; distributes publications; makes referrals to other sources of information; permits on-site use of collection. Publications and loans of materials are available to the membership, which is open to anyone for a fee. Workshops and reproduction services are available to anyone for a fee. Other services are free and available to anyone. Facilities of the Council are accessible to the handicapped. In addition, special exhibits and arts workshops are designed for the handicapped.

**Contact:** Ms. Liza Plaster, Executive Director

**Approval Date:** 10/84

**Latest Information Date:** 1/86

**Index Terms:** Arts resources; Chinese art; Dance; Music; Theater; Teacher training; Operas; Music theater; Folk art; Literature (fine arts); Historic preservation; Special education; Performing arts; Visual arts; Architecture; Crafts; Art management; Fund raising.

## 69

### California Institute of the Arts
### Library

24700 McBean Parkway
Valencia, CA 91355
Tel.: (805) 255-1050                   PUB69-15008

**Areas of Interest:** The arts, including the fine arts, design, dance, theater, music, film/video, and photography.

**Holdings:** 63,827 books; 6,777 bound journals; 543 current subscriptions; 11,100 scores; 805 films; 8,240 exhibition catalogs; 12,131 recordings; 68,452 slides; 6,559 microfilms; 482 video tapes; access to DIALOG data bases.

**Information Services:** Answers inquiries; provides reference and copying services; makes interlibrary loans; makes referrals to other sources of information; permits on-site use of collections. Services are free to members of Total Interlibrary Exchange (a local multitype library cooperative); others are charged for copying services. Services are primarily for faculty, students, and staff.

**Approval Date:** 10/85

**Latest Information Date:** 10/85

**Index Terms:** Arts; Art education; Dance; Music; Photography; Video tapes; Fine arts; Performing arts; Motion pictures; Cinematography; Design; Videodiscs; OCLC; Libraries.

## 70

### Center for Arts Information

625 Broadway
New York, NY 10012
Tel.: (212) 677-7548                   PUB69-17811

Funded by the National Endowment for the Arts, the New York State Council on the Arts, foundations, corporations, and individuals, the Center serves as a clearinghouse and referral service for nonprofit arts on sources of services and funds for arts organizations and artists.

**Areas of Interest:** Resource information for performing and visual arts, architecture, film, video, literature, museums, and historical societies; fund raising

for the arts; arts administration and programming; location of available arts services; guidelines and eligibility for state and federal grants.

**Holdings:** Over 5,500 reference books, pamphlets, directories, reports, and files; over 300 periodical titles; 500 service and funding agency files; 250 subject files.

**Publications:** Directories and guides, including *Artist Colonies, Film Service Profiles, International Cultural Exchange, Jobs in the Arts and Arts Administration, Money for Artists, New York City Arts Funding Guide, A Quick Guide to Loans and Emergency Funds, Video Service Profiles;* and *Wherewithal: A Guide to Resources for Museums and Historical Societies in New York State;* management aids; memos. A publications price list is available.

**Information Services:** Answers inquiries; provides advisory, consulting, reference, literature-searching, abstracting, and indexing services; provides information on R&D in progress; distributes publications; makes referrals to other sources of information; permits on-site use of collections. Fees are charged for some services.

**Approval Date:** 3/84

**Latest Information Date:** 1/86

**Index Terms:** Information services; Consulting services; Information resources; Performing arts; Visual arts; Architecture; Motion pictures; Video art; Fund raising; Nonprofit organizations; Literature (fine arts); Arts; Directories; Historical societies; Art management; Information analysis centers; Federal aid programs; New York (State); Museums (institutions).

## 71

### College Art Association of America (CAA)

149 Madison Ave.
New York, NY 10016
Tel.: (212) 889-2113                   PUB69-20233

CAA is a membership organization comprising scholars, teachers, artists, critics, museum curators and administrators, art dealers, collectors, art and slide librarians, and students.

**Areas of Interest:** Teaching and practice of art and art history

**Publications:** *The Art Bulletin* and *Art Journal* (both quarterly); *CAA Newsletter;* listings of position vacancies at colleges, universities, museums, community art center, galleries, art publishers, etc.

**Information Services:** Answers inquiries; provides a job placement service; conducts annual meetings; distributes publications. Publications are provided to nonmembers for a fee, but listings of position vacancies are available to individuals only.

**Contact:** Ms. Minerva Navarrete, Business Manager

**Approval Date:** 1/84

**Latest Information Date:** 1/86

**Index Terms:** Art resources; Art education; Visual arts; Art history.

## 72

### Colorado Springs Fine Arts Center

30 West Dale St.
Colorado Springs, CO 80903
Tel.: (303) 634-5581                PUB69-21072

The Center has a membership of 3,000 individuals and businesses within the community. Membership is open and solicited from the general public. Activities include art exhibitions, three film series, art classes for children and adults, performing arts programs, community weekend arts programs, and art lectures. International activities include mounting exhibits with international sources and there are plans to mount tours for European institutions consisting of Spanish colonial and Native American art.

**Areas of Interest:** Dance; music; theater; media arts; performing arts; visual arts; special education; comprehensive arts education; fund raising; museum programs.

**Holdings:** Spanish colonial folk art and American Indian art; particularly Southwest tribes; fine arts collection of nineteenth- and twentieth-century American art; art library of about nineteen thousand volumes.

**Publications:** Scholarly publications based primarily on collections; exhibition gallery sheets and catalogs.

**Information Services:** Answers inquiries; provides reference services; conducts seminars and workshops; lends materials; permits on-site use of collections. Services are free and available to qualified individuals. Facilities of the Center, including an art gallery, a museum, an in-house theater, and a library, are accessible to the handicapped, with appropriate ramps, elevators, and modifications to restrooms and drinking fountains. In addition, a permanent Tactile Gallery exhibits rotating displays for the blind and visually impaired, complete with braille labels.

**Contact:** Mr. Paul M. Piazza, Director

**Approval Date:** 10/84

**Latest Information Date:** 1/86

**Index Terms:** Arts resources; Dance; Music; Theater; Media arts; Historic preservation; Performing arts; Visual arts; Comprehensive arts education; Museum programs; Fund raising; American Indian art; Spanish colonial art.

## 73

### Design International

P.O. Box 1803
Ross, CA 94957
Tel.: (415) 457-8596                PUB69-19883

Partially funded through a grant from the National Endowment for the Arts, Design International is an alliance of designers, students, and others involved in design and its application seeking to educate the profession and the public in a humanistic approach to the art and appreciation of design.

**Areas of Interest:** Design arts, including architecture, ceramics, enameling, mosaic, computer graphics, costume design, fashion design, fiber art, film animation, glass art, graphic design, illustration, industrial design, interior design and space planning, jewelry design, landscape architecture, painting, paper art and printmaking, photography, sculpture, film and theatrical set design, textile design, and wearable art.

**Holdings:** Slides of competition entrants in twenty-one categories of design, with computerized information on the collection.

**Publications:** Quarterly journal; *Annual Compendium* of prize-winning designs; seminar papers.

**Information Services:** Conducts design seminars and forums in the United States and abroad; distributes publications internationally. Services are available to anyone and may be provided for a fee.

**Contact:** Connie Carnell, Executive Director

**Approval Date:** 5/84

**Latest Information Date:** 1/86

**Index Terms:** Women designers; Architecture; Enamels; Mosaics; Fashion design; Textile arts; Fine arts; Paintings; Art glass; Graphic design; Computer graphics; Industrial design; Interior design; Jewelry design; Landscaping; Printmakers; Photography; Sculpture; Metal working; Competition; Grants; Arts resources.

## Driftwood Valley Arts Council (DVAC)

425 5th St.
Columbus, IN 47201
Tel.: (812) 379-4192        PUB69-20343

DVAC serves as a private nonprofit organization assisting the community in enjoying a balanced program of cultural activities through information services, clerical assistance, research services, grantsmanship, coordination and scheduling services, ticket sales, administrative services, and advocacy and funding assistance. Membership comprises individuals and both profit and nonprofit organizations interested in or associated with artistic, cultural, educational, humanitarian, or scientific activities in Bartholomew County and the surrounding region.

**Areas of Interest:** Artistic and cultural activities in Bartholomew County and the surrounding region, including dance, music, theater, indigenous and folk arts, landscape design, visual arts, architecture, design arts, crafts, literature, and historic preservation; teacher training; museum programs; arts management; fund raising.

**Holdings:** Library of about sixty-five volumes of arts management resource material, national directories, and other items; publications of member organizations and other newsletters, bulletins, etc.

**Publications:** *Arts News* (monthly newsletter).

**Information Services:** Local artists are offered technical assistance, grant writing seminars, a clearinghouse for dates, and distribution of a monthly cultural calendar and the newsletter. DVAC staff and volunteers will also answer questions and make referrals to other sources of information in response to inquiries from the public on local cultural activities, organizations, and sites. The Council's facilities are accessible to the handicapped.

**Contact:** Mrs. Sandra Springstun, Executive Director

**Approval Date:** 11/84

**Latest Information Date:** 1/86

**Index Terms:** Arts resources; Cultural activities; Dance; Music; Theater; Folk art; Landscaping; Visual arts; Architecture; Design; Handicrafts; Literature (fine arts); Historic preservation; Teacher training; Museum programs; Art management; Fund raising; International arts activities; Handicapped arts services.

## Federated Art Associations of New Jersey, Inc.

720 Lawrence Ave.
Westfield, NJ 07090
Tel.: (201) 232-7623        PUB69-19942

Federated Art Associations of New Jersey consists of sixty member groups united to provide communication and exchange of ideas among arts organizations. Membership is open to all incorporated, nonprofit visual arts groups. Individuals and ineligible groups may join with full privileges except for voting and holding office.

**Areas of Interest:** Visual arts; media arts; arts administration and management, including methods of incorporation and achieving tax-exempt status; arts education; legislation affecting artists; identification of visual artists and visual arts organizations in New Jersey; identification of qualified visual arts judges and jurors or visual arts competitions; identification of radio and television stations, newspapers, and periodicals in New Jersey interested in visual arts; rural and urban beautification.

**Publications:** *Views* (quarterly); *Directory of Visual Art Organizations in New Jersey* (1983 and 1984); *Judge and Jury Selector* (updated periodically); project reports.

**Information Services:** Provides advisory, consulting, and reference services; conducts seminars, art exhibits, panel discussions, art demonstrations, and slide programs; distributes publications. Some services are free or offered at reduced cost to members. Facilities are accessible to the handicapped.

**Contact:** Mrs. Jane Whipple Green, Director

**Approval Date:** 1/84

**Latest Information Date:** 1/86

**Index Terms:** Visual arts; Media arts; Art management; Art education; Art and society; Art associations; International arts activities; Handicapped arts services; Legislation; Tax exemption; Beautification; Communication; New Jersey; Arts resources.

## Foundation for the Extension and Development of the American Professional Theatre (FEDAPT)

165 West 46th St., Suite 310
New York, NY 10036
Tel.: (212) 869-9690        PUB69-18087

FEDAPT is a national not-for-profit service agency offering comprehensive arts management expertise and one-on-one consultancies, workshops, seminars, and publications to professional theaters, dance companies, and performing arts centers throughout the country.

**Areas of Interest:** Board development, marketing, and fund raising assistance for theaters, dance companies, and performing arts centers.

**Publications:** Five publications on arts management, board development, etc.

**Information Services:** Answers inquiries; provides advisory, consulting, and reference services; conducts seminars and workshops; distributes publications; makes referrals to other sources of information. Services are available at a fee to administrators, managers, students, and others.

**Approval Date:** 9/84

**Latest Information Date:** 1/86

**Index Terms:** Performing arts; Dance; Counseling; Theater; Information services; Art management; Theater as a profession; Actors; Professional associations.

## 77

### Grand Center Association

3615 Grandel Square
St. Louis, MO 63108
Tel.: (314) 533-0900          PUB69-20342

Funded in part by federal, state, and local government agencies and private organizations, the Association is a nonprofit affiliate of St. Louis's City Center Redevelopment Corporation. It was founded to ensure that Grand Center, an eight-block National Historic District focused on Grand Avenue between Delmar Boulevard and Lindell Boulevard, becomes the cultural and entertainment heart of the St. Louis metropolitan area through the planning, promotion, and stimulation of a wide variety of entertainment and cultural activity in the area.

**Areas of Interest:** Classical and popular arts, including music, theater, visual arts, architecture, and design arts; historic preservation and renovation; the continuous building of audiences for quality artistic endeavors in renovated urban areas; arts management; fund raising.

**Information Services:** Answers inquiries; provides advisory, consulting, and reproduction services; distributes audiovisual materials for the use of elemen-

tary and secondary students and teachers. Services are available to anyone at cost.

**Contact:** Ms. Robin Greenberg, Associate Director or Thom Digman, Executive Director

**Approval Date:** 11/84

**Latest Information Date:** 1/86

**Index Terms:** Arts resources; Cultural activities; Music; Theater; Visual arts; Architecture; Design; Historic preservation; Renovation; Art management; Fund raising.

## 78

### Indian Arts and Crafts Association (IACA)

P.O. Box 40013
Albuquerque, NM 87196
Tel.: (505) 265-9149          PUB69-20563

**Location:** 4215 Lead St. SE.

A national nonprofit trade organization of Native American craft persons, collectors, museums, traders, and dealers, IACA seeks to protect, preserve, and promote handmade authentic Native American creations.

**Areas of Interest:** Native American crafts; southwestern Indian jewelry and turquoise; Kachina dolls; Navajo weaving; pottery.

**Holdings:** Information on the areas above.

**Publications:** Bimonthly newsletter; directories, technical reports, brochures on such subjects as turquoise, weaving, Kachina dolls, and pottery.

**Information Services:** Answers inquiries; provides reference and current-awareness services; conducts seminars and workshops; conducts wholesale markets for retailers only, twice a year (spring—Denver, CO; fall—Scottsdale, AZ); makes referrals to other sources of information. Services are primarily for members and buyers, but others will be assisted. Fees may be charged for services.

**Approval Date:** 7/84

**Latest Information Date:** 1/86

**Index Terms:** Arts resources; American Indian crafts; American Indian art; Arts and crafts movement; Jewelry, Turquoise; Kachinas; Weaving; Pottery; Trade associations.

**79**

### International Association of Auditorium Managers (IAAM)

500 North Michigan Ave., Suite 1400
Chicago, IL 60611
  Tel.: (312) 661-1700        PUB69-4438

**Areas of Interest:** Auditorium, arena, stadium, and coliseum management, and including convention complexes, exhibition halls, performing arts centers, etc.

**Holdings:** Statistical compendium of public assembly facilities; small collection of books.

**Publications:** *Auditorium News* (monthly); membership directory, material on career opportunities, advertising for the trade.

**Information Services:** Answers inquiries; conducts auditorium management seminar, industrial trade show and conference, and seven regional meetings. Services are provided at cost to some users and free to others.

**Approval Date:** 8/84

**Latest Information Date:** 1/86

**Index Terms:** Professional associations; Stadiums; Auditorium administration; Auditoriums; Theaters; Management development; Career opportunities; Career development; Trade conferences; Arenas; Convention facilities; Performing arts centers.

**80**

### Library of Congress
### American Folklife Center
### Archive of Folk Culture

10 First St. SE.
Washington, DC 20540
  Tel.: (202) 287-5510        PUB69-7000

Hours: 8:30 a.m. – 5 p.m., Mon. – Fri.; closed Sat., Sun., and holidays.

**Areas of Interest:** Folk music, folklore, and ethnomusicology worldwide, with concentration on the United States; U.S. oral history.

**Holdings:** About 125,000 specimens of folk music and folklore on field-recorded cylinders, discs, wires, and tapes (80 percent from the United States, 60 percent English-language traditions); about 50,000 pages of manuscript and typescript materials relating to folk music, folklore, oral history, and other subjects.

**Publications:** Series of documentary recordings of folk music and folklore (available from the Library's Recording Laboratory); over 175 free reference and finding aids on these subjects (list available).

**Information Services:** Answers inquiries; provides reference services; makes referrals. Reading room and listening facilities (some listening by appointment) are available. The Archive participates in an intern program.

**Approval Date:** 2/84

**Latest Information Date:** 1/86

**Index Terms:** Folklore; Folk music; Ethnomusicology; Oral history; Libraries; Folk culture.

**81**

### Michigan Arts Forum

2735 West Warren St.
Detroit, MI 48208
  Tel.: (313) 898-6340        PUB69-20202

A coordinating council for seventy-five statewide arts support organizations, the Forum serves as an advocate for the arts on a statewide basis and encourages cooperation among its member organizations.

**Areas of Interest:** Support of the arts in Michigan; arts management.

**Publications:** Newsletter; directories.

**Information Services:** Answers inquiries; distributes its newsletter; provides speakers. Services may be subject to a fee and are available to anyone.

**Contact:** Shirley Harbin, President

**Approval Date:** 1/84

**Latest Information Date:** 1/86

**Index Terms:** Arts resources; Michigan; Arts management; Art commissions; State encouragement of the arts.

**82**

### Mid Atlantic States Arts Consortium

11 East Chase St., Suite 1-A
Baltimore, MD 21202
  Tel.: (301) 539-6656        PUB69-19931

Sponsored by the official state arts councils in Delaware, the District of Columbia, Maryland, New Jersey, New York, Pennsylvania, Virginia, and West Virginia, the Consortium assists in the development of the arts and provides support to artists, arts organizations, and arts institutions in the eight-state area. Activities include a performing arts touring program and a computerized arts information system.

**Areas of Interest:** Dance; music; theater; opera and music theater; indigenous and folk arts; performance art; visual arts; crafts; multidisciplinary programs.

**Holdings:** Arts resource directories; computerized mailing lists.

**Information Services:** Answers inquiries; provides mailing lists and arts resource directories to the public at cost for nonprofit uses.

**Contact:** Executive Director

**Approval Date:** 4/84

**Latest Information Date:** 1/86

**Index Terms:** Dance; Music; Theater; Operas; Music theater; Folk art; Performance art; Visual arts; Handicrafts; Touring programs; International arts activities; Information systems; Computerized mailing list; Mid-Atlantic United States; Arts resources.

## 83

### Montana Institute of the Arts Foundation

P.O. Box 1456
Billings, MT 59103
Tel.: (406) 245-3688             PUB69-20509

**Location:** 2405 Montana Ave.

A nonprofit organization, the Foundation offers recreational, educational, and informational services to individual artists.

**Areas of Interest:** Arts; crafts; writers; photographers; fiber arts; weavers.

**Holdings:** Collection of items done by Montana painters and other artists.

**Publications:** *Montana Arts* (magazine issued three times a year).

**Information Services:** Answers inquiries; conducts seminars, workshops, and an arts festival; makes referrals to other sources of information. Information services are provided free to anyone; other services are provided for a membership fee.

**Approval Date:** 10/84

**Latest Information Date:** 1/86

**Index Terms:** Arts resources; Handicrafts; Writers; Photographers; Weaving; Montana; Paintings.

## 84

### Museum of Contemporary Art

237 East Ontario St.
Chicago, IL 60611
Tel.: (312) 280-2660             PUB69-16706

A nonprofit organization, the Museum acts as an international forum for contemporary and modern visual arts.

**Areas of Interest:** Contemporary and modern visual art and art performances.

**Holdings:** Permanent collection of twentieth-century works of art; artists' book collection; slide files of Chicago artists; reference library of printed material, videotapes and audiotapes; photography archives, slides, and MCA exhibition archives.

**Publications:** Exhibition catalogs.

**Information Services:** Displays exhibitions of twentieth-century American and international art in all media, including works by Chicago artists; conducts lectures, gallery talks, symposia, film showings, an educational outreach program, and docent, senior citizen outreach, volunteer, and intern programs; maintains a Museum store; permits on-site use of collection.

**Contact:** Lisa Skolnik, Director of Public Relations

**Approval Date:** 11/85

**Latest Information Date:** 11/85

**Index Terms:** Museums (institutions); Modern arts; Visual arts; Contemporary art; Arts resources.

## 85

### National Assembly of Local Arts Agencies (NALAA)

1785 Massachusetts Ave. NW., Suite 413
Washington, DC 20036
Tel.: (202) 483-8670             PUB69-19888

An organization of 540 members that is partially funded by the National Endowment for the Arts, NALAA promotes the causes of local arts agencies through building national and statewide advocacy networks, participation in national policy committees and panels whose work impacts local arts groups, advocacy activities before the U.S. Congress, and a variety of information services and training programs.

**Areas of Interest:** Information useful to the administration, funding, and networking of community-based arts organizations.

**Publications:** Monthly bulletin; *Connections* (quarterly newsletter); reviews, standards, directory, FYI sheets.

**Information Services:** Answers inquiries; provides reference services and information on research in progress; analyzes data; conducts seminars and workshops; distributes publications; makes referrals to other sources of information. Services are available for a fee to nonmembers and free or at a reduced fee to members.

**Contact:** Ms. Elizabeth B. Adams, Program Director

**Approval Date:** 4/85

**Latest Information Date:** 4/85

**Index Terms:** Arts resources; Professional associations; Arts centers; Art management; Financial support; Community/local involvement; Community/local service programs; Information services.

## 86

**National Association for Campus Activities (NACA)**

P.O. Box 6828
Columbia, SC 29260
  Tel.: (803) 782-7121      PUB69-20216

**Location:** 3700 Forest Dr.

NACA is an association of higher education institutions that provides cocurricular activities for the educational enrichment of their campus communities, and persons and businesses selling, marketing, or promoting services and products necessary for such activities. It provides assistance for member institutions to establish and produce quality campus activities programming by providing education, information, and resources for students and administrators and to facilitate cooperative consumer efficiency and marketplace effectiveness.

**Areas of Interest:** Campus activities programming; ethics and standards for administrators of campus activities programming; arts management.

**Holdings:** Computerized membership list generating mailing labels.

**Publications:** *Campus Activities Programming* (nine issues a year); *Profile* (monthly newsletter containing listings for jobs in student affairs, campus programming, residence life, and related industries); *NACA School Directory* (annual); *Associate Member Directory/Entertainment Roster* (semiannual).

**Information Services:** Provides reference services; conducts seminars, workshops, and conferences; distributes publications and mailing labels; makes referrals to other sources of information. Services are available at cost to members.

**Contact:** Mr. Steve Slagle, Executive Director

**Approval Date:** 1/84

**Latest Information Date:** 1/86

**Index Terms:** Campuses; Arts resources; Cultural activities; Cultural programs; Dance; Music; Theater; Art management; Ethics; Standards; Computerized mailing list.

## 87

**National Council on the Aging, Inc. (NCOA)**
**National Center on Arts and the Aging**

600 Maryland Ave. SW., West Wing 100
Washington, DC 20024
  Tel.: (202) 479-1200 Ext. 387     PUB69-20209

Aided by a grant from the National Endowment for the Arts, the Center seeks to make the arts more accessible to older citizens.

**Areas of Interest:** Participation of older Americans in the arts, including dance, music, theater, indigenous and folk arts, performance art, visual arts, and crafts; quality arts programs by and for older Americans; contributions of older persons to the nation's cultural heritage; human development and life enrichment through the arts; cooperative efforts between the arts and aging fields; comprehensive arts education; special education; music, dance, and art therapy; museum programs; arts management; fund raising; funding sources.

**Holdings:** Literature in the above areas.

**Publications:** Program profiles, handbooks, and other materials. A publications price list is available.

**Information Services:** Answers inquiries; provides advisory, consulting, reference, current-awareness services and information on research in progress; evaluates and analyzes data; conducts seminars and workshops; distributes publications; makes referrals to other sources of information; Permits on-site use of collection. Services are available to anyone; some are subject to a fee.

**Contact:** Ms. Priscilla B. McCutcheon, Director

**Approval Date:** 1/84

**Latest Information Date:** 1/86

**Index Terms:** Arts resources; Arts and the aged; Dance; Music; Theater; Folk art; Special education; Musicotherapy; Performance art; Comprehensive art education; Handicrafts; Museum programs; Dance therapy; Art management; Fund raising; Visual arts; Cultural heritage.

## 88

### National Foundation for Advancement in the Arts (NFAA)

100 North Biscayne Blvd.
Miami, FL 33132
　Tel.: (305) 371-9470　　　　　　　PUB69-19973

A privately funded organization, NFAA awards cash grants to young artists in their formative years through various structured programs and sponsors the Arts Recognition and Talent Search (ARTS), which provides cash awards and scholarships for high school seniors.

**Areas of Interest:** Young artists active in dance, music, theater, writing, and the visual arts.

**Publications:** Newsletter; annual reports; catalogs of programs and exhibits.

**Information Services:** Answers inquiries; provides advisory services; conducts seminars and workshops; distributes publications; makes referrals to other sources of information. NFAA's Scholarship List Service provides the names of all registrants to the arts program to colleges and universities nationally. Facilities of NFAA are accessible to the handicapped.

**Contact:** Dr. Grant Beglarian, President

**Approval Date:** 1/84

**Latest Information Date:** 1/86

**Index Terms:** Dance; Music; Theater; Literature (fine arts); Visual arts; Young artists; Grants; Handicapped arts services; Arts resources.

## 89

### National Gallery of Art
### Center for Advanced Study in the Visual Arts

6th St. and Constitution Ave. NW.
Washington, DC 20565
　Tel.: (202) 842-6480　　　　　　　PUB69-20210

The Center promotes the study of the history, theory, and criticism of art, architecture, and urbanism from a variety of approaches by historians, critics, and theorists of art, as well as by scholars in related disciplines of the humanities and social sciences. Funded by private foundations, its fellowship programs bring together a community of scholars from the United States and abroad to study the developed visual arts of the world in all historical periods. The Center participates in international conferences and conducts cooperative projects with foreign groups.

**Areas of Interest:** History, theory, and criticism of the visual arts, including painting, sculpture, architecture, landscape architecture, urbanism, graphics, film, photography, decorative arts, and industrial design; critical studies leading to the formation of esthetic theories.

**Holdings:** The Center has the support and use of the National Gallery of Art's collections and library.

**Publications:** *Research Reports* and *Sponsored Research* (both annual); seminar papers.

**Information Services:** Conducts seminars, shop talks, colloquia, lectures, and symposia for specialists in specific fields. The Center's publications are available for sale through the publications office of the National Gallery of Art. The Center's facilities are accessible to the handicapped.

**Contact:** Henry A. Millon, Dean

**Approval Date:** 2/84

**Latest Information Date:** 1/86

**Index Terms:** Arts resources; Visual arts; History; Criticism; Painting; Sculpture; Architecture; Landscape architecture; Urban research; Graphic arts; Motion pictures; Photography; Decorative art; Industrial design; Historic preservation; Fellowships; International arts activities; Handicapped arts services.

## 90

### National Guild of Community Schools of the Arts, Inc.

P.O. Box 583
Teaneck, NJ 07666
　Tel.: (201) 836-5594　　　　　　　PUB69-19891

**Location:** 545 Cedar Lane, Room 7

An association of 132 nonprofit, nondegree-granting schools and ninety individuals in the United States and Canada, the Guild acts as a central clearinghouse for information, communications, and research. Applications for membership are accepted from nonprofit, nondegree-granting arts education institutions but must be approved by a majority vote of the board based upon evaluation by its membership committee.

**Areas of Interest:** Education in dance, music, opera and music theater, drama, music therapy, performance art, visual arts, and dance therapy; educational administration; arts management; fund raising; arts education for the culturally deprived, senior citizens, inmates of prisons, and the mentally and physically handicapped; scholarship and financial aid programs in community schools of the arts.

**Publications:** *Guildnotes* and *Employment Opportunities* (both monthly); statistical reports; member profile surveys; standards for certificate programs; directories; conference papers; manuals.

**Information Services:** Answers inquiries; provides advisory, technical assistance, and reference services; evaluates and analyzes data; conducts seminars, workshops, and regional and annual meetings and conventions; distributes publications; makes referrals to other sources of information. Referral services and some technical assistance are free to anyone; other services are free to members and at cost to others. Facilities of most member schools are accessible to the handicapped and a number offer instruction to visually impaired students through braille and large-print media.

**Contact:** Ms. Lolita Mayadas, Executive Director

**Approval Date:** 4/85

**Latest Information Date:** 4/85

**Index Terms:** Arts resources; Art education; Dance; Music; Dance therapy; Art management; Handicapped arts services; Technical assistance; Educational administration; Scholarships; Financial support; Community schools.

## 91

### New England Foundation for the Arts

678 Massachusetts Ave.
Cambridge, MA 02139
Tel.: (617) 492-2914                    PUB69-17967

The Foundation is a regional consortium of the six New England state arts agencies with funding from these states as well as from the National Endowment for the Arts and private contributors. Foundation funding is directed to organizations that present performances, exhibitions, and media events to community audiences throughout the region for projects meeting specific programmatic guidelines.

**Areas of Interest:** Touring programs in the performing, visual, and media arts; regional arts research and information center; technical assistance to arts organizations.

**Holdings:** Computerized data bases available are: Arts Presenter and Performer Master Files; Visual Arts/Media Mailing List; State Arts Agencies' Mailing Lists; and Arts Facilities Directories.

**Publications:** *New England Touring Program Guide-*

lines and Rosters and *Visual Arts/Media Rental Program* (annual directories); *The Arts and the New England Economy* (2d ed., 1981); *Presenting Performances: A Handbook for Sponsors* (4th ed., 1982; a slide tape version is also available); *All in Order: Information Systems for the Arts* (1981); *Art Work: Artists in the New England Labor Market* (1983); *Arts Go To School* (1983).

**Information Services:** Answers inquiries; provides consulting and advisory services; conducts seminars and workshops; evaluates and provides arts data; sells publications and data base lists; makes referrals to other sources of information.

**Approval Date:** 3/84

**Latest Information Date:** 1/86

**Index Terms:** New England; Performing arts; Visual arts; Touring programs; Theater; Music; Dance; Operas; Grants; Financial support; Cultural organizations; Cultural administration; Personnel development.

## 92

### New York Public Library at Lincoln Center
### General Library of the Performing Arts

111 Amsterdam Ave.
New York, NY 10023
Tel.: (212) 870-1600 (Recorded announcement
                            of hours)
      (212) 870-1630 (Information)
      (212) 870-1627 (Dance and Drama Section)
      (212) 870-1625 (Music Section)
      (212) 870-1624 (Orchestra Collection)
      (212) 870-1629 (Record Section)    PUB69-16052

The New York Public Library at Lincoln Center is the "Library and Museum of the Performing Arts" of the New York Public Library.

**Areas of Interest:** Performing arts, including dance, drama, and music; theater; cinema; radio; television; circus; puppets; orchestral sets.

**Holdings:** The Dance and Drama Section has books, periodicals, current clippings, and published plays on theater history and criticism, acting, auditions, cinema, radio, television, circus, puppets, theater production, ballet, ballroom dance, ethnic dance, modern dance, dance music, and dance pedagogy. The Music Section has books on all phases of music composition, history, performance, and theory, current clippings and concert programs, reference books and periodicals, and scores of all periods and types, including folk, instrumental, musical comedy, opera, orchestral, sacred, and vocal. The Recording

Section has comedy, folk, jazz, and popular music, monologues, plays, sound effects, sound tracks and dialects, and classical repertory, as well as new and unusual music (all available for borrowing or for listening in the Library). A Special Collection of orchestral sets for nonprofessional orchestras in the New York metropolitan area is maintained (rental by annual fee).

**Information Services:** Provides ready reference; presents free programs in various performing arts categories; makes interlibrary loans through the New York State Interlibrary Loan system; provides coin-operated, self-service, quick-copy facilities; lends materials (with New York Public Library card); permits on-site use of collections. Services are available to anyone and are provided free, except for the library card, for which nonstate residents must pay a nominal fee.

**Contact:** Mr. George L. Mayer, Coordinator

**Approval Date:** 6/85

**Latest Information Date:** 6/85

**Index Terms:** Libraries; Museums (institutions); Dance; Music; Cinematography; Radio communication; Drama; Television arts; Theater; Performing arts; Puppet plays; Circus; Entertainment; Music history; Acting; Musical composition.

---

**93**

---

### New York Public Library at Lincoln Center Performing Arts Research Center (PARC)

111 Amsterdam Ave.
New York, NY 10023
  Tel.: (212) 870-1670 (Administrative Office)
     (212) 870-1657 (Dance Collection)
     (212) 870-1650 (Music Division)
     (212) 870-1663 (Rodgers and Hammerstein
         Archives of Recorded Sound)
     (212) 870-1639 (Billy Rose Theater
         Collection)    PUB69-19837

**Areas of Interest:** Performing arts, including dance, drama, and music; theater; cinema; radio; television; circus; puppets; orchestral sets.

**Holdings:** (1) The Dance Collection includes books, periodicals, manuscripts, microfilm, audiotapes, videotapes, films, clippings, scenic and costume designs, photographs, prints and drawings, programs, posters, and scrapbooks covering all types of dance, including ballet, ethnic, folk, national, modern, and social dance, and every aspect of dance, including economic, educational, historical, religious, theatrical, and therapeutic aspects. Many special collec-

tions of companies and individuals are also maintained. (2) The Music Division has books, libretti, periodicals, scores, sheet music, manuscripts, microforms, photographs, and prints of musicians (portraits only). All types of music are collected comprehensively, including American, chamber, popular, music of the dance, jazz, folk, opera, and orchestral music. The collections include complete works of composers, criticism, harmony, and theory, as well as many special collections of rare books and manuscripts and a microfilm archive of manuscripts from other libraries. (3) The Rodgers and Hammerstein Archives of Recorded Sound has sound recordings in every format from the earliest days to the present, with emphasis on the performing arts. Every type of sound is represented, including speech and drama, nature sounds, languages, dialects, and sound effects. Special collections include many historical archives in areas of musical theater, opera, jazz, Jewish, and instrumental music. (4) The Billy Rose Theater Collection has books, promptbooks, original stage and costume designs, photographs, programs, floor plans, lighting plans, architectural blueprints, and scripts (published plays and film scripts are in the General Library of the Performing Arts and Central Collection of The Research Libraries of the New York Public Library). All aspects of live theater, cinema, TV, radio, circus, magic, minstrel shows, puppetry, vaudeville, and wild west shows are included. The Theater on Film and Tape Collection has film and videotape of live theatrical performances and discussions with theater professionals. Special collections include the memorabilia of many important performing artists, producers, designers, and directors as well as the White and Vandamm studio photographs covering much of the New York stage from 1910 to 1961. (5) As part of the New York Public Library, the Center is a member of METRO and Research Libraries Group (RLG) and has access to and helps maintain the Research Libraries Information Network (RLIN) data base.

**Information Services:** Provides materials for in-depth research in all formats, including sound recordings, audiotapes, videotapes, films, and microforms; provides supervised reproduction services, except for audiovisual formats; makes interlibrary loans through the New York State Interlibrary Loan (NYSILL) and RLG systems. Services are available to anyone wishing to do research, particularly professionals, advanced students, and writers in the performing arts. Materials do not circulate.

**Contact:** Mr. Thor E. Wood, Chief

**Approval Date:** 4/85

**Latest Information Date:** 4/85

**Index Terms:** Performing arts; Libraries; Dance; Dance therapy; Dance history; Music; Musical composition; Manuscripts; Rodgers and Hammerstein Archives of Recorded Sound; Speech; Drama; Languages; Sound recordings; Bill Rose Theater Collection; Theater; Motion pictures; Television arts; Radio arts; Circus; Conjuring; Puppet plays; Cinematography; Online information retrieval systems.

---

## 94

### Performing Arts Management Institute (PAMI)

408 West 57th St.
New York, NY 10019
Tel.: (212) 245-3850                    PUB69-19493

PAMI is sponsored by the accounting firm of Lutz and Carr and *Arts Management* newsletter.

**Areas of Interest:** Management of cultural institutions and programs in every area of the arts.

**Information Services:** Provides advisory services; conducts seminars and informational programs. Services are available for a fee to anyone.

**Contact:** Mr. Alvin Reiss

**Approval Date:** 2/85

**Latest Information Date:** 2/85

**Index Terms:** Performing arts; Art management; Cultural administration.

---

## 95

### Pierpont Morgan Library

29 East 36th St.
New York, NY 10016
Tel.: (212) 685-0008                    PUB69-19543

**Areas of Interest:** History; art history; literature; printing.

**Holdings:** The most extensive collection of medieval and Renaissance manuscripts in North America; about five thousand drawings by artists born before 1800 (Old Masters); incunabula; tens of thousands of autograph manuscripts, letters, and documents, with especially strong collections in French literature, Renaissance Italy, Reformation Germany, the Tudor and Stuart periods in England, the American Revolution, and the early years of the republic; the most comprehensive collection of bookbindings in America, dating from the ninth century to the twentieth; a collection of music manuscripts second in size only to that of the Library of Congress in America; about seventy thousand books printed after 1501;

extensive collection of printed children's books, ranging in date from 1487 to the twentieth century; early Italian and Flemish paintings; ancient, medieval, and Renaissance sculpture; medieval gold work and enamels; majolica; porcelain; faience; Assyrian and Babylonian seals; cuneiform tablets; Egyptian, Greek, and other papyri; world's largest collection of Gilbert and Sullivan manuscripts and printed materials.

**Publications:** Books, catalogs, facsimiles, pamphlets, and cards relating to the materials in the collections.

**Information Services:** Answers inquiries; provides reference and literature-searching services and microfilms, photographs, color slides, and Ektachrome copies of original materials in the collections; makes referrals to other sources of information; permits on-site use of collections. Services are free and available to bona fide scholars, graduate research students, curators, librarians, collectors, and dealers.

**Contact:** Ms. Barbara Paulson

**Approval Date:** 2/85

**Latest Information Date:** 2/85

**Index Terms:** Manuscripts; Music manuscripts; Rare books; Children's books; Drawings; Paintings; Sculpture; Art objects; Medieval history; Renaissance period; Literature (fine arts); American history; British history; German history; French history; Italian history; Art history.

---

## 96

### Rhode Island Alliance for Arts in Education (RIAAE)

c/o Rhode Island Dept. of Education
22 Hayes St.
Providence, RI 02908
Tel.: (401) 277-2648                    PUB69-19950

A nonprofit organization, RIAAE fosters arts programs in Rhode Island schools through advocacy, technical assistance, and networking programs and serves as a statewide clearinghouse for arts education information.

**Areas of Interest:** Dance; music; theater; media arts; opera and music theater; indigenous and folk arts; literature; music therapy; landscape design; performance art; visual arts; architecture; crafts; design arts; dance therapy; art therapy; teacher training; curriculum design; special education; comprehensive arts education; multidisciplinary studies; museum programs; fund raising.

**Publications:** *AERIS—Arts Education in Rhode Island*

*Schools* (quarterly newsletter).

**Information Services:** Answers inquiries; provides advisory, consulting, and reference services; evaluates data; conducts seminars and workshops; provides speakers; distributes newsletter; makes referrals to other sources of information. Services are free and open to any individual or group concerned with arts in education.

**Contact:** Mr. Richard D. Latham, Region 1 Chairperson

**Approval Date:** 1/84

**Latest Information Date:** 1/86

**Index Terms:** Dance; Music; Theater; Teacher training; Media arts; Curriculum design; Operas; Music theater; Folk art; Literature (fine arts); Special education; Musicotheraphy; Landscaping; Performing arts; Visual arts; Architecture; Comprehensive arts education; Handicrafts; Design; Museum programs; Dance therapy; Fund raising; Art therapy; Technical assistance; Arts resources.

## 97

**Sierra Arts Foundation**

P.O. Box 2814
Reno, NV 89505
Tel.: (702) 329-1324          PUB69-20213

**Location:** 135 North Sierra St.

An organization with an open membership of about 1,000 individuals and 120 corporations, the Foundation serves to promote, strengthen, and expand the region's cultural activities and to provide a home for the area's arts. Activities include a Washoe County-funded Arts-in-Education program and a regional Very Special Arts Festival.

**Areas of Interest:** Visual, performing, and participatory arts; arts management; comprehensive arts education; special education; teacher training.

**Holdings:** Computerized mailing list.

**Publications:** *Encore!* (monthly newsletters); *How Do I Feel? What Do I Need?: A Guide to Understanding and Assisting Disabled People; Arts Resource Guide.*

**Information Services:** Answers inquiries; provides advisory, consulting, reference, and reproduction services; evaluates and analyzes data; conducts seminars and workshops; distributes publications, data compilations; its mailing list, and audiovisual educational materials; provides speakers; makes referrals to other sources of information. Services are provided free or at cost to nonprofit arts organizations and nonprofit organizations presenting arts-related

events. The Foundation's facilities are accessible to the handicapped.

**Contact:** Fran Harvey, Director of Community Services

**Approval Date:** 1/84

**Latest Information Date:** 1/86

**Index Terms:** Arts resources; Visual arts; Performing arts; Teacher training; Special education; Comprehensive arts education; Art management; Community art projects; Cultural activities; Handicapped arts services; Community involvement; Computerized mailing list.

## 98

**Smithsonian Institution**
**John F. Kennedy Center for the Performing Arts**
**National Committee on Cultural Diversity in the Performing Arts**

Washington, DC 20566
Tel.: (202) 872-0466, 254-6470, or
          254-6471          PUB69-19221

A standing advisory unit to the Chairman of the Board of Trustees at the John F. Kennedy Center for the Performing Arts, the Committee promotes visibility, accessibility, and respectability for cultural diversity in the performing arts through advocacy, research, technical assistance, networking, talent searching, training, information and advisory services, new and experimental productions and performances, community outreach planning and programs, special audience development designs, and the commissioning of new works in the performing arts.

**Areas of Interest:** Minorities in the performing arts; cultural diversity in the performing arts; the cultural, racial, geographical, and sociological entities of artists as an aspect of excellence in the performing arts; arts administration, including program planning, career counseling, audience development, proposal writing, organizational design, budgeting and fund raising, public relations, booking, cooperative management, promotion, long-range planning, and organizational development.

**Information Services:** The Committee maintains a permanent communication network of minority artists and organizations and supporters of cultural diversity; provides technical assistance, consulting, and advisory services; serves as a national research unit and clearinghouse on minorities and cultural diversity in the performing arts; monitors and evaluates programs; and conducts national workshops, seminars, conferences, forums, and lecture series.

41

Services are available to minority artists, arts administrators, and arts organizations.

**Contact:** Dr. Archie L. Buffkins

**Approval Date:** 2/85

**Latest Information Date:** 2/85

**Index Terms:** Performing arts; Minorities in the performing arts; Cultural pluralism; Art management; Cultural programs; Cultural planning; Counseling; Theater attendance; Proposal writing; Budgeting; Fund raising; Public relations; Promoting; Long-range planning; Organization development; Technical assistance; Outreach programs.

### 99

**Smithsonian Institution**
**National Museum of American History**
**Department of Social and Cultural History**

Constitution Ave. between 12th and 14th Sts. NW.
Washington, DC 20560
　　Tel.: (202) 381-6230　　　　　　PUB69-8429

**Areas of Interest:** Material culture of everyday life in the United States from settlement to the present; ethnic and Western U.S. cultural history, especially the Southwestern United States; American dress; domestic architecture, and interior furnishings; musical instruments made or used in America; ceramics and glass; development of printing presses, tools, and reproduction processes; history of news reporting in America; recreation, entertainment, education, restaurants, labor, and merchandising; history of American textile industry and American textiles; American political history, history of photography.

**Holdings:** American costumes (women's, men's, children's), including women's dress from the eighteenth century to the present; American domestic furnishings (1700-1900); Anglo-American ceramics and lighting devices; domestic utensils and pottery; musical instruments, including seventeenth- and eighteenth-century keyboard instruments; rural and folk artifacts, religious artifacts, sports equipment, entertainment memorabilia, phonograph records, school equipment, labor memorabilia, general store artifacts, hand tools; printing presses and tools, principally eighteenth and nineteenth century; European and American prints from 1500 to the present; American and European textiles and textile machinery and implements; American political memorabilia; first ladies' gowns; American reform movements; photographs; cameras.

**Publications:** The staff publishes scholarly monographs and popular publications, some of which ap-

pear in the series *Smithsonian Studies in History and Technology.*

**Information Services:** The staff identifies objects and artifacts, provides consultation about the collections, and provides information to the public. Researchers may have access to the study collections by prior appointment.

**Approval Date:** 6/85

**Latest Information Date:** 6/85

**Index Terms:** History; Musical instruments.

### 100

**Southeast Michigan Arts Forum**

2735 West Warren St.
Detroit, MI 48208
　　Tel.: (313) 898-6340　　　　　　PUB69-20248

An arts council for the seven counties of southeast Michigan sponsored by local government agencies, the Forum conducts music workshops for children, forums on tourism and the arts, and the Detroit Very Special Arts Festival. It has a membership of 1,600 in the United States and abroad, holds membership in international organizations, participates in international conferences; sponsors foreign artists in the United States and U.S. artists abroad, conducts cooperative projects with foreign groups, maintains foreign affiliations, and is planning future international projects.

**Areas of Interest:** Dance; music; theater; media arts; opera and music theater; indigenous and folk arts; literature; visual arts; architecture; crafts; design arts; comprehensive arts education; special education; teacher training; museum programs; arts management; fund raising; multidisciplinary programs.

**Publications:** *Southeast Michigan Arts Forum Directory*; pamphlet on arts and the handicapped; bibliographies; reprints.

**Information Services:** Answers inquiries; provides services; conducts seminars and workshops; distributes publications in the United States and abroad; provides speakers; makes referrals to other sources of information in the United States and abroad. Except for publications, services are free and all are available to anyone.

**Contact:** Shirley Harbin, Director

**Approval Date:** 1/84

**Latest Information Date:** 1/86

**Index Terms:** Arts resources; Southeast Michigan; State encouragement of the arts; Dance; Music;

Theater; Teacher training; Operas; Music theater; Folk art; Literature (fine arts); Visual arts; Architecture; Comprehensive arts education; Handicrafts; Design; Museum programs; Art management; Fund raising; International art activities; Handicapped arts services; Special education.

## 101

### Texas Arts Council

121 East 8th St., Suite 1103
Austin, TX 78701
Tel.: (512) 474-8495                    PUB69-20341

Funded in part by the National Endowment for the Arts and the Texas Commission on the Arts, the Council is organized to promote, develop, and support local arts agencies and programs in Texas in cooperation with concerned local, state, and federal agencies. Membership, which currently comprises over one hundred arts councils and agencies, thirty-five individuals, and a number of corporate sponsors, is open to anyone.

**Areas of Interest:** Community arts organizations in Texas; arts management; fund raising.

**Holdings:** Computerized membership data.

**Publications:** Bimonthly newsletter, annual directory, resource manuals.

**Information Services:** Answers inquiries; provides advisory and reference services; evaluates and analyzes data; conducts seminars and workshops; provides speakers; distributes publications and data compilations; makes referrals to other sources of information. Services are free and available to anyone.

**Contact:** Mr. Peter Fox, President

**Approval Date:** 1/84

**Latest Information Date:** 1/86

**Index Terms:** Arts resources; Community art projects; Art management; Fund raising.

## 102

### Visual Arts Research and Resource Center Relating to the Caribbean (VARC)
### Caribbean Cultural Center

408 West 58th St.
New York, NY 10019
Tel.: (212) 307-7420                    PUB69-20229

Funded in part by the National Endowment for the Arts, the National Endowment for the Humanities,

the New York State Council on the Arts, and private foundations, VARC identifies, compiles, and disseminates information on the traditions and culture of the Caribbean Basin. Its purpose is the promulgation of cross-cultural understanding. Membership (currently numbering about two hundred) is open to the public. Activities include sponsorship of Caribbean artists and performers in the United States and participation in international conferences. Further international activities and special services for the handicapped are planned.

**Areas of Interest:** Caribbean culture, including dance, music, theater, indigenous and folk arts, performance art, visual arts, and crafts; history of the Caribbean; African roots of Caribbean culture; comprehensive arts education; museum programs; multidisciplinary studies.

**Holdings:** Audio and video tapes of the First Annual Orisa Tradition Conference (1981, Ife, Nigeria); audiovisual library.

**Publications:** *Caribe* (quarterly); *Folktales of the Yoruba People* (illustrated booklet for children, parents, and teachers); exhibition catalogs.

**Information Services:** Answers inquiries; provides advisory and reference services; conducts seminars and workshops; provides speakers; distributes publications; makes referrals to other sources of information; permits on-site use of collections. Although services are free, donations are suggested.

**Contact:** Ms. Marta Moreno Vega, Executive Director

**Approval Date:** 1/84

**Latest Information Date:** 1/86

**Index Terms:** Arts resources; Caribbean Area; Dance; Music; Theater; Folk art; Literature (fine arts); Performance art; Visual arts; Comprehensive arts education; Handicrafts; Museum programs; Cultural history; Cultural centers; Cultural heritage; Lecturers; Cultural exhibitions.

## 103

### Western States Arts Foundation

207 Shelby St., Suite 200
Santa Fe, NM 87501
Tel.: (505) 988-1166                    PUB69-20247

The nonprofit, tax-exempt Foundation manages, directs, coordinates, and supports arts events and activities in the western United States and Hawaii. Its principal objectives are to increase opportunities for the public to experience the arts, expand and develop professional opportunities for artists living and working in the West, and to strengthen the capabilities of artists and arts organizations to accomplish their purposes. The Foundation is a regional alliance of the state acts agencies of Arizona, Colorado, Idaho, Montana, Nevada, New Mexico, Oregon, Utah, Washington, and Wyoming. It operates programs of regional scope, including exhibitions, tours, awards, literary development, networking, technical assistance, and private sector consulting.

**Areas of Interest:** Professional development and training for artists and arts professionals in the dance, music, theater, media arts, opera and music theater, indigenous and folk arts, literature, visual arts, architecture, crafts, and design arts; needs assessment and training in computer technology as it relates to arts organizations; fund raising; arts management; multidisciplinary studies.

**Holdings:** Computerized mailing lists of sponsors and organizations by arts discipline.

**Publications:** *National Arts Jobbank* (biweekly newspaper listing positions available in the arts across the country); books, handbooks, exhibition and tour catalogs, annual reports, pamphlets, directories, data compilations, program guides.

**Information Services:** Answers inquiries; provides advisory, consulting and reference services; evaluates and analyzes data; conducts seminars and workshops; distributes publications and mailing lists; makes referrals to other sources of information. Except for publications, mailing lists, seminars, and workshops, services are free to artists and arts organizations in the ten-state region. All services are available to others at cost.

**Contact:** Mr. Terry Melton, Executive Director

**Approval Date:** 4/84

**Latest Information Date:** 1/86

**Index Terms:** Arts resources; Western United States; Professional development; Artists; Professional training; Dance; Music; Theater; Operas; Music theater; Folk art; Literature (fine arts); Visual arts; Architecture; Handicrafts; Design; Art management; Fund raising; Job placement; State encouragement of the arts; Needs assessment.

## 104

### Wisconsin Center for Film and Theater Research

Vilas Communication Hall
821 University Ave.
University of Wisconsin
Madison, WI 53706
  Tel.: (608) 262-9706          PUB69-15234

Film and manuscript archive: 816 State St., Madison, WI 53706, (608) 262-0585.

Cosponsored by the University of Wisconsin and the State Historical Society of Wisconsin, the Center serves as a national repository of primary source materials relating to the performing arts in America and their role in social and cultural history.

**Areas of Interest:** History of the theater, motion pictures, radio, and television in the United States in the twentieth century.

**Holdings:** Over 200 manuscript collections (correspondence, business records, legal documents, etc.); 4,000 feature films; 5,000 television episodes; 2,500 short subjects; 1,000 cartoons; over two million still photographs and graphics; diaries, typescripts, screen plays, shooting scripts, prompt books, press books, scores, play bills, posters, other promotional materials, and blueprints and plans of stage machinery, theaters, costume designs, etc.

**Information Services:** Answers inquiries and permits on-site use of collections free. Free reference service is limited according to time and effort required. Xerox copies and photoduplication of still photographs are available where restrictions allow. Services are for serious researchers.

**Approval Date:** 4/85

**Latest Information Date:** 4/85

**Index Terms:** Performing arts; Social history; Cultural history; Theaters; Motion pictures; Radio broadcasting history; Television arts; United States; History; Archives.

## 105

### Womankraft Corp.
### Community Artists Project (CAP)

902 East Hampton St.
Tucson, AZ 85719
  Tel.: (602) 622-1506          PUB69-20562

CAP is a consortium of five nonprofit organizations, including Arizona Women's Caucus for Art, Tucson Craft Guild, Southern Arizona Clay and Glass Cooperative, Tucson Women's Commission Arts and Media Task Force, and Womankraft, the administrative organization. It receives funding for specific projects from various sources, including the City of Tucson, Senior NOW, the National Endowment for the Arts, the Arizona Commission on the Arts, private donations, and others.

**Areas of Interest:** Art experiences and events for the disadvantaged; creative living; training for artists in teaching skills; collaborative art works.

**Holdings:** Catalogs, press books, videotapes, and back issues of *"Proto"* (an arts/culture/people section in a community magazine).

**Publications:** Show catalogs, play programs, special event programs, small press poetry editions, magazine articles.

**Information Services:** Answers inquiries; provides advisory and reference services; conducts seminars, workshops, and special performance programs; distributes publications; makes referrals to other sources of information. Services are generally free, except for special art events, and primarily for senior citizens and other special groups, but others will be assisted.

**Approval Date:** 7/84

**Latest Information Date:** 1/86

**Index Terms:** Arts resources; Community art projects; Artistic expression; Creative arts; Artists as teachers; Art education; Education of the disadvantaged.

## 106–107

### Wyoming Council for the Humanities

P.O. Box 3972, University Station
Laramie, WY 82071
   Tel.: (307) 766-6496 or 766-3142     PUB69-21080

**Location:** 1800 Willett Dr., Room 40

Supported by the National Endowment for the Humanities, the Council makes regrants to humanities groups and individuals in Wyoming.

**Areas of Interest:** The humanities in Wyoming; grant writing.

**Holdings:** Funded fellowship reports; resource materials.

**Publications:** Newsletter, calendar of events, directories.

**Information Services:** Answers inquiries; provides advisory, reference, and literature-searching services; evaluates data; conducts seminars and workshops; distributes audiovisual and resource materials; makes referrals to other sources of information. Except for resource materials, services are free and all are available to anyone.

**Contact:** Ms. Laura McLean, Program Assistant

**Approval Date:** 2/85

**Latest Information Date:** 2/85

**Index Terms:** Arts resources; Humanities; Grant writing; Wyoming.

# Arts Education Programs

## 108

### Art Resources in Teaching (A.R.T.)

111 East Wacker Dr., Suite 510
Chicago, IL 60601
Tel.: (312) 856-1338          PUB69-20227

An organization of about two hundred members in the United States and other countries, Art Resources in Teaching brings art experience into the Chicago public school system at the elementary level and provides scholarships to needy and talented students to the Art Institute of Chicago, with which it is affiliated.

**Areas of Interest:** Visual arts, including photography, architecture, printmaking, and sculpture; crafts; media arts; teacher training; comprehensive arts education.

**Publications:** Teacher guides and accompanying slide filmstrips.

**Information Services:** Answers inquiries; provides reproduction services; distributes publications and audiovisual materials for elementary students and teachers in the United States and referrals to other sources of information. Information and referral are free to anyone; all services are free to Chicago public schools. Except for loans, which are restricted to the Chicago public schools, other services are available for a fee to anyone.

**Contact:** Amy Greenwood, Executive Director

**Approval Date:** 1/84

**Latest Information Date:** 1/86

**Index Terms:** Arts resources; Art education; Visual arts; Photography; Prints (graphic art); Sculpture; Handicrafts; Teacher training; Comprehensive arts education; Architecture; Scholarships.

## 109

### Arts Unlimiting, Inc.

1605 East 86th St.
Indianapolis, IN 46240
Tel.: (317) 253-5504 or 253-5505          PUB69-19922

Sponsored by the Indiana Department of Public Instruction, the Indiana Arts Commission, and the National Committee, Arts for the Handicapped, Arts Unlimiting, Inc. is an open membership organization of parents, teachers, service providers, and artists. It provides arts-related training and information to organizations and individuals interested in providing services to disabled persons, fosters cooperation among organizations and individuals with similar concerns, informs the public as to the need for and benefit of creative arts opportunities for disabled persons, and develops and expands arts programming integrating disabled and nondisabled persons.

**Areas of Interest:** Drama, dance, music, and visual arts for the handicapped; special education; teacher training.

**Publications:** Journal articles, teaching materials, reprints.

**Information Services:** Answers inquiries; provides advisory and technical assistance services; conducts seminars and workshops. Services are free and available to anyone.

**Contact:** Ms. Sue Moreland, Executive Director

**Approval Date:** 1/84

**Latest Information Date:** 1/86

**Index Terms:** Dance; Music; Visual arts; Handicapped arts services; Special education; Teacher training; Arts resources; Drama.

## 110

### Atlanta College of Art (ACA)

1280 Peachtree St.
Atlanta, GA 30309
Tel.: (404) 898-1159          PUB69-20351

Sponsored by the Atlanta Arts Alliance, ACA offers a four-year professional course of study for persons wishing to pursue a career in the visual arts and visual arts educational opportunities for the general public. In addition, it maintains a visiting artist program, sponsors exhibitions of the works of U.S. artists abroad and foreign artists in the United States, conducts cooperative projects with foreign groups, maintains foreign affiliates, and, in keeping with its interest in more foreign involvement, is planning future international projects. There are currently 750 ACA alumni and 200 ACA associates.

**Areas of Interest:** Visual arts; design arts; arts education.

**Holdings:** Art books, artist books, sound recordings, video tapes, artist periodicals, rare books.

**Information Services:** Answers inquiries; provides reference services; conducts seminars, workshops, classes, exhibitions, and film screenings; makes interlibrary and direct loans; provides speakers; makes referrals to other sources of information in the

United States and abroad; permits on-site use of collections. Direct loan of materials is available only to ACA Associates and Museum personnel and is provided for a fee. Fees are also charged for continuing education courses. Other services are free and available to anyone. ACA's facilities are accessible to the handicapped.

**Contact:** Ms. Ofelia Garcia, President

**Approval Date:** 1/84

**Latest Information Date:** 1/86

**Index Terms:** Visual arts; Design; Art education; Continuing education; International arts activities; Handicapped arts services; Arts resources.

## 111

### Austin Parks and Recreation Department
### Adaptive Programs Section

P.O. Box 1088
Austin, TX 78767
  Tel.: (512) 453-5084       PUB69-20228

The Section administers a community-based recreation program providing opportunities for leisure experiences and the development of skills for making effective use of leisure time for handicapped persons. The program stresses choice, involvement, and self-direction while providing experiences that contribute to the physical, mental, and social development of disabled individuals. The Section also administers a Very Special Arts Festival, partially funded by the National Committee, Arts for the Handicapped.

**Areas of Interest:** Programs for the handicapped in dance, music, and crafts; special education; music therapy; teacher training; multidisciplinary programs.

**Publications:** Taped newsletter for the visually imparied; workbook; table games.

**Information Services:** Answers inquiries; provides advisory services; makes referrals to other sources of information. Services are available to anyone subject to staff time and availability considerations. Facilities of the Section are equipped with TTY equipment and are accessible to the handicapped.

**Contact:** Patsy M. Siegismund, Supervisor of Adaptive Programs

**Approval Date:** 1/84

**Latest Information Date:** 1/86

**Index Terms:** Arts resources; Handicapped arts services; Handicapped and the arts; Dance; Music; Teacher training; Special education; Musicotherapy; Handicrafts.

## 112

### California College of Arts and Crafts (CCAC)
### Office of the President

5212 Broadway
Oakland, CA 94618
  Tel.: (415) 653-8118       PUB69-20340

With an alumni organization of about three thousand members in the United States and other countries, CCAC offers bachelors' and masters' degree programs in the fine arts. It holds memberships in international organizations, participates in international conferences, sponsors exhibits abroad, sponsors foreign artists in the United States, conducts cooperative projects with foreign groups, and, in keeping with its interest in more foreign involvement, is planning future international projects.

**Areas of Interest:** Visual arts; crafts; design arts; art therapy; literature; comprehensive arts education; museum programs; fund raising; multidisciplinary studies.

**Holdings:** CCAC's Meyer Library has over 27,000 volumes and 232 current periodical subscriptions. Special collections include antique textiles, the Jo Sinnell Industrial Design Collection, and a CCAC historical collection that contains items from the 1915 Pan Pacific Fair in San Francisco.

**Publications:** *CCAC Review* (quarterly journal); *CCAC Bulletin* (list of course offerings and descriptions); *CCAC Viewbook* (visual information on CCAC); curricula, teaching materials, journal articles, state-of-the-art reviews, critical reviews, directories, reprints.

**Information Services:** Answers inquiries; provides advisory, consulting, reproduction, and magnetic tape services and audiovisual materials for elementary and secondary students and teachers; conducts seminars and workshops; provides speakers; makes interlibrary and direct loans; distributes publications in the United States and abroad; makes referrals to other sources of information in the United States and other countries; permits on-site use of collections. Services are provided free to CCAC students and selected institutions and at cost to others. Facilities are accessible to the handicapped. A variety of personal aids are available for disabled students.

**Contact:** Mr. Neil J. Hoffman, President

**Approval Date:** 4/84

**Latest Information Date:** 1/86

**Index Terms:** Arts resources; Visual arts; Handicrafts; Design; Art therapy; Literature (fine arts); Comprehensive arts education; Museum programs; Fund raising; Art management; International arts activities; Handicapped arts services.

## 113

### Center for Understanding Media, Inc.

69 Horatio St.
New York, NY 10014
Tel.: (212) 929-1448          PUB69-15132

**Areas of Interest:** The Center specializes in projects involving education, communication, and the arts. It founded a graduate program in Media Studies at the New School for Social Research.

**Publications:** The Center has published ten books dealing with the creative role of the new media in education and has produced a series of films based on great American short stories that was broadcast in 1977 on public television.

**Information Services:** The Center conducts seminars and conferences on independent filmmaking, film and television criticism, filmmaking by young people, children's film, television festivals, and reading and alphabet reform.

**Approval Date:** 6/85

**Latest Information Date:** 6/85

**Index Terms:** Communication; Teacher education; Arts; Television arts; Cinematography; Video tapes; Performing arts; Curriculum development; Audiovisual aids; Motion picture criticism; Children's films; Sociological research; Photography; Motion pictures; Mass communication; Literacy; Alphabet reform; Arts resources.

## 114

### Colorado Arts for the Handicapped, Inc.

P.O. Box 26292
Colorado Springs, CO 80936          PUB69-19917

Colorado Arts for the Handicapped, Inc. is a nonprofit organization conducting activities for all ages and all handicapping conditions in public schools and all other facilities in Colorado dealing with the disabled. In addition, training is provided for classroom and special education teachers, volunteers, arts specialists, and other interested groups.

**Areas of Interest:** Arts experiences for the handicapped, including dance, music, drama, and visual arts; art therapy; dance therapy; music therapy; special education; teacher training; multidisciplinary activities.

**Publications:** Materials designed and printed specifically for individual workshops. A resource book of project and activity descriptions is being compiled.

**Information Services:** Answers inquiries; provides advisory and consulting services; conducts workshops; provides speakers. Services are free to Colorado-affiliated sites. The cost of transportation, consultant fees, and lodging are charged to all other interested groups and users.

**Contact:** Ms. Sherry R. Mills, Executive Director

**Approval Date:** 3/85

**Latest Information Date:** 3/85

**Index Terms:** Colorado; Arts for the handicapped; Art experiences; Dance; Music; Theater; Visual arts; Art therapy; Musicotherapy; Special education; Teacher training; Dance therapy; International arts activities; Handicapped arts services; Arts resources.

## 115

### Creative Arts in Education

305 Great Neck Rd.
Waterford, CT 06385
Tel.: (203) 443-7139          PUB69-20344

A division of the Eugene O'Neill Theater Center funded in part by federal and state agencies, private corporations, and foundations, Creative Arts in Education is the umbrella organization for several projects, among them Artists-in-the-Schools, the National Youth Theater Institute, the National Theater Arts Institute, Theatre Arts in Deaf Education, training internships, and sponsorship of foreign artists in the United States. It is a broad-based arts in education program that has been designated by both federal and state governments as a demonstration model. Its projects use creative arts disciplines to help diverse groups, from school children to prison inmates, to learn, work, and communicate more effectively, while cultivating in them an interest in and understanding of theater.

**Areas of Interest:** Theater; dance; music; media arts; indigenous and folk arts; performance art; visual arts; crafts; arts management; comprehensive arts education; special education; curriculum design; teacher training; multidisciplinary programs.

**Holdings:** Collections in the above areas.

**Publications:** *Creative Arts in Education Activities Guide; Speaking and Listening; Teaching Made Easy and Fun; 16 Toes* (anthology of children's poetry).

**Information Services:** Answers inquiries; provides advisory, consulting, and reference services; conducts seminars and workshops; provides speakers; makes referrals to other sources of information; permits on-site use of collections. Services are available for a fee to the membership, which is open to any school or agency.

**Contact:** Lynn Britt, Director

**Approval Date:** 1/84

**Latest Information Date:** 1/86

**Index Terms:** Arts resources; Dance; Music; Theater; Media arts; Folk art; Performance art; Visual arts; Art management; Comprehensive arts education; Special education; Curriculum design; Teacher training; International arts activities; Handicapped arts services.

## 116

### Cultural Council of Santa Cruz County

6500 Soquel Dr.
Aptos, CA 95003
   Tel.: (408) 476-2313 or 688-5399    PUB69-21069

Funded by a number of federal, state, and local governments and by private sources, the Council provides an Artists-in-Residence program for county schools, makes grants to cultural organizations and individual artists located in the county, provides management and marketing services to local arts organizations, and works on cultural facilities development.

**Areas of Interest:** Dance, music, theater, media arts, opera and music theater, indigenous and folk arts, literature, performing arts, visual arts, and crafts education; special education; teacher training; curriculum design; arts management; fund raising; multidisciplinary studies; comprehensive arts education.

**Holdings:** About one hundred books on arts management, grants, and the arts in education.

**Publications:** *Spectra Resource Catalog* (information on artists and their programs for schools); *Spectra Curriculum Guide* (curriculum for arts education); *Partners in the Arts* (handbook on starting an arts education program); *Cultural Action Plan* (an arts plan for the county).

**Information Services:** Answers inquiries; provides advisory and reference services; evaluates data; conducts seminars and workshops; lends materials; provides speakers; distributes publications and data compilations; makes referrals to other sources of information; permits on-site use of collections.

**Contact:** Ms. Beverly Grova, Executive Director

**Approval Date:** 10/84

**Latest Information Date:** 1/86

**Index Terms:** Arts resources; Dance; Music; Theater; Teacher training; Media arts; Curriculum design; Operas; Music theater; Folk art; Literature (fine arts); Historic preservation; Special education; Performing arts; Visual arts; Comprehensive arts education; Crafts; Art management; Fund raising.

## 117

### Educational Testing Service
### National Assessment of Educational Progress (NAEP)

CN 6710
Princeton, NJ 08541-6710
   Tel.: (800) 223-0267    PUB69-17460

Administered by ETS and funded by the National Institute of Education, NAEP provides comprehensive information on the educational achievement of young Americans in elementary, middle, and secondary school, as well as adults.

**Areas of Interest:** Educational evaluation.

**Holdings:** Data base of respondent-level data from various learning areas, including reading, writing, mathematics, science, literature, music, art, citizenship, and social studies.

**Publications:** Periodic newsletter, technical and non-technical reports, data compilations, reprints, objectives booklets, assessment exercises, papers. A publications list is available.

**Information Services:** Answers inquiries; provides advisory and public-use data tape services; conducts seminars; distributes publications. Services are free, except for publications and tapes, and available to anyone.

**Approval Date:** 3/84

**Latest Information Date:** 1/86

**Index Terms:** Educational evaluation; Student evaluation; Educational needs; Reading; Writing; Mathematics; Science; Literature (fine arts); Music; Arts; Citizenship education; Social studies; Career development; Vocational education; Academic achievement; Online information retrieval systems.

## 118

**Indianapolis Museum of Art**
**Education Division**

1200 West 38th St.
Indianapolis, IN 46208
  Tel.: (317) 923-1331      PUB69-20352

**Areas of Interest:** Fine arts; fine arts conservation; fine arts education.

**Holdings:** 45,000 pre-Columbian to modern works of art; 80,000 slides covering art from prehistoric times to the present; arts reference library of 21,000 volumes.

**Publications:** *Perceptions* (annual); collection catalogs; exhibition catalogs; journal articles; cultural resource kits.

**Information Services:** Answers inquiries; provides advisory consulting for art conservation, literature-searching, and current-awareness services; conducts lectures, symposia, art education and art appreciation classes, exhibitions, film screenings, tours, and concerts; lends materials; distributes publications; makes referrals to other sources of information; permits on-site use of study collections. Except for publications, which are available for a fee, services are generally offered free to members and at a fee to others.

**Contact:** Ms. Helen Ferrulli, Director of Education

**Approval Date:** 1/84

**Latest Information Date:** 1/86

**Index Terms:** Arts resources; Museums (institutions); Fine arts; Art preservation; Art education.

## 119

**Let's-Play-to-Grow**

1350 New York Ave., Suite 500
Washington, DC 20005
  Tel.: (202) 628-3630      PUB69-19923

Let's-Play-to-Grow is sponsored by the Joseph P. Kennedy, Jr. Foundation, with additional support from the Department of the Interior's Bureau of Indian Affairs and other public and private organizations, agencies, institutions, facilities, corporations, and groups. There are 200 Let's-Play-to-Grow clubs, each involving parents, siblings, and grandparents of children with handicaps as well as professionals and volunteers in ongoing programs of shared play and recreational activities. The national office par-

ticipates in international conferences, conducts cooperative projects with foreign groups, sponsors performances abroad, maintains relationships with international organizations and foreign affiliates, and distributes materials abroad. Let's-Play-to-Grow is interested in more foreign involvement and is planning future international projects concerning families of disabled children.

**Areas of Interest:** Enhancement of the relationships among the members of families of physically handicapped, developmentally disabled, or mentally retarded persons; enhancement of the physical and social development as well as the independent recreational skills of persons with special needs; improvement of parents' confidence in their own ability to help special family members through play; improvement of the attitudes of professionals and volunteers working with special persons; mobilization of community resources to provide essential physical education and recreational services for disabled persons; recreational therapy; art therapy; dance therapy; music therapy; special education; teacher training; curriculum design; museum programs; fund raising; participation by the handicapped in the arts, including dance, music, theater, media arts, opera and music theater, indigenous folk arts, performance art, visual arts, design arts, crafts, and multidisciplinary activities.

**Publications:** Materials available include kits in English and Spanish consisting of play guides and other teaching aids, a planning guide, a club leader manual, a resource guide, supplementary guides on individual activities, posters, a fact sheet, a supply catalog, and a brochure. A price list is available.

**Information Services:** Answers inquiries; provides advisory and consulting services; conducts seminars and workshops; sells and lends materials; provides speakers; makes referrals to other sources of information in the United States and abroad. Except for materials, services are free and all are available to handicapped people of all ages and disabilities and to their families.

**Contact:** Ms. Linda Schulz, Director

**Approval Date:** 1/84

**Latest Information Date:** 1/86

**Index Terms:** Dance; Music; Theater; Teacher training; Media arts; Handicapped persons; Operas; Folk music; Music theater; Literature (fine arts); Special education; Music therapy; Performance art; Visual arts; Handicrafts; Design; Museum programs; Dance therapy; Art therapy; Fund raising; Arts resources; Developmental disabilities; Mentally handicapped; Physically handicapped; Recreational therapy.

## 120

### Maine Art Education Association (MAEA)

7 Manley St.
Augusta, ME 04330
Tel.: (207) 685-4923                    PUB69-21071

Sponsored by the Maine State Commission on the Arts and the Humanities and the State Department of Education, MAEA is concerned with the professional development of its 137 members and with the promotion of art education at all levels.

**Areas of Interest:** Education in literature, performing arts, visual arts, architecture, crafts, and design art; special education; teacher training; curriculum design; art therapy; art management; fund raising; multidisciplinary programs; museum programs; comprehensive arts education.

**Holdings:** Computerized membership data.

**Publications:** Quarterly newsletter.

**Information Services:** Answers inquiries; provides advisory and reference services; conducts seminars, workshops, and an annual conference; lends materials; provides speakers; distributes its newsletter; makes referrals to other sources of information; permits on-site use of collection. Services are available for a fee to anyone.

**Contact:** Ms. Corliss Chastain, Vice President

**Approval Date:** 11/85

**Latest Information Date:** 11/85

**Index Terms:** Arts resources; Maine; Teacher training; Curriculum design; Literature (fine arts); Special education; Performing arts; Visual arts; Architecture; Comprehensive arts education; Crafts; Design; Museum programs; Art therapy; Art management; Fund raising.

## 121

### Minnesota Alliance for Arts in Education (MAAE)

P.O. Box 13039
Minneapolis MN 55414
Tel.: (612) 376-1197                    PUB69-19935

**Location:** 109 Pattee Hall, University of Minnesota

Sponsored by the National Endowment for the Arts, other national arts organizations, state and local arts organizations, and private corporations and foundations, MAAE is an organization of about four hundred individual and organizational members fostering arts programs in Minnesota schools from kindergarten through grade 12. It initiates legislation; monitors laws and policies affecting arts education; promotes public awareness through print, radio, and television media; sponsors and assists local arts education programs; and is a statewide clearinghouse for arts education. Special programs include Arts Development for Elementary Teachers, providing inservice training and classroom demonstrations through a master art teacher in residence, and the MAAE Accessible Arts Project, providing technical support and funding to Minnesota schools, agencies, community groups, hospitals, and arts and education organizations to make the arts available to the handicapped.

**Areas of Interest:** Dance; music; theater; media arts; opera and music theater; indigenous and folk arts; performance art; visual arts; architecture; teacher training; curriculum design; literature; special education; music therapy; comprehensive arts education; fund raising; arts education program administration.

**Publications:** *Artbeat* (quarterly newspaper); *Arts in Minnesota Schools: A Selection of Excellence; All the Arts for All the Kids;* workbook for project development; journal articles; project reports; resource guides; etc. A brochure listing publications and advocacy materials is available.

**Information Services:** Answers inquiries; provides advisory, consulting, reference, and current-awareness services; conducts seminars and workshops; provides speakers; distributes publications; makes referrals to other sources of information. Fees are charged for workshops and most publications; other services are generally free. Grants for arts accessibility for the handicapped are restricted to Minnesota schools and nonprofit organizations; other services are generally available to anyone.

**Contact:** Ms. Margaret Hasse, Executive Director

**Approval Date:** 1/84

**Latest Information Date:** 1/86

**Index Terms:** Dance; Music; Theater; Teacher training; Media arts; Curriculum design; Operas; Music theater; Folk art; Literature (fine arts); Special education; Musciotherapy; Performance art; Visual arts; Comprehensive art education; Fund raising; Lecturers; Arts and education; Handicapped arts services; Arts resources.

**122**

**Monterey Peninsula Museum of Art
Museum on Wheels Program**

559 Pacific St.
Monterey, CA 93940
Tel.: (408) 373-2061 or 372-7591      PUB69-21070

Funded by a number of federal and state agencies, local schools, and private sources, the Program provides a mobile folk art collection of 200 items representing 45 countries in the elementary and middle schools of the central coast area of California.

**Areas of Interest:** Education and teacher training in indigenous and folk art and crafts.

**Holdings:** The Program draws on the Folk Art Collection of the Museum, which consists of about thirty-five hundred pieces, and on the Museum's Folk Art Library of about four hundred volumes.

**Publications:** Teacher packets.

**Information Services:** Answers inquiries; conducts seminars and workshops. Information services are available to the public free, as is access to the Museum collections themselves. The Program's traveling exhibits are available to schools in the region for a fee. Facilities of the Museum are accessible to the handicapped.

**Contact:** Kay Cline, Program Director

**Approval Date:** 10/84

**Latest Information Date:** 1/86

**Index Terms:** Arts resources; Comprehensive arts education; Teacher training; Folk art; Crafts; Museum programs; Visual arts.

**123**

**Montgomery County (MD) Public Schools
Department of Aesthetic Education
Interrelated ARTS Program**

Connecticut Park Center
12518 Greenly Dr.
Silver Spring, MD 20906
Tel.: (301) 942-8081      PUB69-19974

Begun as Project ARTS (Arts Resource Teachers in Schools) with federal funding but now fully supported by the Montgomery County school system, the Interrelated ARTS Program provides demonstration teaching and teacher training directed at infusing the arts into the general curriculum and identifying gifted and talented elementary students in the arts.

**Areas of Interest:** Program design and program materials for interrelating the arts with elementary school general curriculum.

**Publications:** *Newsletter* (two-three issues a year); instructional support kits.

**Information Services:** Answers inquiries free; distributes instructional support kits at cost. Services are intended primarily for educational groups but are available to anyone.

**Contact:** Coordinator

**Approval Date:** 9/84

**Latest Information Date:** 1/86

**Index Terms:** Arts and education; Dance; Music; Theater; Curriculum design; Teacher training; Operas; Music theater; Visual arts; Arts resources; Comprehsnsive art education; Instrumental music.

**124**

**National Association for Creative Children and Adults (NACCA)**

8080 Springvalley Dr.
Cincinnati, OH 45236
Tel.: (513) 631-1777      PUB69-16658

A nonprofit organization, NACCA is dedicated to helping people become the best they can be by understanding and applying the research on creativity.

**Areas of Interest:** Personal development; common sense problem solving; creativity; personality development; self-discovery; giftedness; talent.

**Holdings:** Library on the areas above.

**Publications:** *The Creative Child and Adult Quarterly; It's Happening to Creative Children and Adults* (newsletter); *The Gifted Child Quarterly; The Creative Cat; How to Teach Ourselves to be Good to One Another; Crossroads of Talent; Creativity and Giftedness: An Acrostic for Home and Classroom* (workbook); *Isaacs' Three Way Developmental Growth Check List for Giftedness-Talent-Creativity.* A publications list is available.

**Information Services:** Answers inquiries; provides advisory, abstracting, indexing, current-awareness, and duplication services; evaluates data; conducts conferences, training courses, and creativity workshops; distributes publications; permits on-site use of collection by appointment. Services are provided at cost to all users.

**Approval Date:** 8/85

**Latest Information Date:** 8/85

**Index Terms:** Education of the gifted; Creativity; Creative development; Creative ability; Problem solving; Psychology; Arts; Music; Writing; Teacher training; Inservice education; Creative thinking.

## 125

**National Committee, Arts with Handicapped (NCAH) (former)**
**Very Special Arts (VSA) (current)**

Education Office
The John F. Kennedy Center for the Performing Arts
Washington, DC 20566
Tel.: (202) 332-6960 (voice)
(202) 293-3989 (TTY)          PUB69-19054

Funded by the U.S. Department of Education, VSA is the national coordinating agency for arts and the handicapped programs. Its mission is to assure that disabled individuals have equal opportunity to participate in programs that demonstrate the value of the arts in the lives of all individuals and provide opportunities for the integration of disabled people into society.

**Areas of Interest:** Music, dance, drama, and art for the handicapped.

**Holdings:** Resource library containing articles, publications, curricula, and audiovisual materials.

**Publications:** *The Articulator* (monthly newsletter); pamphlets, reports, program descriptions, conference papers and proceedings, guides, collection of drawings and captions by disabled children, collection of essays, manual, brochure, etc. A publications list is available. All publications are available in nonprint form or large print.

**Information Services:** Answers inquiries; provides advisory, reference, and current-awareness services; provides information on research in progress; conducts seminars and workshops; distributes publications and data compilations; makes referrals to other sources of information. Services are free, except for some publications, and available to anyone.

**Approval Date:** 8/84

**Latest Information Date:** 1/86

**Index Terms:** Handicapped persons; Art education; Curriculum development; Technical assistance; Community involvement; Interagency cooperation; Music; Dance; Drama; Program development; Information dissemination.

## 126

**New Mexico Very Special Arts Festival (VSAF)**

P.O. Box 1293
Albuquerque, NM 87103
Tel.: (505) 766-4888          PUB69-20238

Sponsored by the National Committee Arts with the Handicapped, VSAF provides a noncompetitive forum for disabled and other children and youth to celebrate and share their accomplishments in the visual and performing arts with interested audiences.

**Areas of Interest:** Arts for handicapped children, youth, and adults, including dance, music, theater, media arts, indigenous and folk arts, literature, performance art, visual arts, architecture, crafts, and design arts; dance therapy; art therapy; music therapy; special education; teacher training; curriculum design; comprehensive arts education; museum programs; historic preservation; arts management; fund raising; multidisciplinary studies.

**Publications:** Curriculum guide for teaching the arts and making them accessible to all.

**Information Services:** Answers inquiries; provides advisory, consulting, reference, and current-awareness services; provides speakers; conducts seminars and in-service training program; makes referrals to other sources of information. Services are available at cost to anyone. Facilities of the VSAF are accessible to the handicapped. Large print and braille materials and TTY facilities are available on a referral basis.

**Contact:** Ms. Beth Rudolph, Coordinator

**Approval Date:** 11/84

**Latest Information Date:** 1/86

**Index Terms:** Arts resources; Handicapped children; Children; Youth; Dance; Music; Theater; Teacher training; Curriculum design; Folk art; Literature (fine arts); Historic preservation; Special education; Musciotherapy; Performance art; Visual arts; Architecture; Comprehensive art education; Handicrafts; Design; Museum programs; Dance therapy; Art therapy; Fund raising; Festivals; Handicapped arts services.

## 127

### New York City Board of Education
### Learning to Read Through the Arts

c/o P.S. 9
100 West 84th St.
New York, NY 10024
Tel.: (212) 787-0470, 787-7582,
or 787-7585                           PUB69-20339

Funded by the National Diffusion Network, U.S. Department of Education, Learning to Read Through the Arts offers intensive, individualized reading instruction through the integration of a total art program with a total reading program. Interaction between the program and such cultural institutions as the Staten Island Museum, the Bronx Museum of the Arts, El Museo Del Barrio, the New York Aquarium, the Brooklyn Museum, and Ballet Hispanico of New York is an important aspect of the program. Learning to Read Through the Arts holds memberships in international organizations, participates in international conferences, conducts cooperative projects with foreign groups, and, in keeping with its interest in more foreign involvement, is planning future international projects.

**Areas of Interest:** Use of the arts in teaching reading, including dance, music, theater, media arts, opera and music theater, indigenous and folk arts, performance art, visual arts, crafts, and design arts; teacher training; curriculum design; special education; bilingual education; museum programs; multidisciplinary programs.

**Holdings:** Several articles are listed with the Educational Resources Information Center (ERIC). Information about replicating sites at the Learning to Read Through the Arts Program throughout the United States, Puerto Rico, and the Virgin Islands are entered in the National Diffusion Network Computerized Data Base System, Teachers College, Columbia University, New York, NY.

**Publications:** Teacher training handbooks, curriculum guides, and other teaching materials; journal articles, abstracts, indexes, bibliographies, data compilations, project reports, evaluation reports, reprints.

**Information Services:** Answers inquiries; provides advisory, consulting, reference, and current-awareness services and audiovisual materials for elementary and secondary students and teachers; evaluates and analyzes data; conducts seminars and workshops; provides speakers; distributes publications. Except for consulting and current-awareness services and the provision of speakers, services are free and all are available to administrators, supervisors, and teachers of kindergarten through 12th grade who wish to use the program for remedial, developmental, or enrichment purposes as well as to educators working with special education or bilingual students.

**Contact:** Ms. Mary Jane Collett, Director

**Approval Date:** 4/84

**Latest Information Date:** 1/86

**Index Terms:** Arts resources; Reading instruction; Dance; Music; Theater; Media arts; Operas; Music theater; Folk art; Landscaping; Performance art; Visual arts; Handicrafts; Design; Teacher training; Curriculum design; Special education; Museum programs; International arts activities.

## 128

### Performing Tree, Inc.

1320 West 3d St.
Los Angeles, CA 90017
Tel.: (213) 482-8830 or 625-6285      PUB69-20337

Performing Tree is a community-based, private, nonprofit educational organization dedicated to children and their need for art, music, dance, and theater as essential elements in their basic education. It offers educational performances, student workshops, teacher training sessions, preplanning, arts consultancies, artists-in-residence programs, and educational materials to help teachers teach the arts. In addition, Performing Tree operates an arts-in-education program for the Department of Defense Dependent Schools (DoDDS) in West Germany.

**Areas of Interest:** Dance; music; theater, media arts; opera and music theater; indigenous and folk arts; visual arts; architecture; crafts; comprehensive arts education; teacher training; curriculum design; special education; museum programs; multidisciplinary programs.

**Publications:** *Learning Through Mime/Creative Dramatics; Learning Through Dance/Movement; Puppets and Learning; Guide to the Performing and Visual Arts; Artist's Handbook; Fourth R: Strengthening Your Instruction Program Through the Arts.*

**Information Services:** Answers inquiries; provides advisory and consulting services; evaluates and analyzes data; conducts workshops; distributes publications. Services are available for a fee to parents, educators, and artists.

**Contact:** Ms. Beth L. Cornell, Executive Director

**Approval Date:** 1/84

**Latest Information Date:** 1/86

**Index Terms:** Dance; Music; Theater; Media arts; Operas; Music theater; Folk art; Visual arts; Architecture; Handicrafts; Comprehensive art education; Teacher training; Curriculum design; Special education; Museum programs; Arts resources.

## 129

### Recreation Center for the Handicapped, Inc.

207 Skyline Blvd.
San Francisco, CA 94132
Tel.: (415) 665-4100          PUB69-19941

The Center provides recreation, socialization, education, and rehabilitation programs for individuals with special needs. Activities include adapted recreation/leisure services, a therapeutic swimming pool, a gym, independent living skills training, transportation, meals, a theater ensemble of disabled and able actors, membership in international organizations, and participation in international conferences. The Center is currently planning future international projects.

**Areas of Interest:** Physical education, recreation, and arts participation for the mentally and physically handicapped, the elderly, and the house-bound.

**Publications:** Proposals, grant applications, reports, program materials, manuals, handbooks, reprints of reports and journal articles, papers, films, filmstrips, information packets. A price list is available.

**Information Services:** Answers inquiries; provides advisory and reference services; conducts seminars and workshops; provides speakers; distributes publications in the United States and abroad; makes referrals to foreign and domestic sources of information. Some publications may be subject to a fee; other services are free. All are available to anyone. All facilities are accessible to the handicapped.

**Contact:** Janet Pomeroy, Director

**Approval Date:** 1/84

**Latest Information Date:** 1/86

**Index Terms:** Handicapped and the arts; Theater; Music; Drama; Visual arts; Handicapped arts services; Physical education; Recreation centers; Video art; Mentally handicapped; Physically handicapped; Aged; International arts activities; Outreach programs; Community involvement; Lecturers; Arts resources.

## 130

### Smithsonian Institution Traveling Exhibition Service (SITES)

900 Jefferson Dr. SW
Arts and Industries Bldg., Room 2170
Washington, DC 20560
Tel.: (202) 357-3168          PUB69-20206

SITES organizes and circulates exhibitions on art, history, and science to institutions in the United States and abroad. Its Education Department develops innovative hands-on and interactive exhibitions in new formats.

**Areas of Interest:** Museum programs and exhibitions.

**Publications:** Books, training materials, catalogs, posters. SITES's Education Department produces kits, games, curriculum packets, project books, workbooks, and children's and how-to books.

**Information Services:** Exhibitions are available to qualifying institutions at cost plus outgoing shipping fees. Publications are available to anyone for a fee.

**Contact:** Peggy A. Loar, Director

**Approval Date:** 1/84

**Latest Information Date:** 1/86

**Index Terms:** Arts resources; Museum programs; Exhibitions; Touring exhibitions; Arts; History; Science; Folk art; Visual arts; Historic preservation; Architecture; Comprehensive art education; Handicrafts; Design; International arts activities.

## 131

### Studio in a School Association

131 Livingston St., Room 610
Brooklyn, NY 11201
Tel.: (718) 596-5074 or 596-8322          PUB69-21068

Sponsored by individuals, foundations, and corporations, with support from The New York City Board of Education and Department of Cultural Affairs, the Association provides public school children with art experiences through an Artists-in-Residence program, exhibits the art works of both children and artists, and provides staff development for New York City teachers.

**Areas of Interest:** Visual arts education; curriculum design; special education; teacher training.

**Publications:** Teaching materials.

**Information Services:** Answers inquiries; conducts seminars and workshops; makes referrals to other sources of information. The program is intended for visual artists, educators, and children.

**Contact:** Mr. Thomas Cahill, Executive Director

**Approval Date:** 11/84

**Latest Information Date:** 11/84

**Index Terms:** Arts resources; Art education; Special education; Visual arts; Teacher training; Curriculum design.

## 132

**Sun Foundation Center for Advancement in the Sciences, Art and Education**

R.R. 2
Washburn, IL 61570
Tel.: (309) 246-8403          PUB69-21084

The Center is an organization of 250 members, staff (4), and professional artists, scientists, and educators mobilizing financial and human resources to increase access to the arts, sciences, health, and education. Eighty-five percent of its funding comes from public contributions and earned income and 15 percent from grants.

**Areas of Interest:** Integrative programs in the arts, including music, theater, performing arts, visual arts and crafts, the sciences, and health. Activities include sponsorship of state and national conferences, performances, workshops, classes, school programs, seminars, school residencies, Suzuki School of Music, a Science Center (natural science), teacher training, curriculum design, fund raising, and multidisciplinary programs.

**Holdings:** Science specimens (400 natural science); Plains Indian collection (75 artifacts and specimens); 150 volumes, 200 reports, slide collection (natural sciences and Plains Indians).

**Publications:** Project reports; one film; newsletters.

**Information Services:** Answers inquiries; provides reference services; conducts seminars and workshops; distributes film in the United States and abroad; provides speakers; makes referrals to other sources of information; permits on-site use of collections. Charges are made of workshops, speakers, and materials. Other services are free, unless extensive. All are available to anyone.

**Contact:** Ms. Joan Ericksen, Co-Director

**Approval Date:** 12/84

**Latest Information Date:** 1/86

**Index Terms:** Arts resources; Art education; Teacher training; Curriculum design; Fund raising.

## 133

**University Film and Video Association (UFVA)**

c/o Department of Cinema and Photography
Southern Illinois University
Carbondale, IL 62901
Tel.: (618) 453-2365          PUB69-14152

UFVA is an international professional organization of more than seven hundred fifty persons concerned with the arts and sciences of film and video. The membership includes university and college professors, makers of film and video works (from the avantgarde to commercial, industrial, and feature films), media archivists and librarians, educational institutions and business concerns, and film-video students.

**Areas of Interest:** Uses of film and video for purposes of instruction, communication, and expression throughout the world; encouragement and fostering of production and study of film and video in educational institutions.

**Holdings:** Materials for the Film, Video Research in Progress (FVRP) research resources dissemination service, including a collection of recent research reports, conference papers, and other scholarly written materials.

**Publications:** *Journal of Film and Video* (quarterly); *Digest of University Film and Video Association* (bimonthly newsletter); UFVA Monograph series; *UFVA Membership Directory* (biannual); brochure.

**Information Services:** Answers inquiries; provides advisory and reference services; distributes data compilations and publications; makes referrals to other sources of information. Services are available to anyone and are generally free; major projects are contracted.

**Approval Date:** 1/84

**Latest Information Date:** 1/86

**Index Terms:** Motion pictures; Motion picture production; Audiovisual aids; Cinematography; Motion pictures history; Media arts; Television arts; Video art; Motion picture criticism; Television criticism; Television production; Educational films; Educational television.

## 134

### University of Montana
### School of Fine Arts

Performing Arts Building
Missoula, MT 59812
Tel.: (406) 243-4970                    PUB69-20336

The School of Fine Arts offers the only professional training in the arts in Montana and serves as a cultural resource by offering a touring repertory theater, a touring movement company, music ensembles, solo performances, seminars and workshops, and art exhibits in an eight-state region. It holds memberships in international organizations, participates in international conferences, sponsors performances and exhibits abroad, sponsors foreign artists and performers in this country, conducts cooperative projects with foreign groups, and, in keeping with its interest in more foreign involvement, is planning future international projects.

**Areas of Interest:** Dance; music; theater; opera and music theater; visual arts; performance art; crafts; design arts; comprehensive arts education, including the training of arts educators and professional artistic training in painting, sculpture, ceramics, performance art, acting, directing, design-technical theater, costuming, dance, performance music, theory, composition, and music history.

**Holdings:** The Permanent Art Collection has one of the largest Native American collections in the Northwest; a significant collection of major Western works by such artists as C. M. Russell, J. H. Sharp, E. S. Paxson, and R. E. DeCamp; several hundred lithographs by Daumier and Forain; and a sizeable collection of modern prints.

**Information Services:** Answers inquiries; provides advisory and reference services; evaluates and analyzes data; conducts seminars and workshops; provides speakers; makes referrals to other sources of information in the United States and foreign countries. Except for seminars and workshops, services are generally free and all are available to anyone. Facilities are accessible to the handicapped and equipment enhancing sound for the hearing impaired is planned.

**Contact:** Sr. Kathryn A. Martin, Dean

**Approval Date:** 1/84

**Latest Information Date:** 1/86

**Index Terms:** Arts resources; Dance; Music; Theater; Operas; Music theater; Visual arts; Performance art; Handicrafts; Design; Comprehensive art education; Professional training; Painting; Sculpture; Ceramics; Acting; Music history; Art management; International arts activities; Handicapped arts services; Montana.

## 135

### Visual Studies Workshops (VSW)

31 Prince St.
Rochester, NY 14607
Tel.: (716) 442-8676                    PUB69-19915

Sponsored by the National Endowment for the Arts and the New York State Council on the Arts, VSW is an organization of 2,300 members offering educational programs, studio and research facilities, exhibitions, publications, and supportive services to artists, scholars, institutions, and others interested in the visual arts. It participates in international conferences and sponsors exhibitions abroad, and is currently interested in more foreign involvement. Membership is available to anyone.

**Areas of Interest:** Photography; video arts; independent film; artists' book production and publication; performance art; visual arts; design arts; comprehensive arts education; teacher training; curriculum design; historic preservation; museum programs; arts management; multidisciplinary studies.

**Holdings:** 12,000 illustrated, reference, and artists' books; 1,300 periodical titles; 27,000 original prints by 2,200 picture makers; several thousand snapshots, albums, and scrapbooks; over a million negatives; 85,000 lantern slides, posters, and audio tapes; files on over 4,000 artists, critics, historians, arts organizations, and picture making processes.

**Publications:** *Afterimage* (ten issues a year); books, journal articles, state-of-the-art reviews, teaching materials, critical reviews.

**Information Services:** Answers inquiries; provides advisory, consulting, reference, current-awareness, and reproduction services; evaluates and analyzes data; conducts summer institutes, seminars, workshops, lectures, exhibitions, and other educational programs; lends materials; provides audiovisual materials to elementary and secondary students and teachers; provides speakers; distributes publications and data compilations in the United States and abroad; makes domestic and foreign referrals; permits on-site use of collections. Many lectures, seminars, and exhibitions are free to the public. Other facilities and services are available on a fee basis to persons working seriously in the visual arts.

**Contact:** Mr. Nathan Lyons, Director

**Approval Date:** 10/85

**Latest Information Date:** 10/85

**Index Terms:** Photography; Video arts; Motion pictures; Media arts; Teacher training; Curriculum design; Historic preservation; Performing arts; Visual arts; Art education; Design; Teacher training; Art management; International arts activities; Educational programs; Museums; Arts resources.

## 136

**Young Audiences, Inc.**

115 East 92d St.
New York, NY 10020
Tel.: (212) 831-8110                    PUB69-19893

Funded by private foundations, corporations, the Music Performance Trust Fund, schools, PTAs, and individuals, Young Audiences, Inc. provides professional performances in music, dance, and theater in schools.

**Areas of Interest:** Bringing the live performing arts to children through music, dance, and theater; arts in education; curriculum design.

**Publications:** Quarterly newsletter; annual report; The Young Audiences Program Booklets; A Guide for Performing Artists (*The Young Audiences Program: An Overview; The Young Audiences Performance; The Young Audiences Workshop; The Process of Designing Young Audiences Programs;* and *The Young Audiences Residency*).

**Information Services:** Provides in-school performances, workshops, and residencies.

**Contact:** Warren H. Yost, National Executive Director

**Approval Date:** 4/85

**Latest Information Date:** 4/85

**Index Terms:** Arts resources; Performing arts; Art education; Curriculum design; Children; Dance; Music; Theater; Arts and education.

# Dance Organizations

## 137

### American College Dance Festival Association (ACDFA)

c/o Prof. Betsy M. Carden
82 Livingston St.
Brooklyn, NY 11201
Tel.: (718) 522-1851                PUB69-17915

ACDFA sponsors college dance festivals to provide an opportunity for college dancers to have their work adjudicated and critiqued by established professionals and to provide workshops and performing experiences.

**Areas of Interest:** College dance festivals.

**Information Services:** Answers inquiries; conducts seminars and workshops; provides aid in sponsoring college dance festivals; makes referrals to other sources of information. Services are available to anyone on payment of membership fee. Festival concerts are open to the public.

**Approval Date:** 2/85

**Latest Information Date:** 2/85

**Index Terms:** Performing arts festivals; College dance festivals.

## 138

### American Dance Festival (ADF)

P.O. Box 6097, College Station
Durham, NC 27708
Tel.: (919) 684-6402                PUB69-19932

ADF is a modern dance producing service organization serving the needs of dance, dancers, and choreographers. Activities include a six-week school, young dancers' school, jazz workshop, professional workshops, sponsorship of domestic and foreign artists in performance in the United States, the Young Companies and Composers in Residence Project and other choreography projects, a Community Outreach Program, national television performance productions, the Samuel H. Scripps American Dance Festival Award, the National Competitive Scholarship Auditions, and a poster commission to a visual artist. ADF is currently conducting cooperative projects with foreign groups and is planning future connections with France, China, and Japan.

**Areas of Interest:** Modern dance; choreography; dance production; dance theater design and dance floor construction; music; jazz; theater arts; opera and music theater; media arts; dance education; dance criticism; dance medicine; multidisciplinary studies.

**Holdings:** Technical specifications of over five hundred theaters in the United States and abroad; over three hundred pages of dance floor construction data; ADF archival documents and historical materials.

**Publications:** Technical Assistance Project quarterly newsletter; specifications, critical reviews, data compilations.

**Information Services:** Answers inquiries; provides technical assistance and reference services; conducts training programs, dancers' schools, dance critics' conferences, community classes, public discussions, dance demonstrations, and workshops in dance education, jazz, body therapy, and dance medicine; provides speakers; distributes publications and ADF television productions; makes referrals to other sources of information; permits on-site use of collections. Except for technical assistance, training programs, schools, and some workshops, services are free. All are available to anyone.

**Contact:** Mr. Charles Reinhart, Director

**Approval Date:** 1/84

**Latest Information Date:** 1/86

**Index Terms:** Modern dance; Choreography; Dance production; Theater; Music; Media arts; Operas; Music theater; Dance festivals; Cultural heritage; Historic preservation; Dance education; Dance therapy; Technical assistance; Community service programs; Outreach programs; International arts activities; Dance floor construction; Information resources; Arts resources.

## 139

### American Dance Guild

570 Seventh Ave.
New York, NY 10018
Tel.: (212) 944-0557                PUB69-17808

Partially sponsored by the New York State Council for the Arts, the Guild provides a forum for exchange of ideas and methods among dancers, choreographers, teachers, and students.

**Areas of Interest:** Dance; dance education.

**Holdings:** Collection of 500 volumes.

**Publications:** *Newsletter* (six issues a year). A publications list is available.

**Information Services:** Answers inquiries; provides advisory and consulting services; conducts seminars, workshops, and conferences; makes referrals to other sources of information; permits on-site use of collections. Publications are sold; other services are free and available to anyone.

**Approval Date:** 5/84

**Latest Information Date:** 1/86

**Index Terms:** Dance; Dance education; Professional associations; Performing arts; Information exchange.

## 140

**Congress on Research in Dance (CORD)**

c/o Dance and Dance Education Department
New York University
35 West 4th St., Room 675
New York, NY 10003
Tel.: (212) 598-3459                    PUB69-21081

Comprises 615 individual and institutional members. CORD provides opportunities for the exchange of ideas among dance scholars and scholars working in dance-related fields.

**Areas of Interest:** Intellectual aspects of dance; dance scholarship; dance-related fields, including anthropology, body sciences, education, film, history, music, nonverbal communication, philosophy, sociology, theater, and the visual arts.

**Publications:** *Dance Research Journal* (semiannual); *Dance Research Annual; Dance Research Special* (occasional). A publications list is available.

**Information Services:** Conducts seminars and workshops; distributes publications in the United States and abroad. Services are available to the membership, which is open to individuals and organizations in this country and abroad.

**Contact:** Administrative Secretary

**Approval Date:** 8/85

**Latest Information Date:** 8/85

**Index Terms:** Arts resources; Dance research; Nonverbal communication.

## 141

**Dance Notation Bureau (DNB)**

33 West 21st St., 3d Floor
New York, NY 10010
Tel.: (212) 807-7899                    PUB69-16062

Sponsored by its members, National Endowments for the Humanities and the Arts, state arts councils,

and foundations, the Bureau seeks to preserve our dance heritage through graphic notation using Labanotation and other notation systems.

**Areas of Interest:** Dance recording; movement analysis and its notation; Labanotation; computer applications in dance recording; curriculum development for college dance departments; professional training for regisseurs, ballet masters, notators, and reconstructors; history and development of notation systems.

**Holdings:** Labanotation and Benesh notation scores of theatrical (ballet and modern), folk, ethnic, social, and historical dance, and notation of other human and animal movement patterns; comprehensive collection of materials on dance literacy and notation; computerized Labanotation data; research on copyright as pertinent to movement notation.

**Publications:** *Dance Notation Bureau Newsletter* (quarterly); *Dance Notation Journal* (twice a year); books, text materials, dance scores, dance score bibliographies. A publications list is available free on request.

**Information Services:** Conducts seminars and workshops; lends Labanotation scores of dances; distributes publications; arranges for reconstructions of dance from notation scores; permits on-site use of collections. Services are provided to members for a fee and are primarily for teachers, dancers, choreographers, dance companies, institutions of higher education, state and regional arts councils, and scholars. Reference inquiries on holdings are answered free.

**Approval Date:** 9/84

**Latest Information Date:** 1/86

**Index Terms:** Ballet; Choreography; Dance; Computer applications; Dance notation; Graphic methods; Curriculum development; Profesional training; Movement notation; Dance history; Labanotation Research Files.

## 142

**Dance Theater Workshop, Inc. (DTW)**

DTW's Bessie Schonberg Theater
219 West 19th St.
New York, NY 10011
Tel.: (212) 691-6500                    PUB69-20221

Partially funded by federal, state, and local government agencies and private foundations and corporations, DTW provides production facilities and artist sponsorship programs as well as a broad spectrum of preproduction, promotional, and technical services to the community of independent performing artists in New York and throughout the country. Through its production programs, DTW presents over 75 artists and companies in 275 performances each year at its Bessie Schonberg Theater. In addition to its involvement with the local and national performing arts communities, DTW also sponsors foreign artists in performance and, in keeping with its interest in more foreign involvement, is currently planning cooperative projects with foreign groups and sponsorship of performances abroad. DTW comprises about five hundred paid artists and organizational members; membership is open to all individual performing artists and companies and to nonprofit arts service, presenting, and other support organizations.

**Areas of Interest:** Creation of performance opportunities for independent performing artists; development of audiences for the new work of these performing artists; administrative and promotional needs associated with the preproduction period preceding any performance series, including promotional schedules, direct mail, advertising, press relations, graphic design for advertistments and fliers, video documentation, and assistance with budgeting and arts management concerns.

**Holdings:** Comprehensive dance video archive documenting over six hundred works by nearly one hundred fifty different artists and companies; computerized audience and sponsor mailing lists; press lists.

**Publications:** *Poor Dancer's Almanac* (comprehensive survival manual and resource directory for New York dance artists).

**Information Services:** Answers inquiries; provides advisory, consulting, and technical assistance services; conducts seminars and workshops; distributes publications; makes referrals to other sources of information in the United States and abroad; permits on-site use of reference files on performance and rehearsal spaces and arts-related personnel. General informational services are available free to anyone; concrete promotional services are limited to the membership; publications are available for sale at discounted prices.

**Contact:** Mr. David R. White, Executive Producer

**Approval Date:** 1/84

**Latest Information Date:** 1/86

**Index Terms:** Arts resources; Dance; Music; Theater; Performance art; Art management; Fund raising; Promoting; Advertising; Public relations; Technical assistance.

## 143–144

### Foundation for Ethnic Dance, Inc.

17 West 71st St.
New York, NY 10023
Tel.: (212) 877-9565          PUB69-17914

Partially funded by the National Endowment for the Arts and the New York State Council on the Arts, the Foundation supports research and teaching and sponsors the Matteo EthnoAmerican Dance Theater, a professional dance company that tours nationally and internationally.

**Areas of Interest:** Ethnic dance.

**Holdings:** Contemporary and rare books, authentic recorded dance tapes and records, bibliographies, choreographic notes, dance artifacts and props.

**Publications:** Journal articles.

**Information Services:** Answers inquiries; provides advisory, consulting, reference, and literature-searching services; conducts seminars and workshops; evaluates and analyzes data; makes referrals to other sources of information. Services may be subject to a fee and are available to anyone.

**Contact:** Ms. Carola Goya, Associate Director

**Approval Date:** 2/85

**Latest Information Date:** 2/85

**Index Terms:** Performing arts; Folk dancing; Choreography; Dance notation; Teaching; Research; Ethnic groups.

## 145

### International Center for Dance Orthopaedics and Dance Therapy

9201 Sunset Blvd., Suite 317
Hollywood, CA 90069
Tel.: (213) 728-0148          PUB69-19961

**Areas of Interest:** Musculoskeletal problems of classical dancers as well as others engaging in other types of dance activity; orthopedic and medical aspects of dance, including such areas as stress physiology, sports medicine, and arthroscopy.

**Holdings:** Literature collections in the above areas.

**Publications:** *Dance Medicine-Health Newsletter*; abstracts, indexes, directories.

**Information Services:** Answers inquiries; provides advisory, consulting, reference, and current-awareness services and information on research in progress;

conducts symposia; distributes publications; makes referrals to other sources of information; permits on-site use of collections. Services are available at cost to anyone.

**Contact:** Dr. Ernest L. Washington, Medical Director

**Approval Date:** 1/84

**Latest Information Date:** 1/86

**Index Terms:** Dance; Dance therapy; Orthopedics; Stress physiology; Sports medicine; Musculoskeletal disorders; Information dissemination; Medical research; Arts resources.

## 146

**Laban-Bartenieff Institute of Movement Studies, Inc. (LBIMS)**

133 West 21st St., 7th Floor
New York, NY 10011
Tel.: (212) 255-6800                    PUB69-19901

The Institute conducts educational and research programs on human movement as nonverbal expression. It was founded in 1977 by Irmgard Bartenieff, a dancer, teacher, physical therapist, and student of Rudolf Laban who developed a system to analyze and notate movement. Activities include training and certification of professional Laban Movement Analysts working in the United States and abroad as college educators, dance therapists, dancers and choreographers, management consultants, sports and fitness trainers, and social and behavioral scientists. The Institute is also a membership organization, sponsors research and conferences, and offers workshops and seminars.

**Areas of Interest:** Analysis of human movement and nonverbal communication in dance, dance therapy, physical rehabilitation, industrial efficiency and training, management and personnel assessment, psychological assessment, sports performance and training, and fitness.

**Holdings:** Martin Gleisner Collection of photographs of early European modern dance; Irmgard Bartenieff Archive; unpublished research by Laban Movement Analysts and others, books, articles, films, and videotapes on movement behavior.

**Publications:** *Newsletter of the Laban-Bartenieff Institute of Movement Studies, Inc.*, Directory of members.

**Information Services:** Answers inquiries; provides advisory services; conducts workshops; distributes publications; makes referrals to other sources of information; permits on-site use of collections. Workshops are open to students for a fee; referral serv-

ices are free and available to anyone; library-media center is open to members at no charge and to others at a small fee.

**Contact:** Dr. Suzanne Youngerman, Executive Director

**Approval Date:** 4/85

**Latest Information Date:** 1/86

**Index Terms:** Body language; Movement (acting); Non-verbal communication; Movement education; Dance; Dance therapy; Physical rehabilitation; Performing arts; Physical fitness; Exercise (physiology) Physical education; Anthropology; Sports; Educational programs; Teacher training; Research projects; Physical therapy; Arts resources; Psychology.

## 147

**Lloyd Shaw Foundation, Inc.**
**Archives Division**

1620 Los Alamos Ave. SW.
Albuquerque, NM 87104
Tel.: (505) 247-3921                    PUB69-17655

The Foundation seeks to recall, restore, and teach the folk rhythms of the American people.

**Areas of Interest:** American folk dance; square dance; contra dance; round dance; Kentucky running set; English dance; dance history; social dance; ballroom dance; couple dance; dance education; dance calling, prompting, and cueing; folk dance leadership; dancing in the American West and on the frontier; dance recordings.

**Holdings:** Extensive collections of books and periodicals on square, round, and contra dance and recordings of square, round, and contra dance music. The Dance Away Library, a private library, is available to the Archives and consists of over three thousand books, including rare books, periodicals, photographs, microfilms, and other items, as well as the archives of Legacy, a square dance leadership organization. A computer catalog data base is available on site.

**Publications:** Critical reviews, abstracts, indexes, bibliographies, videotapes of dancing, audiotapes of music.

**Information Services:** Answers inquiries; provides advisory, consulting, reference, literature-searching, abstracting, indexing, current-awareness, reproduction, and microform services; conducts seminars and workshops; evaluates and analyzes data; distributes publications and data compilations; makes referrals to other sources of information; permits on-site use of collections. Services are available to anyone for a fee.

**Approval Date:** 8/85

**Latest Information Date:** 8/85

**Index Terms:** Libraries; Archives; Dance; Folk dance; Square dancing; Dance education; American folk dance; Dance history.

---

## 148

**Michigan Dance Association (MDA)**

Bailey Community Center
300 Bailey St., Room 201
East Lansing, MI 48823
Tel.: (517) 351-0454                PUB69-20346

A membership organization of over four hundred groups and individuals, including dancers, choreographers, administrators, therapists, teachers at all levels, and others in the United States and foreign countries, MDA works cooperatively with the total Michigan dance community as well as state and local arts agencies to support and develop dance opportunities for a broad constituency. It provides a forum for the discussion of matters affecting dance and offers services and support for dance in the private and public sectors. Special activities include a Dancers-In-Schools program and a Dance Project for the Handicapped that offers services to handicapped individuals and service providers for the handicapped. MDA holds memberships in international organizations, participates in international conferences, and is interested in more foreign involvement.

**Areas of Interest:** Dance; dance therapy; comprehensive arts education; special education; arts management; fund raising.

**Holdings:** Collections in the above areas.

**Publications:** *MDA Newsletter* (five issues a year); *Dance in Michigan Directory; Dance Education in Michigan; Resource Lists for Children's Dance; Leap, Skip, Twist, and Freeze; Creative Starters; How to Choose a Dance Teacher* (brochure).

**Information Services:** Answers inquiries; provides advisory, consulting, reference, and current-awareness services; conducts seminars and workshops; provides speakers; distributes publications in the United States and abroad; makes referrals to other sources of information, both foreign and domestic. Some services are provided free to members; other services are provided for a fee to all users.

**Contact:** Ms. Jeanette Abeles, Executive Director

**Approval Date:** 1/84

**Latest Information Date:** 1/86

**Index Terms:** Arts resources; Dance; Dance therapy; Comprehensive art education; Special education; Art management; Fund raising; International arts activities; Handicapped arts services.

---

## 149

**Muskegon Community College Dance Program**

221 South Quarterline Rd.
Muskegon, MI 49442
Tel.: (616) 777-0386                PUB69-20345

The Muskegon Community College Dance Program is a two-year dance transfer program offering classes in several styles of dance plus opportunities to perform and study with visiting guest artists. It includes two dance performing groups: the Overbrook Dance Theatre, which performs an annual concert, and the Repertory Dance Tour Company, which presents modern dance performances, lectures, and demonstrations in area schools, institutions, etc. to kindergarten through grade 12 audiences.

**Areas of Interest:** Modern dance; modern jazz dance; ballet; tap dance; social dance; folk, round, and square dance; Afro-American dance; dance choreography and design.

**Holdings:** Dance-related films, video tapes, books, records, and photographs.

**Publications:** Curricula and teaching materials.

**Information Services:** Answers inquiries; provides advisory, consulting, and reference services; conducts seminars and workshops; provides speakers; distributes publications; makes referrals to other sources of information. A dance student scholarship fund donation is requested for information services. The Program's facilities are accessible to the handicapped.

**Contact:** Ms. Judith Brooky, Dance Coordinator

**Approval Date:** 1/84

**Latest Information Date:** 1/86

**Index Terms:** Arts resources; Dance education; Modern dance; Jazz dance; Ballet; Tap dance; Ballroom dance; Folk dance; Round dancing; Square dancing; Afro-American dance; Choreography; Handicapped arts services; Lecturers; Scholarships.

## 150

**National Association for Regional Ballet**

1860 Broadway
New York, NY 10023
Tel.: (212) 757-8460                    PUB69-19697

**Areas of Interest:** Decentralized dance companies; set and costume referral service; choreography; dance company management.

**Publications:** Newsletters, handbooks, bulletins, directories, data compilations.

**Information Services:** Answers inquiries; provides advisory and consulting services; evaluates data; conducts seminars and workshops; distributes publications; makes referrals to other sources of information. Some services are available to anyone while others are restricted to members.

**Approval Date:** 8/85

**Latest Information Date:** 8/85

**Index Terms:** Dance; Choreography; Stage scenery; Dance production; Performing arts; Costume; Theatrical companies management; Ballet; Modern dance; Arts resources.

## 151

**National Association of Dance and Affiliated Artists, Inc. (NADAA)**

P.O. Box 8
San Bruno, CA 94066
Tel.: (415) 583-7662                    PUB69-19952

**Areas of Interest:** Ballet; jazz dance; tap dance; character dance; modern dance; aerobic dance; children's dance; dance technique; dance production; ballroom and disco dancing; care and prevention of dance injuries.

**Holdings:** Textbooks from past NADAA dance workshops.

**Publications:** Workshop announcements; letters to members.

**Information Services:** Answers inquiries; conducts seminars, workshops, lectures, and youth programs.

Some services may be subject to a fee and some may be restricted to members.

**Contact:** Mr. Glenn Shipley, Chairman of the Board

**Approval Date:** 2/84

**Latest Information Date:** 1/86

**Index Terms:** Ballet; Jazz dance; Tap dance; Character dance; Modern dance; Aerobic dance; Children's dances; Dance techniques; Dance production; Ballroom dancing; Disco dancing; Dancing injuries prevention; Arts resources.

## 152–153

**National Dance Institute, Inc. (NDI)**

599 Broadway
New York, NY 10012
Tel.: (212) 226-0083                    PUB69-19976

Funded by individuals, private corporations, and foundations, NDI provides dance instruction programs to public and parochial school children, deaf children, and selected groups of adults, including police men and women. Programs are performance oriented. A major Event of the Year is held annually.

**Areas of Interest:** Education in a broad spectrum of dance forms, including ethnic, modern, and jazz dance in addition to classical ballet, and emphasizing dance as an enjoyable activity with self-conscious stress on dance as an art form; programs in dance education suitable for local community sponsorship.

**Publications:** Dance films.

**Information Services:** Provides advisory and consulting services; conducts dance instruction classes and workshops; distributes films. Services are available at cost to schools and other local community organizations in the United States and abroad.

**Contact:** Ms. Elizabeth Gardella, Executive Director

**Approval Date:** 1/84

**Latest Information Date:** 1/86

**Index Terms:** Dance education; Special education; Folk dance; Modern dance; Jazz dance; Ballet; International arts activities; Handicapped arts services; Performing arts; Visual arts; Arts resources.

# Theater Organizations

## 154

### Actors' Equity Association (AEA)

165 West 46th St.
New York, NY 10036
Tel.: (212) 869-8530          PUB69-17809

Affiliated with the AFL-CIO, AEA is a labor union for performers in the legitimate theater.

**Areas of Interest:** Wages and working conditions of professional actors; professional theater.

**Publications:** *Equity News* (monthly).

**Information Services:** Answers inquiries free from anyone.

**Approval Date:** 2/84

**Latest Information Date:** 1/86

**Index Terms:** Performing arts; Labor unions; Actors; Acting; Theater as a profession.

## 155

### Alliance of Resident Theatres/New York

325 Spring St.
New York, NY 10013
Tel.: (212) 989-5257          PUB69-19911

An organization of 86 nonprofit professional theaters, 50 arts institutions, and 650 individuals, the Alliance serves as the trade association and service organization for the membership. Activities include a theater management internship program and advocacy before certain groups.

**Areas of Interest:** Theater management, including information on accessibility, marketing, public relations, internships, jobs, career development, performance and rehearsal space availability, technical production resources, fund raising, financial management, contracts, and graphics and printing.

**Holdings:** About two hundred fifty volumes; fifteen periodical titles.

**Publications:** *Theatre Times* (seven issues a year); *Ticket Central Calendar* (eight issues a year); books, directories, project reports, handbooks, guides.

**Information Services:** Answers inquiries; provides advisory, technical assistance, and reference services; evaluates and analyzes data; conducts seminars and workshops; provides speakers; distributes publications and data compilations; makes referrals to other sources of information; permits on-site use of collec-

tions. Inquiries are answered free for anyone. Other services may be subject to a fee and may be available to members only. Facilities are accessible to the handicapped.

**Contact:** Kate Busch, Director of Membership Services

**Approval Date:** 2/85

**Latest Information Date:** 2/85

**Index Terms:** Theater management; Information services; Marketing; Public relations; Internships; Employment; Career development; Performance; Theater; Operas; Music theater; Performing arts; Art management; Fund raising; Lecturers; Handicapped arts services; Financial management; Arts resources.

## 156

### American College Theatre Festival (ACTF)

c/o John F. Kennedy Center for the Performing Arts
Washington, DC 20566
Tel.: (212) 254-3437          PUB69-16362

The Festival, an annual event, seeks to honor the most diverse college and university theater productions, to strengthen the rest, and to encourage college students everywhere to take an active part as writers, designers, performers, directors, and as audience in their college theater. Festival productions are presented at local, regional, and national levels, with the final presentations being given at the Kennedy Center in Washington, D.C., by invitation of ACTF. The Festival is produced by the University and College Theatre Association, a division of the American Theatre Association, presented by the John F. Kennedy Center for the Performing Arts, and supported by grants from the Amoco Companies and the U.S. Department of Education.

**Areas of Interest:** Fostering of highest standards in all aspects of college and university theater, including playwriting, directing, acting, designing, etc.; education in theatrical arts.

**Publications:** Brochure describing the Festival and available awards, and containing entry forms.

**Information Services:** Answers inquiries concerning the Festival; conducts workshops in conjunction with the regional festivals.

**Approval Date:** 8/84

**Latest Information Date:** 1/86

**Index Terms:** Performing arts; Performing arts festivals; Playwriting; Awards; College students; Dramatics; Art education; Colleges and universities; Acting.

## 157

### American Dinner Theatre Institute

P.O. Box 2537
Sarasota, FL 33582
Tel.: (813) 365-1754                    PUB69-19960

The Institute is a membership organization of about fifty professional dinner theater owner-operators. Membership is open to current and potential owner-operators. The Institute currently serves a number of foreign members and is interested in expanding its activities abroad.

**Areas of Interest:** Coordination of information on all phases of dinner theater operation.

**Publications:** Newsletter and current production schedule (both monthly); membership directory (annual); cookbook and bartender's guide.

**Information Services:** Answers inquiries; provides advisory and consulting services; makes referrals to other sources of information. Services are free, except for consulting, and available only to current and potential dinner theater producers.

**Contact:** Mr. Marvin H. Poons, Executive Secretary

**Approval Date:** 4/84

**Latest Information Date:** 1/86

**Index Terms:** Dinner theater play production; Information services; International arts activities; Arts resources.

## 158

### American Theatre Association

1010 Wisconsin Ave. NW., 6th Floor
Washington, DC 20007
Tel.: (202) 342-7530                    PUB69-6629

The Association was formerly known as the American Educational Theatre Association.

**Areas of Interest:** Noncommercial theater (national and international), including community, children's, secondary school, university and college, Army theater, and others; theater technology, architecture, literature, history, and criticism.

**Holdings:** Collection of journals, newsletters, bibliographies, technical reports, and standards and specifications. The Association's Archives are maintained

at the New York Public Library, Performing Arts Section, Lincoln Center.

**Publications:** *Theatre Journal* (quarterly); *Children's Theatre Review* (quarterly); *Secondary School Theatre Journal*; *Directory of American College Theatres*; *Summer Theatre Directory* (annual); *Theatre News* (nine times a year); *Children's Theatre Directory* (biannual); annual directory of members, special bibliographies, course guides, and Books of the Theatre Series.

**Information Services:** Answers brief inquiries free; provides consulting services to members; makes referrals to other sources of information.

**Approval Date:** 8/84

**Latest Information Date:** 1/86

**Index Terms:** Drama; Theaters.

## 159

### Children's Theatre Association of America

c/o American Theatre Association
1010 Wisconsin Ave. NW
Washington, DC 20007                    PUB69-19906

An organization of about one thousand teachers, directors, recreation workers, volunteers, writers, publishers, other professionals, and parents interested in children's theater, the Association is a division of the American Theatre Association and serves as an advocate for the use of children's theater and creative drama in education.

**Areas of Interest:** Creative drama in education; children's theater in education; professional children's theater; drama as therapy; creative drama and creative theater for special populations, including the elderly; interdisciplinary arts projects; new scripts; religious drama; research.

**Holdings:** Historical archives of papers and artifacts.

**Publications:** *Theatre News; Children's Theatre Review; CTAA Newsletter;* bibliographies, directories, curriculum aids.

**Information Services:** Answers inquiries; provides advisory, consulting, reference, and current-awareness services; conducts regional workshops and an annual conference; provides speakers; makes referrals to other sources of information. Services are free to the membership.

**Approval Date:** 12/85

**Latest Information Date:** 12/85

**Index Terms:** Arts resources; Drawings; Professional children's theater; Creative drama with the aged; Creative drama in education; Art therapy; Creative art; Interdisciplinary approach; Teacher training; Children's theater; Theater; Education.

## 160

### Children's Theatre Company and School

2400 Third Ave. South
Minneapolis, MN 55404
Tel.: (612) 874-0500                    PUB69-21073

The Children's Theatre Company and School produces six plays a year for young people and families. The School offers academic and theater eduction for students ages nine to twenty-one in a fully accredited private school with emphasis on the performing arts. A Summer Theatre Institute offers an intensive five-week program for students ages twelve to eighteen in both the performing and production aspects of theater. International activities include membership in international organizations.

**Areas of Interest:** Dance; theater; media arts; performing arts; arts management; fund raising; comprehensive arts educationl

**Holdings:** Library of scripts written and produced by the Company, including stories from all over the world as well as original stories developed in-house. There are about one hundred forty scripts currently on file.

**Information Services:** Answers inquiries; provides advisory and consulting services; conducts seminars and workshops; provides speakers; makes referrals to other sources of information. Services may be subject to a fee and are available to anyone. Facilities are accessible to the handicapped.

**Contact:** Ms. Marcy Dowse, Director of Communications

**Approval Date:** 11/84

**Latest Information Date:** 1/86

**Index Terms:** Arts resources; Children's theater; Dance; Theater; Media arts; Performance art; Comprehensive arts education; Art management; Fund raising.

## 161

### Dramatists Guild, Inc.

234 West 44th St.
New York, NY 10036
Tel.: (212) 398-9366                    PUB69-19918

Founded more than sixty years ago, the Dramatists Guild is the only professional association of playwrights, composers, and lyricists in the United States today. Current membership includes over seventy-eight hundred produced and unproduced theater writers.

**Areas of Interest:** All professional and business needs of playwrights, composers, and lyricists.

**Holdings:** Library of standard theater reference text copies of all Guild contracts since 1926, and an extensive collection of members' books and plays; comprehensive files on awards, contests, grants, workshops, residencies, and conferences open to playwrights. All of the above are available to members only.

**Publications:** *The Dramatists Guild Quarterly; The Dramatists Guild Newsletter* (ten issues a year).

**Information Services:** Provides business counseling; answers queries on dramatists, producers, lawyers, agents, contracts, royalties, grants, copyright, contests, conferences, workshops, and theater across the country; makes referrals to other domestic and foreign sources of information. Facilities of the Dramatists Guild are accessible to the handicapped.

**Contact:** Mr. David E. LeVine, Executive Director

**Approval Date:** 8/85

**Latest Information Date:** 8/85

**Index Terms:** Dramatists guild; Arts resources; Music theater; Professional associations; Playwriting; Composers; Lyricists; Information services; Royalties; Copyrights; Handicapped arts services; Grants; International arts activities; Arts resources.

## 162

### Fairmount Theatre of the Deaf

8500 Euclid Ave.
Cleveland, OH 44106
Tel.: (216) 231-8787 (Business)
       (216) 795-7000 (Box Office)    PUB69-20230

Partially funded by state agencies and private organizations, the Fairmount Theatre produces original and published plays in voiced English and sign language, provides specialized educational programming and outreach programming, presents performances locally (at the Cleveland Play House), nationally, and abroad, holds memberships in international organizations, participates in international conferences and drama festivals, has hired foreign performers, and continues to pursue all aspects of international networking.

**Areas of Interest:** Theater for the deaf; performance art; special education.

**Holdings:** About twenty original sign language translation scripts; about fifteen videotape recordings of productions.

**Publications:** Newsletter; teaching materials. Reviews are available on request.

**Information Services:** Answers inquiries; provides advisory services; conducts seminars and workshops; distributes audiovisual materials; provides speakers. Some services may be subject to a fee. All are available to anyone. Theater office facilities include TTY equipment and are accessible to the handicapped.

**Contact:** Peggy Shumate, Administrative Director

**Approval Date:** 1/86

**Latest Information Date:** 1/86

**Index Terms:** Arts resources; Theater of the deaf; Performing arts; Visual arts; Special education; Fund raising; Educational programs; Outreach programs; International arts activities; Handicapped arts services.

### 163

**International Amateur Theatre Association (IATA)**

Vesterbrogade 175
DK-1800 Copenhagen V., DENMARK
Tel.: 01-22 22 45
(Cable) INTERTHEATRE
COPENHAGEN          PUB69-19938

Subsidized by the governments of Denmark, Norway, and Sweden, IATA is an association of national organizations, institutions, colleges, universities, and other bodies in forty countries concerned with international exchanges in the field of nonprofessional theater.

**Areas of Interest:** Amateur theater; community theater; student theater; children's theater; drama in education.

**Publications:** Bulletin (five issues a year); project reports; conference papers.

**Information Services:** Answers inquiries; conducts conferences, workshops, and seminars; provides speakers. Information service is free to groups and individuals engaged in nonprofessional theater and educational drama. Attendance at events is subject to a fee.

**Contact:** Mr. John Ytteborg, Secretary General

**Approval Date:** 1/84

**Latest Information Date:** 1/84

**Index Terms:** Amateur theater; Community theater; Student theater; Children's theater; Drama in education; Theater; Folk art; International arts activities; Performing arts; Arts resources.

### 164

**International Foundation for Theatrical Research**

P.O. Box 4526
Albuquerque, NM 87196
Tel.:(505) 843-7749          PUB69-18748

**Location:** 614 Indian School Rd. NW

**Areas of Interest:** New forms of theatrical expression.

**Publications:** *The Writing and Production of Plays*; reports.

**Information Services:** Answers inquiries; provides literature-searching and reproduction services; distributes publications. Services are available at cost to anyone.

**Approval Date:** 8/85

**Latest Information Date:** 8/85

**Index Terms:** Performing arts; Theatrical research; Experimental theater.

### 165

**International Theatre Institute of the United States, Inc. (ITI/US)**

1860 Broadway, Suite 1510
New York, NY 10023
Tel.: (212) 245-3950          PUB69-13747

ITI/US is the American center of the International Theatre Institute (ITI), an autonomous nonprofit organization formed by UNESCO in 1948, with a network of sixty national centers.

**Areas of Interest:** Promotion of the exchange of knowledge and practice in the theatre arts.

**Holdings:** Library of books, periodicals, plays, yearbooks, house organs, newsletters, programs, press releases, production schedules, brochures, monographs, articles, and newspaper clippings from and about theaters around the world.

**Publications:** *Theatre Notes* (newsletter); *Theatre 1, 2, 3, 4, 5* (discontinued with No. 5); *Contemporary Stage Design-USA; International Directory of Theatre, Dance and Folklore Festivals* (1979; for sale); annual report.

**Information Services:** Answers inquiries; provides advisory services; organizes meetings, conferences, colloquia, and seminars on specific theater subjects; distributes publications; stimulates and services the exchange of theater specialists among countries; makes referrals to other sources of information; permits on-site use of library materials. Services are free and available to those having a serious interest in the theater arts.

**Approval Date:** 2/84

**Latest Information Date:** 1/86

**Index Terms:** International cultural exchange; Performing arts.

## 166

### International Thespian Society

3368 Central Parkway
Cincinnati, OH 45225-2392
Tel.: (513) 559-1996          PUB69-6803

The International Thespian Society is an educational organization which aims to establish and advance standards of excellence in all phases of theater arts, and which strives to create an active and intelligent interest in theater arts in secondary schools.

**Areas of Interest:** Secondary school theater, as well as nonsecondary school organizations interested in the advancement of secondary school theater.

**Holdings:** 12,000 play manuscripts; 1,500 theatre-oriented books; periodicals; computer list of member schools.

**Publications:** *Dramatics Magazine* (monthly, September through May); numerous publications for teachers, directors, and students of theater arts.

**Information Services:** Answers inquiries and provides data regarding all aspects of theater, with primary emphasis on secondary school theater arts; disseminates pamphlets and pertinent facts concerning the Society. Reference services and interlibrary loans are provided to members and associate members only.

**Contact:** Ronald L. Longstreth, Executive Director

**Approval Date:** 8/84

**Latest Information Date:** 1/86

**Index Terms:** Arts resources; Drama; Arts education.

## 167

### League of Historic American Theatres

1600 H St. NW.
Washington, DC 20006
Tel.: (202) 289-1494          PUB69-20594

The League, a nonprofit organization, is dedicated to the preservation and use of America's historic theater buildings.

**Areas of Interest:** Preservation, restoration, programming, management, funding, history, and architecture of historic theater buildings.

**Holdings:** Building documentation materials are available to the public (by appointment) in the Chesley Collection at Princeton University Library.

**Publications:** *National List of Historic Theatre Buildings* (book); monthly bulletin; quarterly newsletter.

**Information Services:** Answers inquiries; provides consulting and reference services; conducts seminars; distributes publications and data compilations; makes referrals to other sources of information. Services are available to anyone, on a limited scale, except the bulletin, newsletter, and consulting services, which are limited to members. The book is for sale to the public.

**Contact:** Deborah Mikula, Executive Director

**Approval Date:** 11/84

**Latest Information Date:** 1/86

**Index Terms:** Theaters; Historic preservation; Historic buildings.

## 168

### Loon and Heron Theatre for Children, Inc.

194 Boylston St.
Brookline, MA 02146
Tel.: (617) 232-1715          PUB69-20218

Funded in part by the National Endowment for the Arts and the Massachusetts Council for the Arts and Humanities, the Loon and Heron Theatre seeks to entertain, educate, and stimulate children of all ages through multicultural and multidisciplinary programs that directly involve the children, both non-handicapped and handicapped.

**Areas of Interest:** Children's theater, including set design, costume design, and puppet theater; curriculum design; teacher training.

**Publications:** Newsletter; book detailing work with special needs groups.

**Information Services:** Answers inquiries; conducts seminars and workshops; distributes publications and curriculum materials. Services may be subject to a fee and are available to anyone, but are most appropriate for schools, community educational organizations, and other children's theaters. Many of the Theatre's programs are accessible to the handicapped.

**Contact:** Sherrod Sturrock, Executive Director

**Approval Date:** 1/84

**Latest Information Date:** 1/86

**Index Terms:** Arts resources; Children's theater; Teacher training; Curriculum design; Performance art; Puppets; Handicapped arts services.

## 169

### National Association for Drama Therapy (NADT)

19 Edwards St.
New Haven, CT 06511
Tel.: (203) 624-2146                    PUB69-20224

NADT is an organization of 200 regular, associate, and student members in the United States and foreign countries. Regular membership is restricted to those who fulfill the minimum requirement of 1,000 hours of professional practice of drama therapy in the last five years. Practitioners who qualify may become Registered Drama Therapists (R.D.T.).

**Areas of Interest:** Uses of creative drama and theater in therapeutic applications with such special populations as the geriatric, child, psychiatric, forensic, and physically handicapped populations; professional ethics and standards in the practice of drama therapy; drama therapy education.

**Holdings:** Computerized mailing list.

**Publications:** Journal articles, standards, curricula, state-of-the-art reviews, directories, bibliographies, reprints. A publications price list is available.

**Information Services:** Answers inquiries; provides advisory and reference services and information on research in progress; conducts an annual conference; distributes publications and its mailing list; provides speakers. Services may be subject to a fee and are available to anyone.

**Contact:** David Read Johnson, President

**Approval Date:** 1/84

**Latest Information Date:** 1/86

**Index Terms:** Arts resources; Drama therapy; Professional associations; Professional training; Psychology; Psychotherapy; Personal growth; Professional standards; Professional ethics; Acting; Comprehensive art education; Theater; International arts activities.

## 170

### National Association of Schools of Theatre (NAST)

11250 Roger Bacon Dr., Suite 5
Reston, VA 22090
Tel.: (703) 437-0700                    PUB69-18647

**Areas of Interest:** Evaluation and accreditation of theater education programs.

**Publications:** Directory.

**Information Services:** Identifies accredited theater education programs. The directory is sold for one dollar.

**Approval Date:** 2/84

**Latest Information Date:** 1/86

**Index Terms:** Performing arts; Theater; Educational programs; Evaluation; Accreditation.

## 171

### Ohio State University
### Theatre Department
### Theatre Research Institute

1089 Drake Union
1849 Cannon Dr.
Columbus, OH 43210
Tel.: (614) 422-6614                    PUB69-18198

**Areas of Interest:** Theater history; literature and criticism; design, including costume and scenery; acting theory.

**Holdings:** Major collections include the Eileen Heckert Collection, Hartman Theatre Collection, Charles Kean Promptbooks and Scrapbooks, Phelps and Sadler's Wells Collection, Turin Ballet Collection, Ellen Tree Diaries and Letters, Ibsen Promptbooks, Toy Theatre Collection, Basoli Scene Designs, Augustin Daly Scrapbooks and Playbills, Marini Costume Designs, Walter Hampden Scrapbooks, Philip Sills Collection, Harmound Theatre Collection, Comedie Francaise Records, Early Nineteenth-Century Austrian Scene Designs, Sanquirico Scene Designs, Armbruster Scenic Studio Collection, Costume Designs from Biblioteca Nazionale Braidense, Edwin Booth Letters, Planche Promptbooks, Surrey Theatre Collection, Oenslager Collection, and Heal Collection. The Institute also maintains a small data base on theatrical subjects with annual listing in a publication.

**Publications:** *Theatre Studies* (annual).

**Information Services:** Answers inquiries; provides reproduction and microform services; distributes publications; permits on-site use of collections. Reproduction and microform services are offered at cost; other services are free. All are available to anyone.

**Approval Date:** 2/84

**Latest Information Date:** 1/86

**Index Terms:** Performing arts; Theater; History; Literature (fine arts); Costume; Stage scenery; Acting.

## 172

**Puppeteers of America, Inc.**

5 Cricklewood Path
Pasadena, CA 91107
  Tel.: (213) 979-5748          PUB69-16316

Puppeteers of America, Inc. is a nonprofit membership organization with thirty-four local groups.

**Areas of Interest:** Puppetry.

**Holdings:** Audiovisual Library; computerized membership data as to specific involvement in the field.

**Publications:** *Puppetry Journal* (quarterly); annual membership directory; brochures.

**Information Services:** Answers inquiries; provides advisory and reference services; conducts festivals and workshops; distributes publications. Services are free to and primarily for members, but others will be assisted.

**Contact:** Ms. Gayle G. Schluter, Chairperson

**Approval Date:** 4/85

**Latest Information Date:** 4/85

**Index Terms:** Puppeteers; Puppets; Puppet plays.

## 173

**Rainbow Company Children's Theatre**

821 Las Vegas Blvd. North
Las Vegas, NV 89101
  Tel.: (702) 386-6553          PUB69-19916

Partially funded by the City of Las Vegas, the Rainbow Company Children's Theatre produces quality theater for a child audience, trains a core group of young children and adolescents in the theater arts at a professional level and offers classes in creative dramatics for children ages three to eighteen. It serves foreign audiences, holds memberships in international organizations, participates in international conferences, sponsors performances abroad, conducts cooperative projects with foreign groups, and, consonant with its interest in more foreign involvement, is planning future international projects.

**Areas of Interest:** Theater; music theater; performance art; special education; arts management; fund raising.

**Publications:** Reprints; brochures.

**Information Services:** Answers inquiries; provides advisory, reference, and current-awareness services; conducts classes, seminars, workshops, and a touring theater program; provides speakers; distributes publications in the United States and abroad; makes referrals to domestic and foreign sources of information. Services are available to anyone; some may be subject to a fee. All facilities are accessible to the handicapped; braille and large print materials are available to the sight-disabled; and the entire program integrates the handicapped and the nonhandicapped in performance.

**Contact:** Brian Strom, Artistic Director

**Approval Date:** 5/85

**Latest Information Date:** 5/85

**Index Terms:** Theater; Music theater; Performing arts; Special education; Art management; Fund raising; Children's theater; International arts activities; Handicapped arts services; Arts resources.

## 174

**Society of Stage Directors and Choreographers**

1501 Broadway, 31st Floor
New York, NY 10036
  Tel.: (212) 391-1070          PUB69-19933

The Society is a national independent labor union representing 1,000 directors and choreographers in the United States and other countries working in the professional American theater.

**Areas of Interest:** Theater directors and choreographers; stage direction and choreography as a career.

**Holdings:** Stage periodicals.

**Publications:** Semiannual journal; membership directory; working rules and guidelines; minimum basic agreements with theaters.

**Information Services:** Answers questions from the public at no charge; conducts seminars and workshops for members and their guests.

**Contact:** Mr. A. Harrison Cromer, Executive Secretary

**Approval Date:** 1/84

**Latest Information Date:** 1/86

**Index Terms:** Labor unions; Directors (performing arts); Choreography; Theater; Stage management; Arts resources.

---

## 175

### Theatre Communications Group, Inc. (TCG)

355 Lexington Ave.
New York, NY 10017
Tel.: (212) 697-5230                    PUB69-19912

TCG is the national service organization for the non-profit professional theatre. In addition to its nearly two hundred fifty member theatres, TCG serves thousands of artists, managers and other theater professionals.

**Areas of Interest:** Theater arts; professional development of theater artists; performing arts management; use of computers in arts management; trends in theater finances and productivity; trends in public and private philanthropy; legislation affecting the performing arts; theater trustee education; new play and playwright development; Hispanic drama; resources and information about professional opportunities for dramatic writers.

**Holdings:** Extensive theater resource library containing books, periodicals, play scripts, reports and surveys, directories, catalogs, bibliographies and a comprehensive computerized data bank on the finances of the nonprofit theater over the last nineteen years; collection of theater playbills (1958-75) is available on microfiche from Greenwood Press; 1976-79 collection is housed at Library of Congress; and recent playbills available at TCG.

**Publications:** *American Theatre* magazine (formerly *Theatre Communications*, issued eleven times annually); *Art SEARCH* (biweekly national employment bulletin); *Plays in Process* (script circulation service for new plays, translations and adaptations; issues twelve scripts annually); wide range of other literary, critical, and resource titles, as well as anthologies, reports, and directories. Publications catalog available.

**Information Services:** TCG provides research, advisory, and referral services through personal interviews, casting, conferences, roundtables, seminars, and specially arranged consultations; provides information and answers inquiries from theater personnel, funding agencies, the media, and the general public; resource library is available by appointment for use by theater personnel; general information is available free of charge and publications are available for sale to any interested party; other services are available only as membership benefits.

**Contact:** Mr. Peter Zeisler, Director

**Approval Date:** 4/85

**Latest Information Date:** 4/85

**Index Terms:** Performing arts; Theater; Art management; Musical theater; Fund raising; Federal aid to the arts; Nonprofit professional theater; Legislation; Employment opportunities; Fellowships; Grants; Awards; State encouragement of the arts; Information exchange; Information services; Arts resources.

---

## 176

### Youth Theatre Unlimited, Inc.

P.O. Box 3295
Hartford, CT 06103
Tel.: (203) 727-4048                    PUB69-19892

**Location:** 65 Kinsley St.

Sponsored by state and local agencies, foundations, and corporations, Youth Theatre Unlimited provides theater training for children, teenagers, adults, elementary and secondary school teachers, and actors wishing to work in the schools and produces a teenage production company featuring serious drama performed by and for teenagers and a summer theater training camp.

**Areas of Interest:** Theater; teacher training; drama.

**Publications:** Teaching materials.

**Information Services:** Answers inquiries; provides advisory services; provides speakers; conducts seminars and workshops. Answers to inquiries are available free; other services are generally subject to a fee. All services are available to anyone.

**Contact:** Mr. Alan Levys, Director

**Approval Date:** 4/85

**Latest Information Date:** 4/85

**Index Terms:** Theater; Teacher training; Drama; Teaching aids; Arts resources.

# Music Organizations

## 177

### Amateur Chamber Music Players, Inc. (ACMP)

633 E St. NW.
Washington, D. 20004
  Tel.: (202) 628-0099         PUB69-19959

ACMP is a voluntary, nonprofit organization of about four thousand members worldwide formed to encourage and facilitate the playing of chamber music by enabling amateurs to meet each other. Membership is open to anyone who plays chamber music or sings for pleasure and wishes to make music with others while traveling in the United States or abroad, or who is interested generally in promoting the playing of chamber music or singing by amateurs.

**Areas of Interest:** Identification of enthusiastic amateur chamber music instrumentalists and singers.

**Holdings:** ACMP archives; letters and diaries of Helen Rice, ACMP founder.

**Publications:** ACMP publishes a *North and Central American Directory* every second year, giving the names, addresses, telephone numbers, instruments, and performance self-grading of members. In alternate years, ACMP issues an *Overseas Directory* listing members in other countries. ACMP also publishes an annual, and occasionally semiannual, newsletter. *Helen Rice—The Great Lady of Chamber Music*, by Rustin McIntosh, M.D., a biography of the ACMP founding secretary, has also been published.

**Information Services:** Distributes publications; makes referrals to other sources of information. Services are available to interested persons upon payment of membership fee.

**Contact:** Ms. Dianne Shearin, Administrative Secretary

**Approval Date:** 1/84

**Latest Information Date:** 1/86

**Index Terms:** Amateur chamber music; Amateur musicians; Singers; Identification; International arts activities; Voluntary organizations; Nonprofit organizations; Arts resources.

## 178

### American Academy of Teachers of Singing

c/o William Gephart, Secretary
75 Bank St.
New York, NY 10014
  Tel.: (212) 242-1836         PUB69-19956

A professional organization of over thirty teachers of singing, the Academy is concerned with establishing and maintaining high professional standards in the teaching of singing and issues pronouncements from time to time on aspects of the teaching of singing and the art of singing.

**Areas of Interest:** Singing and the teaching of singing.

**Publications:** Standards, data compilations. A publications list is available from Earl Rogers, Publications Officer, 920 Riverside Dr., New York, NY 10032.

**Information Services:** Answers inquiries free; distributes publications for a fee. Services are available to anyone.

**Approval Date:** 1/84

**Latest Information Date:** 1/86

**Index Terms:** Singing; Teaching; Singers; Professional standards; Professional associations; Arts resources.

## 179

### American Accordion Musicological Society

334 Broadway South
Pitman, NJ 08071
  Tel.: (609) 589-8308 or 854-6628      PUB69-19903

An organization of 172 members in the United States and other countries, the Society sponsors a composers' competition, holds memberships in international organizations, sponsors domestic and foreign exhibitions and performances, and is planning further international projects.

**Areas of Interest:** History of the accordion and accordion music.

**Holdings:** Society archives; manuscripts of original compositions for the accordion; museum collections related to the history of the accordion.

**Publications:** Reports; recordings.

**Information Services:** Answers inquiries; provides reference services; conducts seminars and workshops; lends materials; makes referrals to other sources of information; permits on-site use of collections. Except for rental fees on manuscripts and taping fees for recordings, services are free and all are available to anyone.

**Contact:** Mr. Stanley Darrow, Secretary

**Approval Date:** 9/85

**Latest Information Date:** 9/85

**Index Terms:** Accordion; Accordion music; History;

Music; Teacher training; International arts activities; Arts resources; Archives; Music manuscripts.

## 180

### American Accordionists' Association

P.O. Box 616
Minneola, NY 11501
Tel.: (516) 746-0145          PUB69-20220

The Association sponsors international, national, and regional competitions and concerts, commissions composers of accordion works, holds membership in international organizations, participates in international conferences, sponsors performances of foreign artists in the United States and U.S. artists abroad, and is interested in more foreign involvement. Professional and association memberships are open; teacher membership is restricted to examination-qualified instructors.

**Areas of Interest:** The accordion; works for the accordion; performance art.

**Publications:** Quarterly newsletter; annual journal.

**Information Services:** Answers inquiries; provides advisory services; conducts seminars and educational symposia; provides speakers; makes referrals to other sources of information. Except for seminars and speakers, which are subject to a fee, services are free and all are available to anyone.

**Contact:** Faith Deffner, President

**Approval Date:** 1/84

**Latest Information Date:** 1/86

**Index Terms:** Accordion; Accordion music; Concerts; Musical societies; Arts resources.

## 181

### American Association for Music Therapy (AAMT)

66 Morris Ave.
Springfield, NJ 07081
Tel.: (201) 379-1100          PUB69-16527

AAMT fosters information and research in the field of music therapy and approves programs of music therapy at institutions of higher learning.

**Areas of Interest:** Uses of music in therapy.

**Holdings:** Materials on music therapy.

**Publications:** *AAMT Journal; AAMT Newsletter;* standards, directories, bibliographies, reprints.

**Information Services:** Answers inquiries; provides registration-certification services; evaluates institutional programs; conducts seminars and workshops; distributes publications.

**Approval Date:** 12/85

**Latest Information Date:** 12/85

**Index Terms:** Musicotherapy; Occupational therapy.

## 182

### American Bandmasters Association (ABA)

2019 Bradford Dr.
Arlington, TX 76010
Tel.: (817) 261-8629          PUB69-19836

Active ABA members include about 225 professional, educational, and military bandmasters with an associate membership of about 79 musical instrument manufacturers and other companies and individuals who contribute to the perpetuation of the concert band and its music. ABA funds, sponsors, and administers an annual band composition contest. It has hosted two joint meetings with the Japanese Band Directors Association (JBDA) and an ABA delegation travelled to Tokyo, Japan, for an ABA/JBDA conference in 1984. The JBDA will meet with ABA again in 1987.

**Areas of Interest:** Concert band music.

**Holdings:** The ABA Research Center is located at the Hornbake (Undergraduate) Library, University of Maryland, College Park, MD.

**Publications:** ABA cosponsors the *Journal of Band Research* (published semiannually by the Troy State University Press, Troy, Alabama).

**Information Services:** Questions are answered and reference services are provided to researchers by the ABA Research Center at the Hornbake Library.

**Contact:** Mr. Jack H. Mahan, Secretary-Treasurer

**Approval Date:** 2/85

**Latest Information Date:** 2/85

**Index Terms:** Music; Concert bands; Bands; International arts activities.

## 183

**American Choral Directors Association (ACDA)**

P.O. Box 6310
Lawton, OK 73506
Tel.: (405) 355-8161                    PUB69-19889

**Location:** 502 Southwest 38th St.

An organization of over twelve thousand choral musicians from schools, colleges, and universities, community and industrial organizations, churches, and professional groups, ACDA promotes the development of choral music performance, composition, publication, and research. Membership is open to any person who is a choral director or who is responsible for choral music on a consultant, supervisory, or administrative basis.

**Areas of Interest:** Choral music in the community, schools, colleges, and universities, and the church; ethnic music; choral direction as a profession; choral standards and repertoire; choral music education.

**Publications:** *The Choral Journal* (monthly from Aug. to June); monograph series; brochure.

**Information Services:** Answers inquiries; conducts festivals, clinics, and workshops; distributes publications; makes referrals to other sources of information. Services are provided at cost to all users.

**Contact:** Gene Brooks, Executive Secretary

**Approval Date:** 8/85

**Latest Information Date:** 8/85

**Index Terms:** Choral music; School chorals; Colleges and Universities; Church music; Music; Ethnic music; Choral directors; Music education; Repertoire; Arts; Professional associations.

## 184

**American College of Musicians**

P.O. Box 1807
Austin, TX 78767
Tel.: (512) 478-5775                    PUB69-18140

**Location:** 808 Rio Grande

The College offers programs and goals for piano teachers and pupils, including a standardized curriculum, a classification scheme for students through seventeen years, competitons, cash prizes, scholarships, and other awards.

**Areas of Interest:** Piano music suitable for teaching; piano teaching; piano examinations, competitions, and awards.

**Publications:** *Piano Guild Notes* (bimonthly); standards, syllabus.

**Information Services:** Answers inquiries and provides literature-searching services free; sells publications. Services are available to anyone.

**Approval Date:** 8/84

**Latest Information Date:** 1/86

**Index Terms:** Piano music; Music teachers; Piano teaching; Piano instruction; Scholarships; Awards; Music education; Curriculum; Piano competitions; Educational tests.

## 185

**American Composers Alliance (ACA)**

170 West 74th St.
New York, NY 10023
Tel.: (212) 362-8900                    PUB69-19895

A membership organization representing about three hundred American composers of concert music, ACA seeks to protect the rights of its members and to promote the use and understanding of their music. Broadcast Music, Inc. acts as ACA's performance royalty collection agency and all members must affiliate with it as well.

**Areas of Interest:** Contemporary American concert music; music copyrights, licenses, and contracts.

**Holdings:** In-house computer for billing and catalogs.

**Publications:** American Composers Edition, Inc., ACA's publishing division, offers thousands of compositions of all styles and instrumentations, in facsimile editions, making available for sale or rental pieces that other publishers, who must print in quantity, cannot afford to handle. In addition, a *Special Edition* series is selected from time to time by a committee of peer judges. A flute series and a percussion series have been published to date. All ACA music is listed by category in catalogs.

**Information Services:** Answers inquiries; provides advisory, reference, and reproduction services; distributes rental materials and publications; makes referrals to other sources of information. Information is available free to anyone. Catalogs are available for postage and handling costs only.

**Contact:** Ms. Rosalie Calabrese, Executive Director

**Approval Date:** 3/85

**Latest Information Date:** 3/85

**Index Terms:** Arts resources; American composers; Contemporary music; Copyrights; Licenses; Royalties; Concert music composers; Contemporary music concerts; Musical societies; International arts activities.

## 186

**American Federation of Musicians of the United States and Canada**

1501 Broadway, Suite 600
Paramount Bldg.
New York, NY 10036
  Tel.: (212) 869-1330      PUB69-5256

**Areas of Interest:** Union representation of musicians; collective bargaining; wage scales.

**Holdings:** Collection of contracts, reviews, books, newsletters, reprints, publication lists, pamphlets, news releases, clippings, photos, motion pictures, tapes, and data compilations.

**Publications:** *International Musician* (monthly).

**Information Services:** Answers inquiries; makes referrals.

**Approval Date:** 8/84

**Latest Information Date:** 1/86

**Index Terms:** Musicians; Labor relations.

## 187

**American Guild of English Handbell Ringers, Inc.**

601 West Riverview Ave.
Dayton, OH 45406
  Tel.: (513) 223-5065      PUB69-19930

An organization of over five thousand members, the Guild conducts two national festivals and six area festivals yearly. It has a number of foreign members, participates in international conferences, and is currently planning future international projects. Membership consists chiefly of handbell choir members and directors, but is open to anyone.

**Areas of Interest:** English handbell ringing.

**Publications:** *Overtones* (six issues a year); ten to twelve selections of handbell music (twice a year).

**Information Services:** Answers inquiries; conducts annual workshop; distributes publications in the United States and abroad. Services are free and available to the membership.

**Contact:** Mr. Andrew L. Flanagan, Executive Director

**Approval Date:** 1/84

**Latest Information Date:** 1/86

**Index Terms:** Handbell ringing; Music; International arts activities; Festivals; Arts resources.

## 188

**American Guild of Organists**

815 Second Ave., Suite 318
New York, NY 10017
  Tel.: (212) 687-9188      PUB69-19979

A nonprofit organization of about twenty thousand members, the Guild is the national professional association for organists and choral conductors. As both an educational and service organization, its goals are to advance the cause of organ and choral music and to set and maintain standards. It has 320 local chapters nationwide. Membership is open to anyone.

**Areas of Interest:** Organ and choral literature, training, performance, and scholarship; church music.

**Publications:** *The American Organist* (monthly).

**Information Services:** Answers inquiries; provides reference and magnetic tape services; conducts seminars, workshops, and performance and composition competitions; distributes its monthly publication in the United States and abroad; makes referrals to other sources of information. Services are available to the membership.

**Contact:** Mr. Daniel Colburn, Executive Director

**Approval Date:** 1/84

**Latest Information Date:** 1/86

**Index Terms:** Organ music; Choral music; Musicology; Music; Teacher training; Literature (fine arts); Historic preservation; Art management; International arts activities; Professional associations; Arts resources.

## 189

**American Music Center (AMC)**

250 West 54th St., Room 300
New York, NY 10019
  Tel.: (212) 247-3121      PUB69-6328

AMC is a nonprofit membership organization founded in 1940 to foster and encourage the composition of contemporary music and to promote its production, publication, distribution, and performance. It is the official U.S. Information Center for American Music.

**Areas of Interest:** All aspects of contemporary American music.

**Holdings:** 20,000 scores; 3,000 sound recordings; composer biographical files on about 3,000 composers; books, journals, newsletters, reprints, publication lists, bibliographies, pamphlets, brochures, etc. The AMC Library is the world's largest circulating collection of American contemporary scores and also contains the National Endowment for the Arts Composer Collection Archive. Its catalog is on the RLIN data base. Much miscellaneous information on composers, organizations, performing ensembles, etc., is on an AMC minicomputer.

**Publications:** *American Music Center Newsletter* (quarterly); *Catalog of the AMC Collections; Volume I* (choral/vocal music; 1975), *Volume II* (chamber music; 1978), *Volume III* (orchestra and band music; 1982), and *Volume IV* (stage works; 1983); *Contemporary Music Performance Directory* (1975); *Composer-Librettist Collection Held at the American Music Center* (1979); annual list of library additions. A publications list is available.

**Information Services:** Answers written and telephone inquiries; prepares analyses; provides consultation services. Library materials are loaned and there are no restrictions on access to information or use of reference sources. In reply to some inquiries, referral is made to other organizations and individuals.

**Approval Date:** 8/84

**Latest Information Date:** 1/86

**Index Terms:** Music.

---

### 190

#### American Music Conference (AMC)

150 East Huron
Chicago, IL 60611
Tel.: (312) 266-7200        PUB69-10751

AMC is the nonprofit educational association of the American music industry. Founded in 1947, its purpose is the promotion of music, especially amateur participation, in the home, school, church, and community. Membership includes manufacturers, wholesalers, and retailers of musical instruments, publishers of printed music, and other music-related associations.

**Areas of Interest:** Music in the United States, especially amateur participation; music industry sales statistics; trends in music.

**Holdings:** Statistics on musical instrument sales and people who play.

**Publications:** *Music USA* (annual review of industry sales statistics, imports and exports, and association activities); *The Role of Music in the Life of Man; The Community Band; New Zoo Music Review* (juvenile poster); *You and the Music Business* (slide and sound presentation for students). A publications list is available.

**Information Services:** Answers inquiries and/or makes referrals to other sources of information; provides consultation service and other aid to organizations with related goals.

**Approval Date:** 8/84

**Latest Information Date:** 1/86

**Index Terms:** American music; Amateur musicians; Music; Musical instruments; Music trade; Sales; Statistics.

---

### 191

#### American Musical Instrument Society (AMIS)

c/o The Shrine to Music Museum
414 East Clark St.
Vermillion, SD 57069
Tel.: (605) 677-5306        PUB69-17248

**Areas of Interest:** Promotion of the study of the history, design, and use of musical instruments in all cultures and from all periods.

**Publications:** *AMIS Newsletter* (three times a year); *AMIS Journal* (annual).

**Information Services:** Answers inquiries free.

**Approval Date:** 8/85

**Latest Information Date:** 8/85

**Index Terms:** Musical instruments; History; Design; Professional associations.

---

### 192

#### American Musicological Society (AMS)

201 South 34th St.
Philadelphia, PA 19104
Tel.: (215) 898-8698        PUB69-19982

An affiliate of the International Musicological Society, AMS is an organization of 3,600 members in the United States and other countries as well as 1,200 institutional subscribers. The membership consists essentially of university faculty and graduate students.

**Areas of Interest:** The various fields of music as a branch of learning and scholarship.

**Publications:** *Journal of the AMS* (three issues a year); semiannual newsletter; *Directory of Members and Subscribers* (annual); studies and documents series; *International Index of Doctoral Dissertations.*

**Information Services:** Answers inquiries; provides information on research in progress; distributes publications in the United States and abroad; makes referrals to other sources of information. Services are free, except for some publications, and available to members and others with a professional interest in musicology.

**Contact:** Mr. Alvin H. Johnson, Executive Director

**Approval Date:** 1/84

**Latest Information Date:** 1/86

**Index Terms:** Musical societies; Music; Operas; Music theater; Arts resources; International arts activities; Musicology.

---

## 193

**American Orff-Schulwerk Association (AOSA)**

c/o Department of Music
Cleveland State University
Cleveland, OH 44115
Tel.: (216) 543-5366          PUB69-19921

An organization of about thirty-two hundred members in sixty-two local chapters in the United States and abroad representing music teachers, music therapists, church musicians, classroom teachers, colleges, universities, libraries, and the music industry, AOSA promotes the music education philosophy of Carl Orff. His book, *Das Schulwerk, Musik fur Kinder,* consists of five volumes of material for the education of children and provides for introduction to the various elements of music by means of singing, clapping, movement, and playing percussion instruments. Activities include a scholarship fund, a memorial fund, cooperative projects with foreign groups, and sponsorship of teachers from abroad in the United States at annual conferences. Membership is open to all interested persons.

**Areas of Interest:** Music education; music therapy; teacher education; curriculum design; special education; comprehensive arts education; folk music.

**Holdings:** The Isabel McNeill Carley Library containing (1) copies of AOSA publications, (2) books,

recordings, and video tapes relating to Orff's philosophy, and (3) other publications of Orff-related materials; a computerized membership list that is available for purchase in the form of mailing labels.

**Publications:** *The Orff Echo* (quarterly); *Orff-Schulwerk: American Odyssey* (film); indexes, reprints, teaching materials, bibliography, membership directory. A list of publications is available.

**Information Services:** Answers inquiries; provides reference services and information on research in progress; conducts workshops; lends materials; distributes publications and audiovisual educational materials in the United States and abroad; makes referrals to both domestic and foreign sources of information; permits on-site use of collections. Information is available free to anyone, and most workshops are open to all. Other services, except for publications, which are for sale to the public, are for members only.

**Contact:** Mrs. Cindi Wobig, Executive Secretary

**Approval Date:** 1/84

**Latest Information Date:** 1/86

**Index Terms:** Music education; Music therapy; Teacher education; Curriculum design; Special education; Comprehensive arts education; Folk music; Orff, Carl; Musical societies; International arts activities; Arts resources.

---

## 194

**American School Band Directors' Association (ASBDA)**

Box 146
Otsego, MI 49078
Tel.: (616) 694-2092, 694-2086, or
694-6342          PUB69-19937

An organization of 1,000 active and former elementary and secondary school band music teachers and 100 publishers, manufacturers, and retailers, ASBDA is concerned with the improvement of band music education. Activities include organization and sponsorship of the annual National High School Concert Band Competition and Festival, research in music curricula, equipment, and facilities, and participation in international conferences. Full membership is by election only and is restricted to elementary and secondary band music teachers with seven years or more experience.

**Areas of Interest:** Band music; band music education; architectural design and construction of school music rooms; equipment used in band music education; music education materials and methods; audiovisual aids; acoustics of band instruments.

**Holdings:** ASBDA archives are housed at the University of Illinois Band Department.

**Publications:** *ASBDA Curriculum Guide;* project reports; directories; recordings.

**Information Services:** Answers inquiries; distributes publications. Services are available for a fee to anyone.

**Contact:** Mr. James J. Hewitt, Office Manager

**Approval Date:** 11/84

**Latest Information Date:** 1/86

**Index Terms:** Band music; Music; Music education; Architectural design; Construction; School music rooms; Educational materials; Teaching methods; Audiovisual aids; Acoustics; International arts activities; Curriculum; Arts resources.

---

### 195

**American Society of Music Arrangers (ASMA)**

P.O. Box 11
Hollywood, CA 90078
Tel.: (213) 871-2762 or 545-4882          PUB69-21076

ASMA is affiliated with the American Federation of Musicians.

**Areas of Interest:** Music arranging, orchestration, and composition.

**Information Services:** Conducts workshops for members and clinics and seminars open to anyone. Services are available for a fee, with a reduction for members.

**Contact:** Mr. Van Alexander, President

**Approval Date:** 11/84

**Latest Information Date:** 1/86

**Index Terms:** Arts resources; Music arrangement.

---

### 196

**American String Teachers Association (ASTA)**

University of Georgia Station, Box 2066
Athens, GA 30612-0066
Tel.: (404) 542-5254 Ext. 48          PUB69-20236

A nonprofit organization of over five thousand members in the United States and other countries, ASTA promotes and encourages professional and amateur string and orchestra study, performance, teacher education, research, and pedagogy. Activities include sponsorship of American artists in concerts abroad, foreign artists in performance in the United States, and maintenance of foreign affiliates. ASTA is interested in more foreign involvement.

**Areas of Interest:** Stringed instruments instruction, performance, technique, maintenance, and repair; teacher training in violin, viola, cello, double bass, and guitar; string ensemble and orchestra; string and orchestra literature.

**Publications:** *The American String Teacher* (quarterly); books on technique and interpretation; graded lists of teaching material; practical aids for teachers. A publications list is available.

**Information Services:** Answers inquiries; conducts seminars and workshops; distributes publications. Services are generally available for a fee to anyone.

**Contact:** Mr. J. Kimball Harriman, Executive Director

**Approval Date:** 1/84

**Latest Information Date:** 1/86

**Index Terms:** Arts resources; Music teachers; Professional associations; Music; Teacher training; Stringed instruments; Violin; Viola; Violoncello; Double bass; Guitar; International arts activities; Orchestras.

---

### 197

**American Symphony Orchestra League**

633 E St. NW.
Washington, DC 20004
Tel.: (202) 628-0099          PUB69-19887

An organization of 4,200 individuals, orchestras, associations, businesses, arts councils, libraries, and publishers in the United States and abroad, the League seeks to foster the artistic excellence and administrative effectiveness of its constituents. Activities include research, training, government affairs and advocacy, public information, in-field consulting, publications, fund raising, field communications, and membership development. Membership is open to any interested person or organization.

**Areas of Interest:** Symphonic music; orchestra management; arts management; financial management; fund raising; comprehensive arts education.

**Holdings:** The League's Orchestra Archives is housed at the George Mason University Library, Fairfax, Virginia. Orchestra Library Information Service (OLIS)—computerized data base of orchestral repertoire.

**Publications:** League publications include *Symphony Magazine* (bimonthly), orchestra management materials, journal articles, directories, data compilations, and reprints.

**Information Services:** Answers inquiries; provides advisory, consulting, technical assistance, and reference services; provides speakers; evaluates and analyzes data; conducts seminars and workshops; distributes publications; makes referrals to other sources of information. General reference services are available free to anyone; there are fees and some restrictions on other services.

**Contact:** Ms. Melanie Jarratt, Reference Coordinator

**Approval Date:** 3/85

**Latest Information Date:** 3/85

**Index Terms:** Symphony orchestras; Music; Art education; Art management; Financial management; Fund raising; Arts resources; Information resources; American Symphony Orchestra League.

## 198

### APM Library of Recorded Sound

502 East 17th St.
Attn: Allen Koenigsberg
Brooklyn, NY 11226
Tel.: (212) 941-6835                    PUB69-18782

The Library is operated by the APM Press, publishers of Antique Phonograph Monthly.

**Areas of Interest:** History of recorded sound; development of the phonograph; patent history.

**Holdings:** Artifacts dating from 1857 to 1930, including five thousand cylinder recordings, 75 antique phonographs, and Edisonia.

**Publications:** In addition to *Antique Phonograph Monthly*, APM Press publishes books, journal articles, critical reviews, abstracts, indexes, directories, bibliographies, and discographies.

**Information Services:** Answers inquiries; provides advisory, consulting, reference, literature-searching, patent-searching, and reproduction services; provides information on research in progress; distributes publications; makes referrals to other sources of information; permits on-site use of collections. Services are available to bona fide scholars and researchers; some are subject to a fee.

**Approval Date:** 8/85

**Latest Information Date:** 8/85

**Index Terms:** Phonographs; Phonograph records; Sound recordings; History; Music; Patents.

## 199

### Association for Recorded Sound Collections (ARSC)

P.O. Box 75082
Washington, DC 20013
Tel.: (703) 684-8244                    PUB69-19900

A nonprofit organization partially funded by the National Endowment for the Humanities and private foundations, ARSC serves the interests and concerns of the private collector, discographer, librarian, archivist, and specialty dealer in all fields of collecting and historical-discographical information.

**Areas of Interest:** Historical classical, jazz, pop, rock, country, folk-ethnic, and spoken-word recordings; archival treatment of vintage recordings; state-of-the-art equipment and techniques for preserving and reproducing vintage recordings.

**Holdings:** ARSC, the Library of Congress, the Rodgers and Hammerstein Archives of Recorded Sound in the New York Public Library at Lincoln Center, the Audio Archives of Syracuse University, the Archive of Recorded Sound at Stanford University, and the Yale Collection of Historical Sound Recordings at Yale University are working together as the Associated Audio Archives to produce a computer-based index of key discographic information on some 615,000 commercial disc recordings issued between 1894 and the introduction of the LP in the mid-1950s that these archives contain. When completed, researchers at each of the participating institutions will have access to microfilm photographs of all 615,000 discs and to a computer-based index keyed to author/composer, title, performer, publisher, and holding institution.

**Publications:** *ARSC Newsletter* (quarterly); *ARSC Journal* (three issues a year); *ARSC Bulletin* (annual); *Rules for Archival Cataloging of Sound Recordings* (jointly with the Associated Audio Archives in 1980).

**Information Services:** Answers inquiries; provides reference services and information on R&D in progress; distributes publications; makes referrals to other sources of information. Services are available to the membership.

**Approval Date:** 3/85

**Latest Information Date:** 3/85

**Index Terms:** Sound recordings; Discography; Recorded sound collection; Sound recording libraries; Classical music; Popular music; Jazz music; Country music; Folk music; Ethnic music; Spoken-word recordings; Historical recordings; Historical preservation; Information exchange; Information dissemination; Research; Cultural awareness; Cultural heritage; Archives; Nonprofit organizations; Arts resources.

## 200

### Association of Concert Bands, Inc. (ACB)

19 Benton Circle
Utica, NY 13501
  Tel.: (315) 732-2737                    PUB69-19947

ACB is an organization of 600 members in the United States and abroad concerned with the promotion of community wind and percussion music organizations. It participates in international conferences, conducts cooperative projects with foreign groups, and holds membership in international organizations. ACB is interested in more foreign involvement and is planning future international projects. Membership is open to anyone.

**Areas of Interest:** Establishment, funding, development, maintenance, and promotion of musical units in the world community.

**Publications:** *Woodwind, Brass and Percussion* (eight issues a year); newsletters, annual membership directory, project reports, journal articles, reprints.

**Information Services:** Answers inquiries; provides advisory, literature-searching, and current-awareness services; evaluates data; conducts annual conferences; distributes publications in the United States and abroad. Services are free to members.

**Contact:** Mr. J. Edward Hacker, Executive Secretary

**Approval Date:** 1/84

**Latest Information Date:** 1/86

**Index Terms:** Concert bands; Musical societies; Brass instrument music; Percussion instrument music; Woodwind instrument music; Music; Historic preservation; Performing arts; International arts activities; Information services; Arts resources.

## 201

### Association of Professional Vocal Ensembles (APVE)

251 South 18th St.
Philadelphia, PA 19103
  Tel.: (215) 545-4444                    PUB69-19940

APVE is an association of 275 individuals, organizations, agencies, and corporations concerned with the growth and quality of professional vocal ensembles and their art. It conducts advocacy activities and research projects, sponsors administrative internships, national conferences, and workshops, and provides consultation and opportunities for media exposure.

**Areas of Interest:** Choral music; vocal art; vocal music business and marketing; professional singers; teacher training; arts management; fund raising.

**Holdings:** Survey data for 1978, 1980, 1981, and 1982.

**Publications:** *Voice* (bimonthly); project reports.

**Information Services:** Answers inquiries; provides advisory, consulting, reference, literature-searching, current-awareness, and reproduction services and information on research in progress; evaluates and analyzes data; conducts conferences and workshops; distributes publications and data compilations; makes referrals to other sources of information. Answers to inquiries, reference services, and referrals are free to all requesters. Other services are subject to a fee.

**Contact:** Ms. Janice F. Kestler, Executive Director

**Approval Date:** 1/84

**Latest Information Date:** 1/86

**Index Terms:** Choral music; Vocal music; Professional vocal ensembles; Music; Teacher training; Performing arts industry; Art management; Fund raising; Economic aspects of music; Vocal ensembles; Marketing; Arts resources.

## 202

### Black Music Association

1500 Locust St., Suite 1905
Philadelphia, PA 19102
  Tel.: (215) 545-8600                    PUB69-19908

An organization of about twenty-five hundred musicians, managers, retail and wholesale record distributors, music industry executives, disc jockeys, and radio station owners, the Association seeks to protect, preserve, and perpetuate Black music and to expand the Black music market. It serves members in foreign countries, participates in international conferences, conducts cooperative projects with foreign groups, maintains foreign affiliations, and is interested in more foreign involvement.

**Areas of Interest:** Black music; media arts; indigenous and folk arts; preservation of materials relating to the history of Black music.

**Publications:** *Innervision* (monthly newsletter).

**Information Services:** Conducts Black music seminars and an annual conference.

**Contact:** Mr. Abner, President

**Approval Date:** 11/85

**Latest Information Date:** 11/85

**Index Terms:** Afro-American music; Media arts; Folk art; Historic preservation; International arts activities; Arts resources.

## 203

### Broadcast Music, Inc. (BMI)

320 West 57th St.
New York, NY 10019
  Tel.: (212) 586-2000          PUB69-19951

BMI, with over sixty-five thousand music writer and publisher affiliates, is concerned with protection of their performing rights and with service to the public by making music as readily available as possible. It licenses a repertoire of over a million compositions for public performance. BMI is a member of the Confederation Internationale des Societes d'Auteurs et Compositeurs, has reciprocal agreements with thirty-nine licensing societies around the world, and participates in regular conferences concerning the problems of international copyright and cooperation between societies.

**Areas of Interest:** Domestic and international music copyright and licensing.

**Holdings:** BMI archives contain rare musical first editions, items of historical interest, and rare sheet music.

**Publications:** *Many Worlds of Music* (quarterly); brochures and pamphlets dealing with music licensing, performing rights, and BMI's function in the music business.

**Information Services:** Answers inquiries; conducts workshops; provides speakers; distributes publications; makes referrals to other sources of information. Information and publications are available to anyone. Workshops are by invitation only for composers, lyricists, and librettists. The archives are open to legitimate scholars on request.

**Contact:** Mr. Edward M. Cramer, President

**Approval Date:** 2/84

**Latest Information Date:** 1/86

**Index Terms:** Performing arts; Music; Copyrights; Licenses; Performing rights; Public lending rights;

International arts activities; Lecturers; Archives; Arts resources.

## 204

### Chamber Music America

215 Park Ave. South
New York, NY 10003
  Tel.: (212) 460-9030          PUB69-19977

Partially funded by the National Endowment for the Arts, the New York State Council on the Arts, and private sources, Chamber Music America is an organization of 1,056 members, including 437 chamber music professional ensembles, 187 presenters, and interested persons, and makes direct grants of about $150,000 a year to performers. International activities include service to foreign members. Chamber Music America is currently interested in expanding its foreign involvement.

**Areas of Interest:** Unification of the chamber music field and the advancement of chamber music in all its forms.

**Holdings:** Collections in the above areas.

**Publications:** *Chamber Music Magazine* (quarterly); *New Music Repertoire Directory; Directory of Summer Workshops, Schools and Festivals; Membership Directory;* manuals, books, research summaries, bibliographies, data compilations, and reprints.

**Information Services:** Answers inquiries; provides advisory and reference services; evaluates data; conducts seminars and workshops; provides speakers; distributes publications; makes referrals to other sources of information in the United States and abroad; permits on-site use of collections. Services are available to the membership, which is open to all interested persons.

**Contact:** Howard Herring, Executive Director

**Approval Date:** 1/84

**Latest Information Date:** 1/86

**Index Terms:** Musical societies; Chamber music; Grants; International arts activities; Fund raising; Public relations; Art management; Consulting services; Arts resources.

## 205

### Charlin Jazz Society

3003 Van Ness St. NW
Washington, DC 20008
  Tel.: (202) 362-0858          PUB69-20355

The Society's purpose is to produce a performing arts series that highlights jazz, America's classical art form, through the use of music, dance, and drama; to train young performers in the art of producing; and to raise scholarship funds for students at the Duke Ellington School of the Arts. The Society achieves its goals through the programs of the Performing Arts Series and the Art Institute of Washington.

**Areas of Interest:** The history, artists, and styles of jazz; the art of producing.

**Information Services:** The Association provides free information to the public regarding current jazz activities in the Washington-Baltimore area and offers consulting services and workshops for a fee. The Society produces entertainment for other businesses and organizations for a fee.

**Contact:** Ms. Linda S. Wernick, Director

**Approval Date:** 1/86

**Latest Information Date:** 1/86

**Index Terms:** Arts resources; Jazz music; Art management; History; Artists.

## 206

### College Band Directors National Association (CBDNA)

c/o University of Texas at Austin
Box 8028
Austin, TX 78713
Tel.: (512) 471-5883                PUB69-19953

An organization of 850 junior college, college, and university band directors, CBDNA serves as a resource and provides support for college and university band programs through development of wind band music and music research projects. Membership is open to college and university band conductors upon application. The Association is affiliated with similar organizations in other countries, conducting cooperative projects, sponsoring performances abroad, and offering reciprocal services to members.

**Areas of Interest:** Wind band music; performance art; teacher training.

**Holdings:** Records and files of the CBDNA and materials relevant to its history are maintained at the Hornbake (undergraduate) Library, University of Maryland, College Park, MD.

**Publications:** *CBDNA Newsletter; CBDNA Journal;* technical reports, project reports, directories, conference papers.

**Information Services:** Answers inquiries; provides reference services; conducts biennial national conferences and annual conducting symposiums; distributes publications; makes referrals to other sources of information; permits on-site use of collections at the Hornbake Library. Services are provided free or at cost to members and at an additional charge to nonmembers.

**Contact:** Mr. Richard L. Floyd, National Secretary-Treasurer

**Approval Date:** 4/84

**Latest Information Date:** 1/86

**Index Terms:** College and university bands; Wind band music; Band music; Music; Teacher training; Historic preservation; Performing arts; International arts activities; Research projects; Arts resources.

## 207

### College Music Society, Inc. (CMS)

1444 15th St.
Boulder, CO 80302
Tel.: (303) 449-1611                PUB69-20245

An organization of about fifty-five hundred members in the United States and other countries, CMS is concerned with the philosophy and practice of music in colleges and universities and holds memberships in international organizations.

**Areas of Interest:** Music instruction in higher education; education for college students considering careers in music; music studies for the general college student; college and university music teaching as a career.

**Publications:** *College Music Symposium* (semiannual); *Bibliographies in American Music* (series of eight titles); *CMS Reports* (series of four titles on women and minorities in music education and music in general education); *Directory of Music Faculties in Colleges and Universities—United States and Canada.*

**Information Services:** Answers inquiries; conducts seminars and workshops; distributes publications. Services are available for a fee to anyone.

**Contact:** Robby D. Gunstream, Executive Director

**Approval Date:** 1/84

**Latest Information Date:** 1/86

**Index Terms:** Arts resources; Music in colleges and universities; Music education; Teacher training;

Operas; Music theater; Folk art; Comprehensive art education; Music teachers; Career in music.

## 208

### Company of Fifers and Drummers

P.O. Box 318
Westbrook, CT 06498          PUB69-18808

**Areas of Interest:** Early American martial music.

**Holdings:** Instruments, uniforms, pictures, out-of-print music books, fife and drum corps artifacts.

**Publications:** *Ancient Times* (quarterly); instruction books, music transcriptions, indexes, directories.

**Information Services:** Answers inquiries; provides advisory and reference services; conducts seminars and workshops; distributes publications; makes referrals to other sources of information; permits on-site use of collections. Services may be subject to a fee and are available to anyone.

**Approval Date:** 2/84

**Latest Information Date:** 1/86

**Index Terms:** Music history; Military music; Fife and drum music; Musical instruments; Uniforms; Musical scores.

## 209

### Council for Research in Music Education (CRME)

c/o School of Music
University of Illinois
Urbana, IL 61801
    Tel.: (217) 333-1027          PUB69-18417

**Areas of Interest:** Music education.

**Holdings:** Doctoral degree requirements at all institutions; extensive collection of music tests, including rating scales, questionnaires, and observational techniques; doctoral dissertations on music education.

**Publications:** Bulletin (quarterly); annual listing of dissertations in progress worldwide; annual listing of doctoral advisers at degree-granting institutions; journal articles, critical reviews, monograph series.

**Information Services:** Answers inquiries; abstracts all research results; provides advisory, reference, and literature-searching services; provides information on research in progress; distributes publications; makes referrals to other sources of information; permits on-site use of collections. Services are free and available to anyone.

**Approval Date:** 3/85

**Latest Information Date:** 3/85

**Index Terms:** Colleges and universities; Music education; Musicology.

## 210

### Country Dance and Song Society of America

505 Eighth Ave., Room 2500
New York, NY 10018
    Tel.: (212) 594-8833          PUB69-12530

The Society is an association of people dedicated to the enjoyment, preservation, and study of English and American traditional dance, music, and song.

**Areas of Interest:** American and English folk dances, both the present traditional forms, including squares, contras, reels, rounds, and step dancing, and the historic forms of these dances, from the seventeenth century "Playford" dances through the nineteenth century; ritual morris and sword dances from England; folk music and song, including traditional regional styles of vocal and instrumental music.

**Holdings:** Collection of about fifteen hundred books, some recordings and tapes, and a few periodicals; the complete library of ballad authority, Evelyn Wells.

**Publications:** *Country Dance and Song* (semiannual); dance records; dance books; newsletter.

**Information Services:** Answers inquiries; provides consulting services; permits on-site use of collection. Services are free, except for extensive consulting services, and available to anyone.

**Approval Date:** 8/84

**Latest Information Date:** 1/86

**Index Terms:** Folk music; Folk dance.

## 211

### Country Music Association, Inc. (CMA)

P.O. Box 22299
Nashville, TN 37202
    Tel.: (615) 244-2840          PUB69-20239

**Location:** 7 Music Circle North

A nonprofit organization of over seven thousand individuals and organizations in the United States and abroad, CMA promotes country music around the world. Activities include membership in international organizations, participation in international conferences, cooperative projects with foreign groups, and maintenance of an office in London, England. In keeping with its desire for more foreign involvement, CMA is planning future international projects.

**Areas of Interest:** Country music; country music industry; recording production in the United States and Europe.

**Holdings:** CMA has established the Country Music Foundation, a nonprofit educational institution that maintains and operates the Country Music Hall of Fame and Museum and the Hall of Fame Library and Media Center, all located in Nashville.

**Publications:** *Close-Up* (monthly magazine); *Reference Guide* (updated lists of publishers, publications, record company personnel, artists, labels, agents, managers, producers, personal managers, talent agencies, recording studios, and promotion/publicity/public relations companies); *Radio Survey* (complete listing of all full- and part-time country music radio stations in the United States and Canada, including call letters, wattage, address, telephone number, frequency, station manager, music director, and other pertinent data); *Arbitron Demographic Profile* (containing demographic information on country music radio listeners); *Broadcast Handbook* (covering broadcast programming, promotion, and sales); "Music for the Times" (nine-minute video presentation). CMA also sponsors the annual CMA Awards Show, nationally televised in October.

**Information Services:** Answers inquiries; provides reference and literature-searching services; conducts seminars and workshops; distributes publications in the United States and abroad. Services are available to members only.

**Contact:** Mrs. Jo Walker-Meador, Executive Director

**Approval Date:** 1/84

**Latest Information Date:** 1/86

**Index Terms:** Country music; Country music industry; Musical societies; Promoting; Advertising; International arts activities; Recording; Arts resources.

## 212

### Country Music Foundation Library and Media Center

4 Music Square East
Nashville, TN 37203
Tel.: (615) 256-1639          PUB69-12581

The Library and Media Center are housed in the Foundation's Country Music Hall of Fame and Museum.

**Areas of Interest:** Country music; Anglo-American folk song; sound recording technology and engineering; music copyright; historical recordings.

**Holdings:** 125,000 recorded discs; 5,000 recorded audiotapes; 13,000 photographs, films, videotapes, manuscripts, etc.; vertical file of 1,200 active files, including clippings; fan club publications; over 6,500 books, 425 periodicals, and a few reports.

**Publications:** *Journal of Country Music* (three issues a year); *Historical Instrument Series*; *Recording Technology Series*; books, bibliographies, discographies, directories.

**Information Services:** Answers inquiries; provides advisory, reference, literature-searching, and reproduction services; makes referrals to other sources of information; permits on-site use of collections. Services are available to anyone by appointment; some may be provided at cost.

**Approval Date:** 1/84

**Latest Information Date:** 1/86

**Index Terms:** Folk music; Sound recordings; Music manuscripts; Phonograph records; Music history; Copyrights.

## 213

### Curtis Institute of Music Library

1726 Locust St.
Philadelphia, PA 19103
Tel.: (215) 893-5265          PUB69-4809

The Library serves the students, faculty, and alumni of the Institute, a full scholarship school for the training of young musicians for careers in performance.

**Areas of Interest:** Performance music (orchestral, opera, keyboard, vocal); solo and chamber repertoire.

**Holdings:** 50,000 volumes, primarily music scores; 6,000 recordings; 40 journal subscriptions; Archives of the Institute, including scrapbooks and clippings; programs and recordings of Curtis recitals. Special collections include the personal library of Leopold Stokowski, including his orchestral transcriptions, scrapbooks, memorabilia, and the Robert Gatewood Collection of all recordings made by Stokowski; the personal music collection of Lynnwood Farnam; the music collection of Charles H. Jarvis; harp compositions and transcriptions of Carlos Salzedo; editions for contrabass by Anton Torello; the personal papers of Mary Louise Curtis Bok Zimbalist, founder of the Institute, including correspondence, photographs, and memorabilia; materials relating to distinguished alumni and faculty of the Institute; a complete run of the Institute's periodical *Overtones*, 1929–40 and 1974.

**Publications:** Annual catalogs of the Institute.

**Information Services:** Answers brief telephone inquiries and written requests concerning material and information unavailable elsewhere; makes interlibrary loans.

**Approval Date:** 8/84

**Latest Information Date:** 1/86

**Index Terms:** Music libraries; Music; Musical scores.

## 214

### Fellowship of Christian Musicians

3100 Fleetwood, B-7
Amarillo, TX 79109
Tel.: (806) 358-2646          PUB69-19955

The Fellowship is a nonprofit organization of about one hundred fifty musicians representing students, educators, and professionals. Membership is open to anyone in the United States or abroad sharing the Fellowship's goals.

**Areas of Interest:** The role of Christianity in the lives of musicians and students of music.

**Holdings:** Computerized membership data.

**Publications:** Newsletter (three issues a year); membership directory.

**Information Services:** Answers inquiries; provides advisory, consulting, and reference services; conducts prayer breakfasts, fellowship meetings, and other events at state and national music conventions, conferences, and clinics; distributes publications; provides speakers; makes referrals to other sources of information. Services are free to the membership.

**Contact:** Mr. Bill Anderson, Executive Secretary

**Approval Date:** 9/84

**Latest Information Date:** 1/86

**Index Terms:** Christianity; Music; Musicians; Operas; Music theater; Musicotherapy; Music education; International arts activities; Lecturers; Arts resources.

## 215

### Foundation for Research in the Afro-American Creative Arts, Inc.

P.O. Drawer I
Cambria Heights, NY 11411          PUB69-19287

**Location:** 115-05 179th St., St. Albans, NY

**Areas of Interest:** Black music; American music; African music.

**Holdings:** Files on over fifteen hundred black musicians; collection of taped interviews with black musicians; computerized indexes to the files and to the Foundation's periodical.

**Publications:** *The Black Perspective in Music* (semiannual); reviews; indexes.

**Information Services:** Answers inquiries at cost; distributes publications for a fee. Services are available to anyone.

**Contact:** Ms. Eileen Southern, Editor

**Approval Date:** 4/85

**Latest Information Date:** 4/85

**Index Terms:** Afro-American music; American music; African music.

## 216

### Indiana University
### Archives of Traditional Music

Indiana University
Maxwell Hall, Room 57
Bloomington, IN 47405
Tel.: (812) 335-8632          PUB69-7265

**Areas of Interest:** Sound recordings of traditional music (tribal music, folk music, Oriental art music, and some popular music) and of verbal data (oral history, folklore, tales, jokes, children's rhymes, and similar material) from many geographic and cultural areas of the world, particularly from North American Indians, Afro-Americans, Latin America, Africa, and Asia (Nepal, Thailand, and Afghanistan); discography; archives and archiving of sound recordings.

**Holdings:** About three hundred fifty thousand items, including some film and videotapes. Field notes, line and brochure notes, and occasional photos accompany some of the recordings. The recordings are on wax cylinders, Webster and Pierce wire, aluminum, acetate, and vinyl discs, and magnetic open-reel and cassette tapes.

**Publications:** *Resound* (quarterly newsletter); *A Catalog of Phonorecordings of Music and Oral Data Held by the Archives of Traditional Music* (Boston: G. K. Hall, 1975); *African Music and Oral Data: A Catalog of Field Recordings*, by Ruth M. Stone and Frank J. Gillis (Bloomington: Indiana University Press, 1976); area catalogs (African, Afro-American, Latin American, Indiana); long-playing record albums with accompanying brochures, issued through Folkways Records; *Native North American Music and Oral Data: A Catalogue of Sound Recordings, 1893-1976*, by Dorothy Sara Lee (Bloomington: Indiana University Press, 1979). A brochure describing the Archives' activities and services is available.

**Information Services:** All recordings are available to the public for use in the Archives. Within restrictions placed upon the recordings by depositors, tape copies and accompanying documentation are available through purchase, exchange, or interlibrary loan. Where restrictions do exist, permission of the depositor must be secured for use of the material in scholarly articles and other publications, commercial records, films, telecasts, or broadcasts. Upon request, information concerning tape recorders and their use in the field is made available. The Archives will also try to locate or secure particular types of recordings for the use of scholars, and it will advise about the suitability of recordings for use in specific studies. Services are limited according to time and effort required and availability of staff.

**Contact:** Ms. Marilyn Graf

**Approval Date:** 2/85

**Latest Information Date:** 2/85

**Index Terms:** Archives; Folk music; Ethnomusicology; Sound recordings; Oral history; Folklore; American Indians; Afro-Americans; Latin America; Africa; Thailand; Afghanistan; Discography; Asia; Nepal.

---

**217**

---

## International Clarinet Society (ICS)

c/o Norman Heim
7402 Wells Blvd.
Hyattsville, MD 20783
Tel.: (301) 422-9006                    PUB69-19954

ICS is a nonprofit organization of about sixteen hundred teachers, professional performers, students, industry personnel, and others interested in the clarinet. It supports projects benefiting clarinet performance; provides opportunity for the exchange of ideas, materials, and information among members; fosters the composition, publication, recording, and distribution of clarinet music; encourages the research and manufacture of a more definitive instrument; and, while avoiding commercialism, encourages communication and cooperation among clarinetists and the music industry throughout the world.

**Areas of Interest:** Composition of music for the clar-

inet; publication and recording of clarinetists and clarinet music; clarinet literature, performance practice, and techniques; acoustics of the clarinet; clarinet manufacture and innovations of design.

**Holdings:** The ICS Research Library is housed at the University of Maryland, College Park, MD, and contains over seventeen hundred titles, scores, and parts.

**Publications:** *The Clarinet* (quarterly); *Bibliography of the Holdings in the ICS Research Library*; books, state-of-the-art reviews, indexes, critical reviews, teaching materials.

**Information Services:** Answers inquiries; conducts seminars and workshops; lends materials; distributes publications; makes referrals to other sources of information; permits on-site use of collections. Services are free to the membership, which is open to anyone.

**Contact:** Norman Heim, Secretary

**Approval Date:** 1/84

**Latest Information Date:** 1/86

**Index Terms:** Music; Teacher training; Performing arts; Clarinet music; Musical societies; Musical composition; Recording; Publications; Clarinet literature; International arts activities; Manufacturing; Arts resources.

---

**218**

---

## International Horn Society (IHS)

c/o Ms. Ruth Hokanson, Executive Secretary
1213 Sweet Brier Rd.
Madison, WI 53705
Tel.: (608) 233-6336                    PUB69-19897

An organization of 2,000 individuals and libraries, IHS conducts horn competitions, awards grants and scholarships to outstanding horn performers, and encourages and commissions composers and arrangers writing music featuring the horn.

**Areas of Interest:** Horn music; music education; research in the horn and horn playing.

**Publications:** *IHS Newsletter* (quarterly); *The Horn Call* (semiannual journal); annual membership directory.

**Information Services:** Conducts workshops; distributes publications. Services are available for a fee to anyone.

**Approval Date:** 4/85

**Latest Information Date:** 4/85

**Index Terms:** Horn music; Music education; Music;

Historic preservation; Grants; Scholarships; International arts activities; Musical societies; Horn players; Arts resources.

## 219

### International League of Women Composers (ILWC)

P.O. Box 42
Three Mile Bay, NY 13693
Tel.: (315) 649-5086          PUB69-17653

ILWC seeks to obtain more commissions, recordings, and orchestral performances for women composers of serious music. In addition, it sponsors a radio series and chamber music concerts of members' works and a composition contest for women student composers.

**Areas of Interest:** Serious music by contemporary women composers.

**Holdings:** A permanent collection of ILWC information concerning its activities, business, and correspondence is on file at the University of Wyoming (Laramie).

**Publications:** Quarterly newsletter; directory listing members' biographies and compositions (published by Greenwood Press).

**Information Services:** Answers inquiries; provides advisory, reference, and current-awareness services; distributes newsletter and data compilations; makes referrals to other sources of information. Services are free to anyone whose purpose is not commercial.

**Approval Date:** 3/84

**Latest Information Date:** 1/86

**Index Terms:** Women composers; Musical societies; Music teachers; Musical composition; Concerts; Chamber music; Information services; Promoting; Women; Music; Hawaii.

## 220

### International Musicological Society (IMS)

P.O. Box 1561
CH-4001 Basle, SWITZERLAND          PUB69-17406

**Areas of Interest:** Musicology; international cooperation in musicological research.

**Publications:** *Acta Musicologica* (semiannual); *Communiques* (semiannual); *Documenta Musicologica* (irregular series of musical and musico-theoretica sources in facsimile); *Repertoire International des Sources Musicales* (catalog of all known musical manuscripts, pieces, theoretical works, and collections); *Repertoire International de Litterature Musicale* (abstracts of musicological literature published since 1967).

**Information Services:** Maintains an international center for listing dissertations and other large musicological projects in preparation; distributes publications for a fee. Services are available to anyone.

**Approval Date:** 3/84

**Latest Information Date:** 1/86

**Index Terms:** Musicology; Ethnomusicology; International organizations; International cooperation; Musical societies; International meetings; Machine readable data bases; Bibliographic data bases; RILM.

## 221

### International Society for Music Education (ISME)

c/o Prof. John Ritchie, Secretary-General
School of Music
University of Canterbury
Christchurch, NEW ZEALAND
Tel.: 482009 Ext. 8907          PUB69-15991

ISME is partially sponsored by the UNESCO International Music Council.

**Areas of Interest:** Music education; teacher training; music therapy; professional musicians; music education research; amateur music; comparative music education; preschool music.

**Publications:** Newsletters; yearbooks *Challenges in Music Education;* journal articles, reprints.

**Information Services:** Answers inquiries; conducts international annual seminars and biennial conferences; distributes publications. Services are free and available to the membership.

**Approval Date:** 3/84

**Latest Information Date:** 3/84

**Index Terms:** Music education; Musicotherapy; Musicians; Music teachers; Teacher training; Research.

## 222

### International Society of Bassists (ISB)

c/o School of Music
Northwestern University
Evanston, IL 60201
Tel.: (312) 492-7228          PUB69-20353

ISB has over fourteen hundred members in the United States and abroad. While most are bassists, membership is open to anyone. ISB holds membership in international organizations, participates in international conferences, and has foreign affiliates.

**Areas of Interest:** The double bass, including performance, repertoire, teaching, making, and repairing.

**Publications:** *International Society of Bassists Magazine* (three issues a year); reports, critical reviews, bibliographies, teaching materials, data compilations.

**Information Services:** Answers inquiries; provides advisory, reference, and literature-searching services; conducts seminars and workshops; distributes publications; makes referrals to other sources of information. Services are free to members.

**Contact:** Mr. Jeff Bradetich, Executive Director

**Approval Date:** 11/84

**Latest Information Date:** 1/86

**Index Terms:** Double bass; Repertoire; Teaching; Music; Teacher training; Literature (fine arts); Comprehensive art education; International arts activities; Arts resources.

---

### 223

### International Trumpet Guild (ITG)

c/o School of Music
Western Michigan University
Kalamazoo, MI 49008
Tel.: (616) 383-8193          PUB69-19943

An organization of about twenty-six hundred performers and teachers in the United States and abroad, ITG promotes communication among trumpet players and seeks to improve professional levels of performance, teaching, and literature. International activities include membership in international organizations, participation in international conferences, sponsorship of foreign artists in performance in the United States, and maintenance of foreign affiliates. Membership is available to anyone.

**Areas of Interest:** Trumpet performance and teaching.

**Publications:** *International Trumpet Guild Journal* (quarterly); membership directory.

**Information Services:** Answers inquiries; provides information on research in progress; conducts seminars and workshops; distributes publications in the

United States and abroad. Services are free, except for publications, and available to anyone with a serious interest in the trumpet.

**Contact:** Dr. Stephen Jones, Secretary

**Approval Date:** 1/84

**Latest Information Date:** 1/86

**Index Terms:** Trumpet music; Music education; Performing arts; International arts activities; Music; Arts resources.

---

### 224

### Lettumplay, Inc.

418 Seventh St. NW.
Washington, DC 20005
Tel.: (202) 724-4493          PUB69-18085

Sponsored by the National Endowment for the Arts, District of Columbia Commission on Arts and Humanities, corporations, and individual memberships, Lettumplay, Inc. provides opportunities for local artists to perform in noncommercial settings and sponsors a jazz studies program, indoor and outdoor concerts, an art exhibition, and an outreach program to support rehabilitation efforts of local penal and mental health institutions, senior citizen complexes, and physically handicapped facilities.

**Areas of Interest:** Jazz and other forms of contemporary music in the Washington area; opportunities for local performing artists.

**Holdings:** Collection of sound recordings by local artists; jazz archives and museum, including photos and memorabilia of jazz greats dating back thirty years.

**Publications:** Newsletter

**Information Services:** Provides advisory and consulting services; conducts seminars, workshops, jazz lectures, and slide presentations; makes referrals to other sources of information; permits on-site use of collections. Services are available at a fee to anyone.

**Approval Date:** 4/84

**Latest Information Date:** 4/84

**Index Terms:** District of Columbia; Jazz music; Performing arts; Musicians; Career opportunities.

**225**

## Library of Congress
## Music Division

10 First St. SE.
Washington, DC 20540
Tel.: (202) 287-5504 (Reference Section)
(202) 287-5507
(Music Reading Room)          PUB69-7898

Hours: 8:30 a.m.-5 p.m. Mon.-Sat.; closed Sun. and holidays.

**Areas of Interest:** Music of western civilization and its history; American music and its documentation; opera; chamber music; manuscripts of master and other composers; correspondence of composers and musicians; early music literature; rare flutes and flute-type instruments.

**Holdings:** About six million items. Copyright deposits of music and books form the bulk of the holdings. In addition, there are extensive collections of rare and early music, rare books, original manuscripts, autograph correspondence, music literature in all non-Asiatic languages, operatic material, Stradivari instruments (for use in endowed concerts), over sixteen hundred flutes and flute-type instruments, and a comprehensive body of flute music and literature. The Division has access to the DIALOG, SDC ORBIT, and RLIN computerized data bases and is building a data base of nonmusic manuscripts in its custody.

**Information Services:** Answers inquiries; makes referrals to other sources of information; provides consulting and reference services; makes interlibrary loans. The collections are accessible for on-site use; certain restricted categories and rare materials are accorded special care and supervision. The Division will supply information on special services made possible through gifts of money administered by the Library Trust Fund Board; these include the composition, dissemination, and performance of chamber music, the commission of new works by prominent composers, the broadcast of concerts held in the Library of Congress under foundation auspices, lectures on music, and financial aid in the publication of historical studies in the field of American music.

**Approval Date:** 5/84

**Latest Information Date:** 1/86

**Index Terms:** Music; Musicology; Musical instruments; Music manuscripts.

**226**

## Massenet Society and Lovers of French Music

4775 Durham Rd. (Route No. 77)
Guilford, CT 06437          PUB69-18550

Membership Information and Dues; 9 Drury Lane, Fort Lee, NJ 07024, (201) 224-4526

**Areas of Interest:** Operas of Jules Massenet (1842–1912); French music in general composed by teachers and students of Massenet.

**Holdings:** Piano-vocal scores of French operas, especially those of Massenet.

**Publications:** Newsletter (semiannual); compendium in two volumes on the operatic works of Massenet.

**Information Services:** Answers inquiries; provides reference services; sponsors concerts and lectures; distributes publications. Services are available for a yearly membership fee of fifteen dollars.

**Approval Date:** 11/85

**Latest Information Date:** 11/85

**Index Terms:** Operas; Massenet, Jules; Musical scores; French composers; Vocal music.

**227**

## Metropolitan Opera
## Central Opera Service (COS)

Lincoln Center
New York, NY 10023
Tel.: (212) 799-3467          PUB69-16332

Sponsored by the Metropolitan Opera National Council, COS is an information center that fosters closer association among civic, community, college, and national opera companies throughout the country and assists them in improving artistic standards, thus encouraging and furthering national interest in opera.

**Areas of Interest:** Opera repertory, productions, scores, translations, scenery, costumes, and publicity; opera companies, income, expenses, attendance, staff, and educational and community programs; opera composers, librettists, performers, administrators, supporting organizations, production methods, and producing organizations in the United States and abroad; nonprofit musical theater; theater architecture and acoustics; national arts service organizations in symphony, theater, and dance; government agencies affecting the arts; laws affecting the arts (copyright, tax, etc.); education in the arts; academic instructions in music, opera, arts administration, etc; U.S. opera statistics on performances, companies, academic workshops, audiences, budgets, etc.

**Holdings:** Collection of files on about thirty thousand operas, including performance records, some catalogs, information on publishers, sets, and costumes, translations, and various editions; about one thousand reference books and sixty-five periodicals on the arts; some reviews, programs, and photographs.

**Publications:** *Central Opera Service Bulletin* (quarterly); latest operatic news items, book reviews, performance listing, journal articles, state-of-the-art reviews, indexes, sixteen directories (e.g., American, Foreign, Contemporary Operas, Opera Producing Companies/Workshops: U.S. and Canada), career guide for young American singers, etc. A publications list is available.

**Information Services:** Answers inquiries; provides reference, literature-searching, and current-awareness services; conducts regional and national conferences and surveys; provides information on research in progress; evaluates data; distributes data compilations and publications; makes referrals to other sources of information. Single inquiries from nonmembers are answered free. Other services are available to members only, but membership is open.

**Approval Date:** 9/84

**Latest Information Date:** 1/86

**Index Terms:** Performing arts; Operas; Theaters; Performance schedules; Musical scores; Orchestration; Costume; Stage scenery; Stage management; Opera repertory; Opera production; Opera companies; Librettists; Opera singers; Educational programs; Artistic standards; Statistical data; Budgets; Music education; Translations; Performing arts festivals; Music theater.

## 228

**Moravian Music Foundation, Inc.**

20 Cascade Ave.
Winston-Salem, NC 27107
Tel.: (919) 725-0651 PUB69-9438

**Areas of Interest:** World Moravian musical activities; hymnology; eighteenth-century music.

**Holdings:** Music manuscripts and prints from the late eighteenth and early nineteenth centuries; 6,000 books and hymnals.

**Information Services:** Permits on-site use of collection by qualified research scholars and students (ad-

vance arrangements required). Copying facilities are available.

**Approval Date:** 9/84

**Latest Information Date:** 1/86

**Index Terms:** Moravian music; Musicology; Hymns; Eighteenth-century music.

## 229

**Music Associates of America (MAA)**

224 King St.
Englewood, NJ 07631
Tel.: (201) 569-2898 PUB69-19967

MAA is a commercial organization serving music publisher and composer clients through the widest possible distribution of information about their catalogs and published works to music makers of all media, including producers, editors, distributors, managers, and performers.

**Areas of Interest:** Catalogs of selected music publishers; personal and professional information on individual composers; commissioning information.

**Publications:** *MadAminA! A Chronicle of Musical Catalogs* (semiannual magazine); "A Paper on Music Publishing in the U.S. Since 1945."

**Information Services:** Answers inquiries; provides advisory and consulting services; distributes publications. Consulting services are restricted to music publisher and composer clients, who pay an annual retainer. The magazine is distributed free to orchestras, opera companies, festivals, the press, concert managers, academic institutions, and distinguished figures in the arts.

**Contact:** Mr. George Sturm, Director

**Approval Date:** 1/84

**Latest Information Date:** 1/86

**Index Terms:** Professional associations; Music publishers; Composers; Information dissemination; Catalogs; Performing rights; Administration; Promoting; Music; Operas; Music theater; Arts resources.

## 230

**Music Critics Association, Inc. (MCA)**

6201 Tuckerman Lane
Rockville, MD 20852
Tel.: (301) 530-9527 PUB69-19975

An organization of about 250 music critics in the

United States and Canada, MCA acts as an educational medium for the promotion of high standards of music criticism in the United States, Canada, and elsewhere in the Americas. International activities include membership in international organizations, participation in international conferences, and cooperative projects with foreign groups. Membership is open to all music critics in the United States and Canada. MCA Educational Activities, Inc., the Association's educational arm, conducts Music Critics Institutes providing supplementary training for professionals in the field each summer.

**Areas of Interest:** Music criticism in the Americas.

**Publications:** Newsletter (three times a year).

**Information Services:** Answers inquiries; conducts summer institutes. Services are available to all music critics, both members and nonmembers. Participation in the institutes is free to selected fellows, chosen on the basis of applications evaluated by committee.

**Contact:** Richard D. Freed, Executive Director

**Approval Date:** 1/84

**Latest Information Date:** 1/86

**Index Terms:** Professional associations; Criticism; Music; International arts activities; Educational programs; Arts resources.

---

### 231

#### Music Distributors Association (MDA)

135 West 29th St.
New York, NY 10001
Tel.: (212) 564-0251                    PUB69-19968

MDA is a membership organization presently comprising thirty-five wholesalers and distributors and thirty-five manufacturers of musical instruments and accessories. Membership is open to any firm headquartered in the United States qualifying as a wholesaler or manufacturer of musical instruments and accessories selling through wholesalers.

**Areas of Interest:** Distribution and wholesale trade of musical instruments and accessories.

**Information Services:** Answers inquiries free for anyone.

**Contact:** Mr. Jerome Hershman, Executive Vice-President

**Approval Date:** 1/84

**Latest Information Date:** 1/86

**Index Terms:** Musical instruments; Wholesalers; Manufacturers; Physical distribution management; Music trade; Arts resources.

---

### 232

#### Music Educators National Conference

1902 Association Dr.
Reston, VA 22091
Tel.: (703) 860-4000                    PUB69-6801

**Areas of Interest:** Music education.

**Publications:** *Music Educators Journal* (nine issues a year); *Journal of Research in Music Education* and *Soundings* (both quarterly); reports, bibliographies, conference proceedings, books, reprints. A publications list is available.

**Information Services:** Answers brief inquiries.

**Contact:** Rebecca Taylor, Editor

**Approval Date:** 9/84

**Latest Information Date:** 1/86

**Index Terms:** Music education.

---

### 233

#### Music Industry Educators Association (MIEA)

c/o School of Music
University of Miami
P.O. Box 248165
Coral Gables, FL 33124                    PUB69-19914

An organization of over sixty-five music educators and a number of students, educational institutions, music industry firms, and others in the United States and Canada, MIEA promotes educational standards, encourages music industry and educator interaction, advises on program development, and sponsors programs in the promotion and recognition of research, scholarship, and outstanding achievement.

**Areas of Interest:** All aspects of education in the music business, including music publishing, record production, talent management, music marketing and promotion, recording techniques, studio arranging, and arts management; curriculum design and development; multidisciplinary studies.

**Holdings:** Tape library.

**Publications:** *MIEA Notes* (quarterly newsletter).

**Information Services:** Answers inquiries; provides advisory, reference, and current-awareness services and information on research in progress; evaluates data; conducts seminars and workshops; provides speakers; distributes newsletter; makes referrals to other sources of information. Distribution of the newsletter is restricted to the membership; other services are generally free and available to anyone.

**Contact:** Mr. James Progris, President

**Approval Date:** 7/85

**Latest Information Date:** 7/85

**Index Terms:** Music trade; Music education; Media arts; Curriculum design; Operas; Music theater; Art management; Music publishing; Recorded music industry; Talent management; Merchandising; Recording; Popular music; Jazz music; International arts activities; Arts resources.

## 234

### Musical Box Society, International

c/o Mrs. Clarence W. Fabel, Secretary
Box 205, Route 3
Morgantown, IN 46160          PUB69-14792

The Society is a historical, educational, and museum organization dedicated to the preservation and restoration of mechanical musical instruments.

**Areas of Interest:** Preservation and restoration of mechanical musical instruments; history of music boxes.

**Holdings:** Collection of books on mechanical musical items; small collection of musical items for a future museum.

**Publications:** Bulletin (technical magazine issued three times a year); nontechnical newsletter (issued six times a year); journal articles.

**Information Services:** Answers inquiries; conducts seminars and workshops. Services are free and available to anyone who writes.

**Approval Date:** 4/85

**Latest Information Date:** 4/85

**Index Terms:** Musical box; Mechanical musical instruments; Restoration; History.

## 235

### Musicians National Hot Line Association

277 East 6100 South
Salt Lake City, UT 84107
Tel.: (801) 268-2000          PUB69-20916

A nonprofit organization of musicians, musical groups, schools, instructors, students, businesses that hire musicians, suppliers of music-related products and services, and music-related occupations, the Association seeks to increase the employment of musicians and related occupations. It acts as a national center for employment information and education and seeks to improve communications between musicians and employers of musicians.

**Areas of Interest:** Musician employment and education; employment opportunities for musicians; musical groups, continuing education for musicians; music supplies and equipment.

**Holdings:** Computerized data base of information on musicians wanting to join bands or musical groups, music instructors looking for music education positions, positions available, etc.

**Publications:** *Hotline News* (bimonthly newsletter); brochures and other materials with such titles as *How to Stay Employed in Music*, *What You Should Know Before You Join a Band*, *How to Start Your Own Band*, *How to Break into Recording*, *How to Select an Agent*, etc.

**Information Services:** Answers inquiries; provides computerized data base searching and matching; distributes publications; operates a telephone hotline; makes referrals to other sources of information. Services are primarily for members, but others will be assisted as time and staff permit.

**Contact:** Mr. Marvin Zitting, Executive Director

**Approval Date:** 10/84

**Latest Information Date:** 1/86

**Index Terms:** Musicians; Arts resources.

## 236

### National Association for Music Therapy, Inc.

1133 15th St. NW.
Washington, DC 20005
Tel.: (202) 429-9440          PUB69-6168

This is a professional association devoted to the progressive development of the uses of music as therapy. Although it is a national society, membership is open to residents of countries other than the United States.

**Areas of Interest:** Use of music to accomplish therapeutic aims in restoring, maintaining, and improving mental and/or physical health of adults and children; certification, education, and standards for the profession.

**Holdings:** Collection of books, journals, abstracts, indexes, publication lists, bibliographies, pamphlets, and correspondence. The Association also maintains the *National Registry Listing*, a registry of persons certified as Registered Music Therapists.

**Publications:** *Journal of Music Therapy* (quarterly), containing research abstracts and a bibliography; *Music Therapy Index, Vol. I* (international interdisciplinary index of related literature published between 1960 and 1975); pamphlets; publications lists.

**Information Services:** Answers brief inquiries; distributes pamphlets free on request; makes referrals to other sources of information.

**Approval Date:** 5/84

**Latest Information Date:** 1/86

**Index Terms:** Musicotherapy.

### 237

**National Association of Composers-USA (NACUSA)**

Box 49652, Barrington Station
Los Angeles, CA 90049          PUB69-19978

Partially funded by ASCAP and the national music fraternity, Mu Phi Epsilon, NACUSA is an organization of over four hundred members in the United States and other countries concerned with advancing the professional, musical, and social status of American composers. It sponsors performances, broadcasts, and publication of members' music; conducts cooperative projects with foreign groups; and annually conducts contests for young performers and composers.

**Areas of Interest:** Modern American music.

**Holdings:** An archive of members' music is being developed at the library of California State University Dominguez Hills, Carson, CA.

**Publications:** *Composer/USA* (quarterly newsletter); members' music; critical reviews.

**Information Services:** Answers inquiries; provides current-awareness services; distributes publications. Information services are generally restricted to members.

**Contact:** Mr. Marshall Bialosky, President

**Approval Date:** 3/84

**Latest Information Date:** 1/86

**Index Terms:** Professional associations; American composers; Contemporary music; Contemporary

music concerts; Contests; Performing arts; International arts activities; Arts resources.

### 238

**National Association of Jazz Educators (NAJE)**

P.O. Box 724
Manhattan, KS 66502
Tel.: (913) 776-8744          PUB69-20225

**Location:** 1335 Anderson

NAJE is concerned with the promotion and teaching of jazz and popular music in schools. Membership, currently consisting of about fifty-five hundred teachers, students, professionals, and others, is open to all persons interested in jazz and jazz education. Special projects include a composition contest, scholarships, research, performances, membership in international organizations, participation in international conferences, maintenance of foreign affiliates, and the planning and encouragement of additional international activities.

**Areas of Interest:** Jazz and popular music; jazz history; jazz literature and repertory; performance of jazz; teacher training; curriculum design; arts management, fund raising.

**Publications:** *The Jazz Educators Journal* (quarterly); *NAJE Newsletter* (two issues a year); recordings.

**Information Services:** Answers inquiries; provides advisory and reference services; conducts seminars, workshops, clinics, student activities, and a national convention; provides speakers; distributes publications in the United States and abroad. Services are available at cost to anyone.

**Contact:** Mr. Matt Betton, Executive Director

**Approval Date:** 2/84

**Latest Information Date:** 1/86

**Index Terms:** Arts resources; Jazz music; Popular music; History; Literature (fine arts); Repertoire; Teacher training; Folk art; Art management; Fund raising; International arts activities; Handicapped arts services; Curriculum design.

### 239

**National Association of Pastoral Musicians (NAPM)**

225 Sheridan St. NW.
Washington, DC 20011
Tel.: (202) 723-5800          PUB69-17945

An affiliate of the U.S. Catholic Conference, NAPM

serves as an ecumenical resource for information about church music in whatever style.

**Areas of Interest:** Church music; liturgy; parish music problem solving; positions for church musicians; repertoire sources; hymn copyrights.

**Holdings:** Contemporary and historical hymns of various denominations. NAPM also maintains a church music job bank for musicians seeking jobs and parish churches seeking musicians.

**Publications:** *Pastoral Music* and *Pastoral Music Notebook* (both bimonthly); *Resources* (annual); books, discographies, hard copy and cassette conference proceedings. In addition, NAPM distributes the English-language edition of *Universa Laus—The Bulletin of Universa Laus International Study Group for Liturgical Music.*

**Information Services:** Answers inquiries; provides advisory, reference, literature-searching, current-awareness, reproduction, and translation services; lends materials; conducts seminars and workshops; evaluates and analyzes data; distributes publications; makes referrals to other sources of information; permits on-site use of collections. Inquiries are answered free; other services may involve payment of a fee. All services are available to anyone.

**Approval Date:** 2/84

**Latest Information Date:** 1/86

**Index Terms:** Professional associations; Church music; Musicians; Musical societies; Hymns; Choral music; Liturgy; Job placement; Continuing education; Problem solving; Job opportunities.

## 240

**National Association of Professional Band Instrument Repair Technicians (NAPBIRT)**

P.O. Box 51
Normal, IL 61761
  Tel.: (309) 452-4257         PUB69-19910

**Location:** 8 Ardith Dr.

An organization of about seven hundred members in the United States and abroad, NAPBIRT seeks to update and upgrade the knowledge and craftsmanship of its members through continuing education programs. It is interested in more foreign involvement and is currently planning future international projects.

**Areas of Interest:** Repair, restoration, rejuvenation, conservation, and maintenance of band instruments.

**Publications:** *Techni-Com* (bimonthly journal); tech-

nical reports, journal articles, membership directory, data compilations.

**Information Services:** Answers inquiries; provides advisory and reference services; conducts seminars and workshops; provides speakers; distributes publications in the United States and abroad; makes referrals to foreign and domestic sources of information. Information services are generally free and available to anyone. Detailed information on band instrument repair is subject to a seminar fee.

**Contact:** Mr. Charles W. Hagler, Executive Secretary

**Approval Date:** 4/85

**Latest Information Date:** 4/85

**Index Terms:** Arts resources; Professional associations; Band instrument repair technicians; Restoration; Historic preservation; Conservation; Maintenance; Musical instruments; Musicotherapy; Handicrafts; Lecturers; Information services; Continuing education; International arts activities.

## 241

**National Association of School Music Dealers (NASMD)**

513 Gillespie St., P.O. Box 1209
Fayetteville, NC 28302
  Tel.: (919) 483-9032         PUB69-19884

An organization of about three hundred members representing retail businesses involved in servicing school music programs, NASMD fosters the exchange of business ideas and promotes and coordinates activities among the industry, education organizations, and the public. Membership is by invitation.

**Areas of Interest:** Music in the schools, emphasizing instrumental music.

**Publications:** Quarterly newsletter.

**Information Services:** Answers inquiries; conducts seminars and workshops; distributes newsletter; makes referrals to other sources of information. Services are free and available to members.

**Contact:** Mr. Vincent McBryde, President

**Approval Date:** 4/85

**Latest Information Date:** 4/85

**Index Terms:** Arts resources; Music education; Music; Instrumental music; Teacher training; Promotion; Awards; Public relations; Professional associations.

**242**

## National Association of Schools of Music

11250 Roger Bacon Dr., No. 5
Reston, VA 22090
   Tel.: (703) 437-0700          PUB69-6682

**Areas of Interest:** Music in higher education; accreditation of schools and departments of music.

**Publications:** *Proceedings of the Annual Meeting; Music in Higher Education* (annual); directory (annual); handbook (biennial).

**Information Services:** Answers inquiries; makes referrals; provides consulting services to members and nonmember institutions.

**Approval Date:** 11/84

**Latest Information Date:** 1/86

**Index Terms:** Arts resources; Music education; Educational evaluation; Accreditation.

**243**

## National Association of Teachers of Singing (NATS)

c/o New York University
35 West 4th St. (778)
New York, NY 10003
   Tel.: (212) 677-5651          PUB69-19964

NATS is a professional organization representing everyone who is concerned with singing and vocal instruction in private studios, conservatories, schools, colleges, and community life. Membership is open to citizens of the United States and Canada whose professional training or experience qualify them as teachers of singing, and whose character is of known probity. There are currently about four thousand members.

**Areas of Interest:** Vocal music; opera and music theater; music therapy, ethical principles in the teaching of singing.

**Publications:** *NATS Bulletin* (five issues a year); newsletter (three issues a year); books; journal articles.

**Information Services:** Conducts national, regional, and chapter meetings, summer workshops, and artist auditions; participates in international conferences; provides speakers; distributes publications; makes biennial awards to young artists. The *NATS Bulletin* is available to anyone by subscription.

**Contact:** Mr. James Browning, Executive Secretary

**Approval Date:** 1/84

**Latest Information Date:** 1/86

**Index Terms:** Professional associations; Vocal music; Operas; Music theater; Musicotherapy; Singing; Teaching; Ethics; International arts activities; Lecturers; Arts resources.

**244**

## National Catholic Bandmasters Association (NCBA)

P.O. Box 1023
Notre Dame, IN 46556
   Tel.: (219) 239-7136          PUB69-19969

NCBA is an organization of about two hundred members who are teachers in band programs in Catholic elementary and secondary schools and colleges. Membership is open to any qualified teachers of band in Catholic schools and Catholic teachers of band in public schools.

**Areas of Interest:** Concert band; wind ensembles; marching band; jazz band; brass ensembles; woodwind ensembles; percussion ensembles; instrumental liturgical music; teacher training; curriculum design.

**Holdings:** Library of music suitable for use in the worship service (about one hundred fifty titles).

**Publications:** *NCBA Newsletter* (monthly); *National Conference Proceedings* (annual); *NCBA Liturgical Music Sourcebook; NCBA Basic Repertoire Listing; Administrators' Guide to the Parochial School Band; NCBA Directory of Instrumental Music Programs in Catholic Colleges and Universities;* liturgical music manuscripts.

**Information Services:** Answers inquiries; provides advisory and reference services; evaluates school music programs; conducts seminars and workshops; lends materials from its collections; distributes publications; makes referrals to other sources of information. Services are free or available at cost and, while intended primarily for members, can be extended to others as time and staff availability permit.

**Contact:** Pam Potter, President

**Approval Date:** 1/84

**Latest Information Date:** 1/86

**Index Terms:** Concert bands; Wind ensembles; Woodwind ensembles; Marching bands; Percussion ensembles; Jazz bands; Liturgical music; Teacher training; Curriculum design; Arts resources.

**245**

## National Council of Music Importers and Exporters (NCMIE)

135 West 29th St.
New York, NY 10001
Tel.: (212) 564-0251
(TELEX) 425102                    PUB69-19965

NCMIE's membership is open to anyone who imports for resale to the trade, to manufacturers, and to exporters.

**Areas of Interest:** International trade in musical instruments and accessories.

**Publications:** Annual calendar of worldwide music trade shows.

**Information Services:** Answers inquiries; makes referrals to out-of-country sources of information. Services are free and available to anyone.

**Contact:** Mr. Jerome Hershman, Executive Vice-President

**Approval Date:** 1/84

**Latest Information Date:** 1/86

**Index Terms:** Musical instruments; International trade; Exports; Imports; Arts resources.

**246**

## National Flute Association (NFA)

P.O. Box 834
Elkhart, IN 46515
Tel.: (817) 387-9472                    PUB69-19949

Alternate address; 805 Laguna Dr., Denton, TX 76201

NFA is an organization of about three thousand individual members and an additional seventy associate members representing commercial firms interested in increasing the standard of excellence in flute performance and teaching and encouraging the composition and publication of flute music. Activities include annual performance and publication competitions and sponsorship of American and foreign artists in performance in the United States.

**Areas of Interest:** Flute performance; composition for the flute; flute literature; flutes and flute manufacture.

**Holdings:** Computerized mailing list. The NFA Library of Flute Music is housed at the University of Arizona in Tucson, representing a large segment of the repertoire that is available for study. In addition, NFA provides support and assistance to the Music Division of the Library of Congress in Washington, DC, in maintaining the Dayton C. Miller Flute Collection, which includes 1,500 flutes and related instruments, a 3,000-volume library, about 4,000 titles of printed music, portraits and autographs of flutists and composers, concert programs, clippings, pamphlets, articles, patent specifications, prints and photographs, sales catalogs and price lists, and eight file drawers of correspondence.

**Publications:** *Newsletter of the National Flute Association* (quarterly); *Catalog of the NFA Library of Flute Music;* membership directory.

**Information Services:** Answers inquiries; provides information on research in progress; conducts seminars, workshops, and an annual conference; makes interlibrary loans; distributes publications and mailing lists. Information is available to anyone. The newsletter is available to schools and libraries by subscription. The mailing list is available by purchase to members and others by special authorization. Other services are generally restricted to the membership.

**Contact:** Ms. Myrna Brown, Executive Coordinator

**Approval Date:** 2/84

**Latest Information Date:** 1/86

**Index Terms:** Flute; Flute music; Flute manufacturers; Musical composition; Publishing; Performing arts; Contests; Literature (fine arts) Music; Teacher training; Historic preservation; Arts resources; Fund raising; International arts activities.

**247**

## National Institute for Music Theater (NIMT)

John F. Kennedy Center for the Performing Arts
Washington, DC 20566
Tel.: (202) 965-2800                    PUB69-16762

NIMT is dedicated to the support of all forms of music theater in the United States. It defines music theater as the theatrical art form in which the singing voice is the primary means of dramatic expression and includes opera, musical theater, operetta, and a variety of experimental, interdisciplinary forms. NIMT is funded in part by the National Endowment for the Arts and by private contributions.

**Areas of Interest:** All aspects of music theater, including the creation and production of new works, helping young professionals, and the generation and distribution of information on current key issues.

**Publications:** *Commentary* (quarterly newsletter); program guidelines; brochures; reports.

**Information Services:** Answers inquiries; sponsors national colloquia on subjects of current concern to the field.

**Approval Date:** 5/85

**Latest Information Date:** 5/85

**Index Terms:** Operas; Performing arts; Music; Financial support; Music and state; State encouragement of the arts; Endowments; Theater.

## 248

### National Music Council (NMC)

c/o ACA
570 Seventh Ave., 20th Floor
New York, NY 10018
    Tel.: (212) 265-8132        PUB69-15976

A nonprofit membership organization, NMC provides a forum for the professional, educational, industrial, and lay musical interests in the United States. It has been selected by the U.S. Department of State to be represented on the U.S. Commission for UNESCO and is the U.S. representative in the International Music Council of UNESCO.

**Areas of Interest:** Music.

**Publications:** *National Music Council Newsletter* (quarterly).

**Information Services:** Answers inquiries or refers inquirers to other sources of information free.

**Approval Date:** 2/84

**Latest Information Date:** 1/86

**Index Terms:** Music United States; Music eduction; Musical societies; Professional ethics; Musicians; Music and state; Legislation; Music trade.

## 249

### National Music Publishers' Association, Inc. (NMPA)

205 East 42nd St.
New York, NY 10017
    Tel.: (212) 370-5330        PUB69-18493

**Areas of Interest:** Music publishing protection; copyright of music; licensing of recorded music.

**Publications:** *NMPA Bulletin* (quarterly; available free); various booklets, pamphlets, and other explanatory material (available free).

**Information Services:** Answers inquiries; distributes publications; conducts seminars and workshops; makes referrals to other sources of information; attempts to locate publishers of copyrighted music if not known. Fees are charged for seminars and workshops, but other services, including most publications, are free and available to anyone.

**Approval Date:** 4/85

**Latest Information Date:** 4/85

**Index Terms:** Trade associations; Music publishers; Copyrights; Licenses.

## 250

### National Opera Association (NOA)

Route 2, Box 93
Commerce, TX 75428
    Tel.: (214) 886-3830        PUB69-19958

A membership organization of professional, educational, and civic opera personnel, NOA (1) aims to promote greater appreciation, more performances, and increased composition of opera; (2) seeks to provide more opportunities for operatic talent; and (3) supports special projects that improve the scope and quality of opera. National auditions for NOA members are held each year to encourage operatic talent and increase regional employment opportunities. Membership is available to individuals and organizations involved in any facet of opera production and promotion, as well as related service companies and enthusiasts.

**Areas of Interest:** All aspects of opera.

**Holdings:** The NOA Score/Tape Library of contemporary American operas is housed at the American Music Center, 250 West 57th St., New York, NY.

**Publications:** *Opera Journal* (quarterly presenting articles on all aspects of opera, along with reviews of new operas and books about opera); *NOA Newsletter* (quarterly); *NOA Membership Directory* (annual); *NOA Monograph Series* (scholarly and practical books on the history and practice of opera).

**Information Services:** Answers inquiries or refers inquirers to other sources of information free; sells publications, data compilations, and mailing lists and labels. Members may participate in the annual conference and auditions and receive a discount on publications.

**Contact:** Ms. Mary Elaine Wallace, Executive Secretary

**Approval Date:** 1/84

**Latest Information Date:** 1/86

**Index Terms:** Professional associations; Operas; Opera singers; Opera producers; Opera composers; Opera directors; Singer auditions; Arts resources.

## 251

### National School Orchestra Association (NSOA)

330 Bellevue Dr.
Bowling Green, KY 42101
 Tel.: (502) 842-7121          PUB69-19948

NSOA is a nonprofit organization of about fourteen hundred members who direct school orchestras or teach in public schools and colleges.

**Areas of Interest:** School orchestra programs; school orchestra literature; school orchestra promotion and problems; public relations and community relations for school orchestra directors; string, woodwind, brass, and percussion pedagogy for large groups; conducting techniques.

**Publications:** Quarterly bulletin; *All State Orchestra Survey Report* (1981); *PR Manual* (1982); *Sure Fire Materials List* (1983); monographs, project reports, journal articles, critical reviews, teaching materials, graded lists.

**Information Services:** Answers inquiries; provides advisory, consulting, and reference services; conducts seminars, workshops, and an annual composition contest; provides speakers; distributes publications; makes referrals to other sources of information. Services are available free or at cost to members of the Association.

**Contact:** James H. Godfrey, President

**Approval Date:** 1/84

**Latest Information Date:** 1/86

**Index Terms:** School orchestras; School orchestra programs; School orchestra literature; Orchestra directors; Music education; Teacher training; Arts resources; Conducting techniques.

## 252

### New Music Distribution Service (NMDS)

500 Broadway
New York, NY 10012
 Tel.: (212) 925-2121          PUB69-19926

NMDS is a musician-run, nonprofit organization for the distribution of all independently produced recordings of new music, new jazz, and electronic music, regardless of commercial potential or per-

sonal taste. It is a division of the Jazz Composers Orchestra Association (JCOA) and is funded by the National Endowment for the Arts, the New York State Council on the Arts, and private foundations.

**Areas of Interest:** Promotion and sale of independently produced recordings of all contemporary American progressive music, including twentieth-century classical music, avant-garde jazz, and progressive rock. NMDS advises the independent producer and all musicians and composers about all phases of record production and manufacturing.

**Holdings:** Extensive mailing list of individuals interested in new music.

**Publications:** Annual catalog of available recordings; *Corrective News* (every 2 1/2 years).

**Information Services:** Answers inquiries; provides advisory services; provides speakers; distributes publications; makes referrals to other sources of information. Services are available to independent record producers, composers, music dealers, and the public.

**Contact:** Yale Evelev, Director of Promotion

**Approval Date:** 1/84

**Latest Information Date:** 1/86

**Index Terms:** Music; Recorded music industry; Distribution services; Promoting; Sales; Contemporary music; Jazz music; Twentieth century classical music; Nonprofit organizations; Arts resources.

## 253

### Ohio State University
### School of Music
### Music Information Retrieval System

c/o Dr. Peter Costanza, Professor
126 Lord Hall, 124 West 17th Ave.
Columbus, OH 43210
 Tel.: (614) 422-6400          PUB69-12722

**Areas of Interest:** Music; music education; music perception; music theory; psychology and sociology of music; acoustics; music testing and measurement.

**Holdings:** Collection of over five thousand indexed reports and fifty thousand documents by author card; access to the University's computerized data base.

**Information Services:** Provides literature-searching, abstracting, indexing, and reproduction services. Services are provided on-site only and are free, except for reproduction services, and available to anyone.

**Approval Date:** 9/85

**Latest Information Date:** 9/85

**Index Terms:** Music; Music education; Musicology.

### 254

## Oldtime Country Music Club of Canada

c/o Bob Fuller, Secretary
1421 Gohier St.
St. Laurent, Quebec, CANADA H4L 3K2
Tel.: (514) 748-7251                   PUB69-14956

**Areas of Interest:** Oldtime country and western music, including bluegrass music, cowboy music, hillbilly music, traditional music, etc.

**Holdings:** Library of records, tapes, and old movies; collection of books relevant to oldtime music.

**Publications:** *Underground-Voice of Oldtime Music* (periodical).

**Information Services:** Provides current-awareness, magnetic tape, and reproduction services; sponsors concerts, family-get-togethers, etc.; distributes publication; makes interlibrary loans; makes referrals to other sources of information; permits access to library. Many services are free to members, and membership is invited.

**Approval Date:** 4/85

**Latest Information Date:** 4/85

**Index Terms:** Folk music; Music.

### 255

## OPERA America

633 E St. NW.
Washington, DC 20004
Tel.: (202) 347-9262                   PUB69-19656

OPERA America is the nonprofit service organization for the professional opera-producing companies in North, Central, and South America.

**Areas of Interest:** Opera; opera composers, librettists, directors, producers, administrators, companies, costumes, and scenery; opera in video media; audience development; fund raising and development; marketing of new operatic works; financial management; operations management; labor relations; opera and public policy; access of the aged and the handicapped to opera; opera education for artists, producers, teachers, and the public.

**Publications:** *Intercompany Announcements* (monthly report); *Management Resource Volume* (annual reference information on national organizations and resources); *Profile: OPERA America and the Professional Opera Companies* (annual report on the professional opera field, including profiles of each of the ninety member companies); *Scenery, Costumes & Musical Materials Directory* (listing of commercial costume houses, scenery studios, and company-owned materials available for rental); *Professional Opera Survey* (financial and statistical data on opera companies); *Season Performance Schedule* (annual); *Perspectives: Creating and Producing Contemporary Opera and Musical Theater* (135-page book of monographs); *Working Ideas: A Resource Guide for Developing Successful Opera Education Programs; Survey of Professional Training/Apprentice Programs; Opera Companies and Shopping Centers: Partners in Community Outreach; 504 Programs That Work.*

**Information Services:** Answers inquiries about the opera field and the professional opera companies; provides advisory, consulting, and reference services; analyzes data; conducts seminars, symposia, conferences, and auditions; distributes publications; makes referrals to other sources of information. Services are provided free to member and correspondent companies. Some services and materials are available to others for a fee.

**Approval Date:** 5/85

**Latest Information Date:** 5/85

**Index Terms:** Performing arts; Operas; Music; Financial support; Educational programs; Composers; State encouragement of the arts; Costume; Opera production; Stage scenery; Statistical data; Surveys; Budgets; Translations; Fund raising; Opera singers; Librettists; Opera producers; Singer auditions; Management training; Information dissemination; Documentation.

### 256

## Organization of American Kodaly Educators (OAKE)

c/o Dr. Robert Perinchief, Executive Secretary
Music Department
University of Wisconsin-Whitewater
Whitewater, WI 53190
Tel.: (414) 472-1341                   PUB69-19919

An organization of about one thousand members representing schools, universities, libraries, and the music industry and including some student members, OAKE promotes the music education principles and practices of Zoltan Kodaly, which emphasize the importance of folk music in teaching music and music literacy in any country. OAKE's commitment is to investigate and articulate for the American situation the combined folk music research techniques, the qualifications of teachers, and methods of Kodaly, for its application to American schools at all levels, from preschool to university. International activities include membership in international organizations, participation in international conferences, and performances abroad. Membership in OAKE is available to interested professionals.

**Areas of Interest:** Music; folk music; performance art; music education.

**Publications:** *Kodaly Envoy* (quarterly bulletin).

**Information Services:** Answers inquiries; conducts seminars and workshops; distributes its bulletin. The bulletin is sent to members only; other services are available to anyone and are provided free.

**Approval Date:** 8/85

**Latest Information Date:** 8/85

**Index Terms:** Music; Music education; Performing arts; Folk music; International arts activities; Teacher training; Arts resources.

## 257

**Percussive Arts Society**

214 West Main
Urbana, IL 61801
  Tel.: (217) 367-4098          PUB69-10334

**Areas of Interest:** Percussion music; acoustics of percussion instruments; music education; musical literature; world musics.

**Holdings:** Over 150 periodical titles.

**Publications:** *Percussive Notes;* reports, bibliographies, news, reviews, product information, etc.

**Information Services:** Answers inquiries; provides reference services; makes referrals to other sources of information.

**Approval Date:** 9/84

**Latest Information Date:** 1/86

**Index Terms:** Music.

## 258

**SESAC Inc.**

10 Columbus Circle
New York, NY 10019
  Tel.: (212) 586-3450          PUB69-20240

An organization of over five hundred publishers and more than fifteen hundred song writers, SESAC licenses performances of copyrighted music by broadcast and nonbroadcast users of music and the mechanical and synchronization uses of its repertory. In addition, it collects license fees and distributes royalties to its members. SESAC has agreements with over forty performance and mechanical licensing organizations throughout the world, makes copyrights from abroad available to its licensees in the United States, participates in international conferences, and is interested in more foreign involvement.

**Areas of Interest:** Protection and representation of performance, mechanical, and synchronization rights in copyrighted musical compositions, on both the domestic and international levels.

**Information Services:** Answers inquiries; provides advisory services; maintains a speakers' bureau and participates in song writing seminars at colleges and universities throughout the country; makes referrals to other sources of information. Services are free and available to affiliated song writers and publishers, licensees, music-oriented groups, and others interested in music programming.

**Contact:** A. H. Prager, Chairman

**Approval Date:** 1/84

**Latest Information Date:** 1/86

**Index Terms:** Music; Musical composition; Licenses; Royalties; Copyrights; International arts activities; Arts resources.

## 259

**Society for Ethnomusicology**

P.O. Box 2984
Ann Arbor, MI 48106
  Tel.: (313) 665-9400          PUB69-19890

The Society is an organization of 2,124 musicologists, anthropologists, students, and institutions in the United States and abroad. Activities include dissemination of knowledge concerning the music of the world's peoples, participation in international conferences, cooperative projects with foreign groups, and maintenance of foreign affiliates. It is interested in more foreign involvement. Membership is open to all interested persons.

**Areas of Interest:** Music and society; music in the life of specific ethnic groups and social classes; comparison of music of individual groups and of different geographical areas; music analysis of non-Western music; anthropology of music; dance; theater; indigenous and folk arts; comprehensive arts education; museum programs; multidisciplinary programs.

**Holdings:** Computerized membership list.

**Publications:** *Ethnomusicology* (three times a year); *Newsletter* (four times a year); books, journal articles, directories, bibliographies, critical reviews, indexes, reprints.

**Information Services:** Answers inquiries; provides advisory, consulting, reference, and microform services; provides speakers; provides information on research in progress; conducts seminars and workshops; distributes publications and membership lists in the United States and abroad; makes referrals to domestic and foreign sources of information. Services are available at cost to anyone.

**Contact:** Mr. William Malm, Office Manager

**Approval Date:** 4/85

**Latest Information Date:** 4/85

**Index Terms:** Arts resources; Ethnomusicology; Musical societies; Ethnic music; Music analysis; Non-Western music; Dance; Theater; Folk art; Museums (institutions); Cultural programs; International arts activities; Music and society; Art education; Computerized membership list; Lecturers; Information services.

## 260

**Society for the Preservation and Encouragement of Barber Shop Quartet Singing in America, Inc. (S.P.E.B.S.Q.S.A.)**
**Old Songs Library**

P.O. Box 575
Kenosha, WI 53140
   Tel.: (414) 654-9111            PUB69-20031

**Location:** 6315 Third Ave.

The Society's purpose is to perpetuate vocal harmony and good fellowship among its members, to encourage music appreciation among members and the general public, to promote charitable projects and maintain music scholarships, and to promote a broad program in music education, particularly in the field of vocal harmony.

**Areas of Interest:** Barbershop quartet singing.

**Holdings:** 800,000 pieces of original sheet music.

**Publications:** *Harmonizer* (bimonthly magazine); directories.

**Information Services:** Answers inquiries; provides

reference, literature-searching, and copying services; conducts workshops; evaluates data; distributes publications; makes referrals to other sources of information; permits on-site use of collection. Services are provided free to members, at cost to others, and are available to anyone.

**Approval Date:** 1/84

**Latest Information Date:** 1/86

**Index Terms:** Barbershop quartets; Music education; Scholarships; Vocal music; Arts resources; Art appreciation; Barbershop harmony.

## 261

**Songwriters Resources and Services (SRS) (former)**
**National Academy of Songwriters**
**(NAS) (current)**

6772 Hollywood Blvd.
Hollywood, CA 90028
   Tel.: (213) 463-7178            PUB69-19936

NAS is a nonprofit arts organization of about three thousand published and unpublished members in the United States and abroad promoting the protection and education of song writers. Special programs include Songsearch, a national competition culminating in an annual concert presentation of the best songs in six categories. Membership in NAS is available to anyone.

**Areas of Interest:** Writing song music and lyrics; song writing for commercials; scoring films; production of recordings; copyright law affecting song writers and song collaborators; marketing songs; contract negotiation; identification of publishers, producers, and artists needing song material; identification of lyricists and composers needing collaborators and musicians available for recordings.

**Holdings:** The Alan and Marilyn Bergman Library of books and periodicals on the history, craft, and business of music. In addition, NAS maintains the Songbank, a register of unpublished songs useful to writers in establishing a prior claim to authorship.

**Publications:** *Open Ears* (bimonthly listing of publishers, producers, and artists needing songs); *NAS Newsletter* (bimonthly); information papers on frequently asked questions of a general nature; pamphlets, cassettes.

**Information Services:** Answers inquiries; provides advisory, consulting, reference, literature-searching, current-awareness, tape, professional counseling, and group legal services; evaluates songs; conducts workshops and professional forums; provides speakers; distributes publications in the United States and abroad; makes referrals to other sources of information; permits on-site use of collections. Some services are provided free or at cost to anyone; others are limited to the membership.

**Contact:** Barbara Marcus, Executive Director

**Approval Date:** 1/84

**Latest Information Date:** 1/86

**Index Terms:** Music; Media arts; Performing arts; Songwriters; Songwriting; Songs; Lyricists; Marketing; Publishing; Contracts; Recording; Composers; Song festivals; Information resources; Copyrights; Contests; Awards; International arts activities; Handicapped arts services; Counseling; Arts resources.

## 262

### Suzuki Association of the Americas, Inc. (SAA)

P.O. Box 354
Muscatine, IA 52761
Tel.: (319) 263-3071                    PUB69-19924

An organization of about eighty-two hundred members in North and South America, SAA promotes the music education methods of Shinichi Suzuki, emphasizing beginning at age three or four, proceeding in very small steps, and encouraging parental participation. SAA is a member of the International Suzuki Association and participates in its conferences and conducts cooperative projects. It also sponsors performances abroad and presents foreign artists in performance in the United States. Membership is open to all.

**Areas of Interest:** Suzuki instruction in violin, viola, cello, flute, wind, piano, harp, oboe, and recorder; concept of the Suzuki method.

**Holdings:** Computerized membership records. The SAA archives are housed at Southern Illinois University at Edwardsville, IL.

**Publications:** *American Suzuki Journal* (six issues a year); membership directory.

**Information Services:** Answers inquiries; provides advisory, consulting, reference, literature-searching, reproduction, and translation services and information on research in progress; conducts seminars and workshops; distributes publications and audiovisual materials in the United States and abroad; makes referrals to both domestic and foreign sources of information; provides speakers. Services are available to the membership.

**Contact:** Mr. Robert K. Reinsager, Executive Director

**Approval Date:** 1/84

**Latest Information Date:** 1/86

**Index Terms:** Music education; Pedagogy; Suzuki, Shinishi; Violin; Viola; Violoncello; Flute; Wind instruments; Piano; International arts activities; Teacher training; Scholarships; Musical societies; Lecturers; Arts resources.

## 263

### Sweet Adelines, Inc.

P.O. Box 470168
Tulsa, OK 74147
Tel.: (918) 622-1444                    PUB69-19899

**Location:** 5334 East 46th St.

An organization of 33,000 members in the United States and other countries, Sweet Adelines, Inc. sponsors regional and international competitions for quartets and choruses.

**Areas of Interest:** Music in four-part harmony, "barbershop" style.

**Publications:** *The Pitch Pipe* (quarterly magazine); sheet music arranged in four-part harmony.

**Information Services:** Inquiries are answered free for anyone. Seminars, workshops, schools, and publications are limited to the membership. Subscriptions available for the magazine.

**Contact:** Ms. Peggy Chambers, Executive Director

**Approval Date:** 4/85

**Latest Information Date:** 1/86

**Index Terms:** Barbershop harmony; Barbershop quartets; Music; International arts activities; Teacher training; Performing arts; Vocal quartets; Vocal music; Arts resources.

## 264

### Thematic Indexes of Renaissance Polyphony

c/o Dr. Harry Lincoln
Music Department
State University of New York at Binghamton
Binghamton, NY 13901
Tel.: (607) 798-2436                    PUB69-19561

**Areas of Interest:** Data processing and computer techniques involved in creating an index system with music input language from which intervallic order and other information can be extracted and by which sixteenth-century Italian polyphonic anonymous works can be identified and borrowings cited.

**Holdings:** Computer data bank of about forty thousand incipits (opening melodies) of Italian polyphony, 1500–1600, with capability of searches as well as printing of themes in staff notation; microfilms of about three hundred fifty madrigal collections from sixteenth-century Italy.

**Publications:** Conference paper reprints.

**Information Services:** Answers inquiries; provides magnetic tape services and printing of musical themes; distributes reprints; permits on-site use of collections. Services are available at cost to anyone.

**Approval Date:** 2/85

**Latest Information Date:** 2/85

**Index Terms:** Renaissance music; Music computer applications.

---

### 265

**Tulane University**
**Howard-Tilton Memorial Library**
**William Ransom Hogan Jazz Archives**

New Orleans, LA 70118
Tel.: (504) 865-5688                  PUB69-9409

**Areas of Interest:** History of New Orleans jazz from the various types of music which antedated and contributed to its development and to the influence of New Orleans styles on the music of other countries.

**Holdings:** Over 30,000 phonograph records, 2,000 reels of tape recordings, 40,000 pieces of sheet music, and 6,000 photos; 59 piano rolls; 32 motion picture films; books; microfilm rolls; videotape rolls; miscellaneous notes; clippings; posters.

**Information Services:** Answers inquiries; provides consulting and reference services; permits on-site use of collection. Fees are charged for duplication services (limited by copyright restrictions) and handling.

**Approval Date:** 4/85

**Latest Information Date:** 4/85

**Index Terms:** New Orleans; Music history; Jazz music; Music libraries; Archives.

---

### 266

**University of Delaware**
**Department of Music**
**Music Resource Center**

Newark, DE 19716
Tel.: (302) 451-8130                  PUB69-20347

**Areas of Interest:** Music.

**Holdings:** About 3,000 recordings; 4,500 music scores; 2,550 books on music; 600 cassette and reel-to-reel tapes; video tapes; periodicals. The collection is particularly strong in recordings of operas and opera singers throughout the history of recorded sound, especially French opera and singers. There is also a collection of large ensemble music for band, orchestra, and chorus.

**Information Services:** Answers inquiries; provides advisory and reference services; lends materials; distributes audiovisual materials to elementary and secondary students and teachers; makes referrals to other sources of information; permits on-site use of collections. Except for reproducing tape copies of University of Delaware concerts and recitals, for which a fee is charged, services are generally free. The Center's primary audience is the Department of Music and the University, but others in the region (Delaware, southern New Jersey, southeastern Pennsylvania, and northern Maryland) are accommodated as time and staffing considerations permit. The Center's facilities, including listening facilities, are accessible to the handicapped.

**Contact:** Mr. J. Michael Foster, Supervisor

**Approval Date:** 1/84

**Latest Information Date:** 1/86

**Index Terms:** Arts resources; Music; Handicapped arts services.

---

### 267

**University of Western Ontario**
**Music Library**

London, Ontario, CANADA N6A 3K7
Tel.: (519) 679-2466 or 3761          PUB69-15183

**Areas of Interest:** Music.

**Holdings:** 24,750 monographs; 3,100 reference books; 4,100 periodical volumes; 1,400 pamphlets; 330 periodical subscriptions; 350 nonperiodical subscriptions; 31,100 scores and parts; 5,150 miniature scores; 14,000 solo music references; 23,000 phonorecords; 150 tapes; 147,000 choral, 2,700 band and orchestra sets (score and 10 parts or more), and 12,400 method books, 1,400 rare books; 8,200 microforms. Primary strengths are the collection of opera manuscripts, scores, books about opera, and related material of the period 1597–1800, and the collection of letters of Gustav Mahler.

**Information Services:** Answers inquiries; provides reference, limited literature-searching, microform, and reproduction services; makes interlibrary loans; makes referrals to other sources of information; permits on-site use of collections. Services are free, except for reproduction services, and available to anyone.

**Approval Date:** 8/85

**Latest Information Date:** 8/85

**Index Terms:** Music libraries; Colleges and universities; Musical scores.

## 268

### Viola d'Amore Society of America

c/o Dr. Myron Rosenblum, Codirector
39-23 47th St.
Sunnyside, NY 11104
  Tel.: (212) 786-1467          PUB69-20212

c/o Mr. Daniel Thomason, Codirector 10917 Pickford Way, Culver City, CA 90230, (213) 837-7596

An organization of about one hundred professional and amateur musicians, teachers, organizations, and others in the United States, Canada, and overseas, the Society seeks to further scholarship dealing with the history of the viola d'amore, promote its performance, encourage contemporary composition, and to make available editions of music written for it. The Society sponsors international congresses, performances abroad, and performances of foreign artists in the United States, and is planning future international projects.

**Areas of Interest:** History of the viola d'amore, including its origins and predecessor instruments found in Turkey, the Middle East, and India; evolution of the viola d'amore; music for the viola d'amore, principally middle Baroque, late Baroque, Classical, Romantic, and Contemporary; performance practices; biography of instrumentalists; discography.

**Holdings:** Small library of music for the viola d'amore.

**Publications:** Newsletter, journal articles, biographies. Editions of music for the viola d'amore is a current publications project.

**Information Services:** Answers inquiries; conducts seminars and workshops; distributes publications in the United States and foreign countries; makes referrals to other sources of information. Services are primarily for members, but scholars and musicians are accommodated where possible.

**Approval Date:** 2/84

**Latest Information Date:** 1/86

**Index Terms:** Arts resources; Viola d'amore; Musical compositions; History; Biographies; Discography; International arts activities; Musical societies.

## 269

### Women Band Directors National Association (WBDNA)

344 Overlook Dr.
West Lafayette, IN 47906
  Tel.: (317) 463-1738          PUB69-19928

An organization of women band directors and supervisors of music in schools at all levels and fifteen industrial members, WBDNA serves women band directors and their students. Activities include the sponsorship of awards, scholarships, and an annual composition contest; participation in national and international conferences; some sponsorship of performances abroad; and cooperative projects with foreign groups. Membership is open to all women band directors and supervisors of music. Affiliate memberships are available to all women connected with band music and student memberships to women college students.

**Areas of Interest:** Band music; performance art; music therapy; teacher training.

**Holdings:** Archives of about eight hundred pieces.

**Publications:** Membership roster (annual); a recommended music list; list of women clinicians; biographies of women band directors; journal articles; project reports, teaching materials.

**Information Services:** Answers inquiries; conducts seminars, workshops, and summer courses; provides speakers; distributes publications. Information is provided free to anyone. Other services are generally available for a fee, but some publications may be restricted to members.

**Contact:** Ms. Gladys Wright, President

**Approval Date:** 1/84

**Latest Information Date:** 1/86

**Index Terms:** Band music; Performing arts; Music; Teacher training; Musicotherapy; Fund raising; Archives; Lecturers; International arts activities; Women and directors; Arts resources.

**270**

## Young Concert Artists, Inc. (YCA)

250 West 57th St.
New York, NY 10019
  Tel.: (212) 307-6655           PUB69-19913

YCA is a nonprofit management and presenting organization funded by the National Endowment for the Arts, the New York State Council for the Arts, foundations, corporations, and individuals. It "discovers" extraordinary young classical musicians through the Young Concert Artists International Auditions each year and launches their careers as professionals through the Young Concert Artists Series in New York and Washington, DC, concert bookings, management services, and materials at no cost to the artists.

**Areas of Interest:** Professional career management of young musicians.

**Publications:** Roster of current young concert artists; brochures on the Young Concert Artists Series in New York and Washington.

**Information Services:** Information is provided only to auspices booking YCA artists. Management services are provided only to artists who are winners of the Young Concert Artists International Auditions, thus becoming members of the YCA roster.

**Contact:** Mrs. Susan Wadsworth, Director

**Approval Date:** 4/85

**Latest Information Date:** 4/85

**Index Terms:** Young concert artists; Professional career management; Music; Performing arts; Arts resources.

# Film Organizations

## Academy of Motion Picture Arts and Sciences National Film Information Service

8949 Wilshire Blvd.
Beverly Hills, CA 90211
Tel.: (213) 278-8990                    PUB69-1831

The Service was established to offer access by mail to the extensive research holdings of the Academy's Margaret Herrick Library to persons outside the greater Los Angeles area.

**Areas of Interest:** History and technology of motion pictures and the motion picture industry.

**Holdings:** The Academy's Margaret Herrick Library contains over sixteen thousand books and periodicals about the motion picture industry, biographical information about industry personnel, cast and technical credits, reviews, photographs, and other pertinent information about 65,000 motion pictures (nearly every motion picture made in the United States since 1915).

**Publications:** Research Guides containing information on the holdings of the Margaret Herrick Library together with a detailed bibliography and sources of films on or by the subjects of the Guides (the films are preserved in U.S. archives and are available for rental in 16mm). Titles currently available in this series include *British Cinema, Frank Capra, Cecil B. DeMille, Lillian Gish, D. W. Griffith, F. W. Murnau, Eugene O'Neill on Film, King Vidor, James Whale, Preston Sturges,* and *Women Directors.*

**Information Services:** Answers inquiries; provides photocopies of reviews, hard-to-find articles, and still photographs in the Library's collections; provides reference and literature-searching services; distributes Research Guides and data compilations; permits on-site use of Library's collections; makes referrals to other sources of information.

**Approval Date:** 2/85

**Latest Information Date:** 2/85

**Index Terms:** Motion pictures.

## American Film Institute (AFI) Louis B. Mayer Library

P.O. Box 27999
Los Angeles, CA 90027
Tel.: (213) 856-7655 or 856-7656       PUB69-19454

**Location:** 2021 North Western Ave.

The Library is partially funded by the National Endowment for the Arts.

**Areas of Interest:** Motion pictures; television; video; cable/satellite; major U.S. and international film festivals; legal, business, and financial aspects of motion pictures; screenwriting; the entertainment industry; photography; theater; costume design; stage plays; short stories and novels made into film/TV shows.

**Holdings:** Over 6,000 books; 150 current periodical subscriptions; unpublished shooting scripts of more than 2,250 American feature films; over 1,000 scripts from current television shows; transcriptions of AFI seminars with professionals from the film and television industries; transcripts of in-depth interviews with pioneers of the film industry; personal papers and manuscript collections of leading film figures; the Columbia Stills Collection (1930–1959); over 25,000 clipping files containing articles, reviews, pamphlets, and other ephemera.

**Publications:** Bimonthly acquisitions lists; script checklist.

**Information Services:** Answers inquiries; provides advisory and reference services; conducts an annual Film/TV Documentation Workshop; makes referrals to other sources of information; permits on-site use of collections. Reference service is free; other services may be subject to a fee. The Library was designed for the faculty, fellows, and staff of AFI but is also available on a noncirculating basis to visiting scholars, researchers, advanced graduate students, and all members of the motion picture and television industries.

**Approval Date:** 1/85

**Latest Information Date:** 1/85

**Index Terms:** Performing arts; Motion pictures; Motion picture film collections; Video art; Motion picture festivals; Newspaper clippings; Motion picture plays; Television scripts; Oral history; Photographs; International motion picture festivals; Motion picture film collections; Television; Cable television systems; Satellite communication systems; Screen writers; Entertainment industry; Costume design; Theater; Theater management; Arts resources.

## American Film Institute (AFI) Resource Center

John F. Kennedy Center
Washington, DC 20566
Tel.: (202) 828-4088                    PUB69-19091

AFI receives some of its funding from the National Endowment for the Arts' Media Arts Program

**Areas of Interest:** Current information on film and television; history of film and television; foreign cinema; genre studies; criticism; literature and film; film and television personnel; screenplays; film and video making.

**Holdings:** About three thousand books and one hundred periodical titles; ten file cabinets of clippings; six file cabinets of other vertical file material, including film festival brochures, information on awards, repertory theaters, and media organizations, newsletters, bibliographies, and filmographies.

**Publications:** Publications of AFI's Education Services include *AFI Education News* (five issues a year), *Factfile* (a continuing series of directories and bibliographies), indexes, catalogs, guides, study materials, and videotapes. A publications list is available.

**Information Services:** Answers inquiries; provides reference service; makes referrals to other sources of information; permits on-site use of collections. Services are free and available to anyone by appointment.

**Contact:** Mr. Stan Umans

**Approval Date:** 2/85

**Latest Information Date:** 2/85

**Index Terms:** Motion pictures; Television films; Video art; Cinematography; Foreign motion pictures; Animation (cinematography); Criticism; Performing arts; Motion picture plays; Video tapes; Information resources; Educational programs; Teaching arts; Bibliographies; Directories; Libraries; Motion picture film collections.

### 274

**American Society of Cinematographers (ASC)**

P.O. Box 2230
Hollywood, CA 90078
Tel.: (213) 876-5080                    PUB69-13100

**Location:** 1782 North Orange Dr.

**Areas of Interest:** Cinematography.

**Holdings:** Small collection of books.

**Publications:** *American Cinematographer* (monthly); *American Cinematographer's Manual; ASC Treasury of Visual Effects, Cinema Workshops,* and *Electronic Production Techniques* (all books); booklet on ASC.

**Information Services:** Answers inquiries; provides advisory and reference services; permits on-site use of

collection. The above services are free and available to anyone. Publications are for sale.

**Approval Date:** 6/84

**Latest Information Date:** 1/86

**Index Terms:** Cinematography.

### 275

**Council on International Nontheatrical Events, Inc. (CINE)**

1201 16th St. NW.
Washington, DC 20036
Tel.: (202) 785-1136 or 785-1137          PUB69-15533

CINE selects short films from the United States for submission to international film events. Film entrants pay a fee.

**Areas of Interest:** Short nontheatrical movie films; television documentaries.

**Publications:** *CINE Yearbook* (annual).

**Information Services:** Answers inquiries; provides reference services. Services are free and available to anyone.

**Approval Date:** 3/85

**Latest Information Date:** 3/85

**Index Terms:** Motion pictures; International motion picture festivals; Documentary motion pictures; Television films.

### 276

**Directors Guild of America, Inc.**

7950 Sunset Blvd.
Hollywood, CA 90046
Tel.: (213) 656-1220                    PUB69-5227

New York office: 110 West 57th St., New York, NY 10019, (212) 581-0370

Chicago office: 520 North Michigan Ave., Suite 436, Chicago, IL 60611, (312) 644-5050

**Areas of Interest:** The Guild is a labor organization representing for collective bargaining in the motion picture and television industry all directors, assistant directors, associate directors, stage managers, unit production managers, production assistants, and technical coordinators.

**Information Services:** Answers inquiries; makes referrals.

**Approval Date:** 11/84

**Latest Information Date:** 1/86

**Index Terms:** Labor unions; Motion picture industry; Directors (performing arts); Television industry.

## 277

**Eastern New Mexico University**
**Film Library**

Portales, NM 88130
Tel.: (505) 562-2622          PUB69-2317

**Areas of Interest:** All subjects.

**Holdings:** 3,600 prints of 16mm films. There is a computerized record of the Library's holdings.

**Publications:** Film rental catalog.

**Information Services:** Provides consulting services to colleges, universities, and public schools on newer media, and demonstrations and lectures on all types of new media equipment and materials; rents films.

**Approval Date:** 6/85

**Latest Information Date:** 6/85

**Index Terms:** Educational films.

## 278

**The Film and Television Study Center, Inc.**

6216 Yucca St.
Hollywood, CA 90028
Tel.: (213) 469-1917          PUB69-15946

The Center coordinates the resources of all major film research, study, and screening activities (non-profit, cultural) in the Los Angeles area, including The Academy of Motion Picture Arts and Sciences, UCLA, USC, Cal Arts, Loyola University, the National Academy of Television Arts and Sciences, the County Museum, and the American Film Institute's Center for Advanced Film Studies. It also engages in major research projects such as *Union Catalogue of Motion Picture & Television Manuscript and Special Collections* (housed in eleven Western states), which was published by G. K. Hall in 1977.

**Areas of Interest:** Films, television, and video education, history, and criticism.

**Holdings:** Vast collections on film and television are held at the member institutions.

**Publications:** Conference proceedings; union catalog; occasional papers.

**Information Services:** Answers inquiries; provides reference services; conducts seminars and work-

shops; distributes some publications (some are available through publishers); makes referrals to other sources of information; permits on-site use of collections. Services are available to serious researchers.

**Approval Date:** 4/85

**Latest Information Date:** 4/85

**Index Terms:** Motion pictures; Cinematography; Video tapes; Television films; Television arts; Motion picture film collections; Cataloging of motion pictures; Television criticism; Motion picture criticism; Preserving; Union catalogs; Education.

## 279

**Film Fund, Inc.**

80 East 11th St., Suite 647
New York, NY 10003
Tel.: (212) 475-3720          PUB69-19898

**Areas of Interest:** Production and use of films, slide shows, and video tapes as creative and educational instruments for social change.

**Holdings:** Mailing list of 5,500 filmmakers, community groups, and foundations.

**Publications:** *Medialog: A Guide to Television, Film and Radio Programs Supported by the National Endowment for the Humanities.*

**Information Services:** Distributes a newsletter for independent filmmakers.

**Contact:** Ms. Maria Colon, Office Manager

**Approval Date:** 6/85

**Latest Information Date:** 6/85

**Index Terms:** Cinematography; Motion pictures; Slides (photography); Video tapes; Political systems; History; Social systems; Social change; Arts resources; Financial support; Social problems.

## 280

**Film Library Information Council**

P.O. Box 348, Radio City Station
New York, NY 10101-0348
Tel.: (212) 956-4211          PUB69-9134

**Areas of Interest:** Nontheatrical films, video tapes, and other nonprint materials suitable for public library, museum, school, and community use.

**Publications:** *Film Library Quarterly.*

**Information Services:** Answers inquiries by mail.

**Approval Date:** 11/84

**Latest Information Date:** 1/86

**Index Terms:** Motion pictures.

## 281

### International Museum of Photography at George Eastman House

900 East Ave.
Rochester, NY 14607
Tel.: (716) 271-3361                    PUB69-3080

Partially funded by federal, state, and local government agencies, the International Museum of Photography at George Eastman House, generally known as George Eastman House, is a museum of the art and technology of photography and cinematography. Activities include membership in international organizations, participation in international conferences, exhibits abroad, and maintenance of foreign affiliations. In keeping with its interest in more foreign involvement, the Museum is currently planning future international projects. Its membership of some two thousand persons in the United States and abroad is open to anyone.

**Areas of Interest:** History of photography; history of the cinema. The Museum's particular strengths lie in nineteenth-century French photography, nineteenth-century American photography, the silent film in America, and German Expressionist film.

**Holdings:** 600,000 still photographs; one million movie stills; 5,000 film titles; 10,000 historic cameras; 24,000-volume library.

**Publications:** *Image* (quarterly); books, reprints, data compilations.

**Information Services:** Answers inquiries; provides limited reference services, and permits on-site use of collections by appointment to the general public free. The Museum provides direct and interlibrary loans, reproduces materials, and distributes publications in the United States and abroad to the general public for a fee. Facilities are accessible to the handicapped.

**Contact:** Mr. Robert Mayer, Director

**Approval Date:** 4/85

**Latest Information Date:** 4/85

**Index Terms:** Cinematography; Photography; Motion pictures history; Engineering history.

## 282

### Library of Congress
### Motion Picture, Broadcasting, and Recorded Sound Division

10 First St. SE.
Washington, DC 20540
Tel.: (202) 287-5840                    PUB69-8457

Hours: 8:30 a.m.-4:30 p.m. Mon.–Sat.; closed Sun. and holidays.

**Areas of Interest:** Films, television and radio programs, and sound recordings representing the full history of these media.

**Holdings:** Over 1.5 million items, including recordings dating from the 1880s, films from the 1890s, radio programs from the 1920s, and television programs from the 1940s; select collection of related books, stills, scripts, and other documentation materials. Acquisitions are via copyright deposit, gift, exchange, and occasional off-air taping for archival purposes. An extensive preservation program is in progress. Except for fragile and unique items, materials are available for individual scholarly research on premises.

**Publications:** Filmographies, discographies, and bibliographies on particular subjects.

**Information Services:** Research activities are served through personal visits, by correspondence, and telephone. Listening and viewing services are available by advance appointment to qualified scholars for specialized research, without charge. Copying services are available for public domain material, or where the necessary permissions have been obtained in writing.

**Approval Date:** 2/84

**Latest Information Date:** 1/86

**Index Terms:** Television programs; Motion pictures; Radio programs; Sound recordings; Documentation; Manuscripts; Photographs.

## 283

### Motion Picture Association of America, Inc.

1600 I St. NW.
Washington, DC 20006
Tel.: (202) 293-1966                    PUB69-20068

The Association's membership consists of the nine largest companies producing and distributing theatrical films and TV material in the United States and around the world.

**Areas of Interest:** Motion picture production and distribution.

**Publications:** Articles, statements, reports.

**Information Services:** Answers inquiries; distributes publications. Services are free and available to anyone.

**Approval Date:** 7/84

**Latest Information Date:** 1/86

**Index Terms:** Cinematography; Motion picture production; Motion picture distribution.

---

### 284

**Museum of Modern Art**
**Department of Film**

11 West 53d St.
New York, NY 10019
Tel.: (212) 708-9400                    PUB69-5968

**Areas of Interest:** Motion pictures as works of art; motion pictures having historical or technical value.

**Holdings:** The collection includes more than eight thousand titles, or twenty-six million feet of film, and consists of feature films, documentaries, and experimental and animated films from all countries that have a major film industry and all periods since 1894. Holdings also include 12,000 books, periodicals, scripts, 30,000 posters, newspaper and magazine clippings, music scores, and special collections of documents relating to cinema. Copies of over three million stills are also available to professional and scholarly researchers. The catalog of films is being entered in a computerized data base.

**Information Services:** Films and related materials are available to qualified researchers on the premises by appointment. Telephone and mail inquiries are handled within the limits of available staff time. Through its circulating film program, the Department provides a rental service of about eight hundred selected titles to educational institutions in the United States and Canada.

**Approval Date:** 4/85

**Latest Information Date:** 4/85

**Index Terms:** Motion pictures; Motion pictures history.

---

### 285

**National Archives and Records Administration**
**Office of the National Archives**
**Special Archives Division**
**Motion Picture, Sound, and Video Branch (NNSM)**

Washington, DC 20408
Tel.: (202) 786-0041                    PUB69-11782

**Areas of Interest:** Motion pictures, sound recordings, and video tapes that (1) were created by or for federal agencies, (2) were acquired by federal agencies in the course of their official functions, or (3) were obtained from nonfederal sources but which contain significant information about federal activities and programs not available in official records (these nonfederal products include newsreels, documentaries based on the holdings of the National Archives, and the sound and video output of national network news divisions).

**Holdings:** The Branch has over one hundred forty thousand reels of motion picture films dating from 1894 to the present that include outtakes, newsreels, documentaries, training films, and a few feature films, and over one hundred five thousand audio and ten thousand video recordings of press conferences, speeches, court proceedings, news broadcasts, and public affairs and entertainment programs dating from 1896 to the present. The Stock Film Library collection contains nondefense government-produced stock motion picture footage (existing unedited footage resulting from film productions that has the potential to be used in other productions).

**Publications:** Various finding aids.

**Information Services:** Reproductions of all the Branch's holdings that are not subject to copyright or other restrictions are available for a fee. Motion pictures may be screened in the Branch's research room from 8:45 a.m. to 5:00 p.m. Monday through Friday. Groups may view motion pictures in the National Archives Theater (prior arrangements are necessary). The motion picture holdings are not available on loan. The Stock Film Library serves as a centralized source of film footage for a fee. Under an agreement between the National Archives and CBS, Inc., the Branch receives, maintains, and makes available for research videotape copies of that network's hard news programs. On request, copies of these programs can be made available at libraries throughout the country under interlibrary loan procedures on a fee basis. The videotapes can also be used in the eleven regional branches of the National Archives and at the Ford, Johnson, and Kennedy Presidential libraries. The Branch also maintains off-the-air copies of NBC and ABC evening television news broadcasts (1976–1982) obtained under separate agreement with the networks and makes video recordings of these programs available for research at the National Archives, the eleven regional branches, and the Ford, Johnson, and Kennedy Presidential libraries. National Public Radio (NPR) news and public affairs broadcasts are also preserved and made available for research five years after date of broadcast under an agreement with NPR.

**Approval Date:** 10/84

**Latest Information Date:** 1/86

**Index Terms:** Archives; Motion pictures; Photographs; Sound recordings; American History.

## 286

**National Board of Review of Motion Pictures, Inc.**

P.O. Box 589
New York, NY 10021
  Tel.: (212) 628-1594          PUB69-17467

The Board seeks to promote an intelligent appreciation of the movies and film history through its publications and annual awards.

**Areas of Interest:** Film history; films; cinema.

**Publications:** *Films in Review* (monthly) with indexes; pamphlets, reprints.

**Information Services:** Answers inquiries; evaluates and analyzes data; distributes publications; makes referrals to other sources of information. Services are provided free to some users and at cost to others.

**Approval Date:** 9/84

**Latest Information Date:** 1/86

**Index Terms:** Motion pictures; Cinematography; Motion pictures history; Motion picture criticism.

## 287

**New Day Films**

c/o Jim Daigle, Manager
853 Broadway, Suite 1210
New York, NY 10003
  Tel.: (212) 477-4604          PUB69-16462

A commercial cooperative of independent filmmakers, New Day Films produces and distributes films about the changing roles of women and men in our society.

**Areas of Interest:** Films on such topics as: abortion;

aging; career education; family relationships; feelings and attitudes; history; sexuality; health; art; identity; Jewish life; labor movement; life stages; marriage; masculinity; parenthood; social roles; values; work; and youth.

**Holdings:** Collection of films.

**Publications:** Films and film catalog.

**Information Services:** Rents and sells films; distributes film catalog; answers inquiries; conducts seminars and workshops. Services are free, except for film rental or sales, and available to anyone.

**Booking Contact:** New Day Films, Inc.
  22 Riverview Dr.
  Wayne, NJ 07470
  (201) 633-0212

**Approval Date:** 5/85

**Latest Information Date:** 5/85

**Index Terms:** Abortion; Aged; Career education; Family relations; Emotions; Attitudes; Judaism; Labor unions; Marriage; Social role; Urban development; Sports; Social studies; Values; Women; Youth; Motion pictures; Health; Sexuality; History; Arts.

## 288

**North American Films, Inc.**

P.O. Box 919
Tarzana, CA 91356
  Tel.: (818) 340-1328          PUB69-13619

**Areas of Interest:** Educational and industrial motion pictures.

**Publications:** Films; data sheets describing the films.

**Information Services:** Rents and sells films. The company also answers questions, provides advisory or consulting services, and makes referrals to other sources of information. Fees may be charged for these services.

**Contact:** Mr. Richard Krown, President

**Approval Date:** 9/84

**Latest Information Date:** 1/86

**Index Terms:** Educational films; Motion pictures.

## 289

**Northwest Film Study Center**

1219 Southwest Park Ave.
Portland, OR 97208
  Tel.: (503) 221-1156          PUB69-19904

An organization of about sixty-five hundred members and sponsored by the Portland Art Association, the Center provides film and video resource information. Activities include sponsorship of film and video festivals, membership in international organizations, participation in international conferences, sponsorship of exhibitions of domestic and foreign films, and cooperative projects with foreign groups. In keeping with its interest in more foreign involvement, the Center is currently planning future international projects.

**Areas of Interest:** Media arts.

**Holdings:** 175 films.

**Publications:** *Animator* (quarterly newsletter); annotated calendar of exhibition programs; film library catalog; critical reviews; directories.

**Information Services:** Answers inquiries; provides advisory, consulting, reference, and literature-searching services; evaluates and analyzes data; conducts seminars and workshops; provides speakers; lends materials; distributes publications and audiovisual materials; makes referrals to other sources of information; permits on-site use of collection. Some services may be subject to a fee and all are available to anyone.

**Contact:** Mr. Bill Foster, Director

**Approval Date:** 4/85

**Latest Information Date:** 4/85

**Index Terms:** Motion pictures; Video art; Exhibitions; Education; Media arts; International arts activities; Information resources; Art resources.

## 290

**Ohio State University
Department of Photography and Cinema
Film & Video Distribution**

156 West 19th Ave.
Columbus, OH 43210-1183
Tel.: (614) 422-5966                    PUB69-13381

Film & Video Distribution promotes and distributes films produced by the Department of Photography and Cinema.

**Areas of Interest:** Educational films covering a variety of subjects, including agriculture, botany, communications, dance, dentistry, education, engineering, fine arts, geology, guidance, history, home economics, journalism, medicine, metallurgy, music, nursing, photography, physics, sociology, speech, sports, vocational guidance, welfare, and zoology. Safety and photography/film/video.

**Holdings:** Over three hundred titles of 16mm films produced by the Department of Photography and Cinema, also available on video. Student films from the 1960s; historical film collections; awards winners from the Columbus Film Festival for research.

**Publications:** Catalog of available films (annual).

**Information Services:** Rents and sells films; answers inquiries regarding film sources.

**Approval Date:** 5/85

**Latest Information Date:** 5/85

**Index Terms:** Educational films.

## 291

**Screen Actors Guild (SAG)**

7750 Sunset Blvd.
Hollywood, CA 90046
Tel.: (213) 876-3030                    PUB69-5225

SAG negotiates and enforces wages and working conditions for actors in the motion picture/television industry. It is a branch of the Associated Actors and Artistes of America and is affiliated with the AFL-CIO.

**Areas of Interest:** Labor relations in the motion picture and filmed television industry; statistics on the income and demographics of professional actors and their associations.

**Holdings:** Collection of SAG contracts (actors' collective bargaining agreements in film and television); statistics on income and demographics of professional actors in America; information on 1980 actors' strike.

**Publications:** *Screen Actor Magazine* (semiannual); *Screen Actor News* (five times a year); news releases; directory of actors' talent agents; regional branch publications.

**Information Services:** Answers inquiries regarding employers and talent representatives in motion pictures and television, and on the terms of various contracts; advises members on rights, responsibilities, and benefits. Executives and contract representatives may be consulted in the following metropolitan areas: Atlanta, Boston, Chicago, Dallas, Denver, Detroit, Miami, Houston, Honolulu, Nashville, New York City, Phoenix, Philadelphia, San Diego, San Francisco, and Washington, D.C.

**Approval Date:** 8/85

**Latest Information Date:** 8/85

**Index Terms:** Actors; Labor relations Motion picture industry.

**292**

## Society for Cinema Studies (SCS)

Janet Staiger, President
Cinema Studies, 400 South Bldg.
New York University
New York, NY 10003
  Tel.: (212) 598-7777       PUB69-19927

SCS is an organization of over five hundred members in the United States and abroad representing faculty and students actively involved in graduate and undergraduate programs in cinema studies as well as persons in other disciplines interested in film.

**Areas of Interest:** Cinema studies; television arts; media arts; visual arts; multidisciplinary studies.

**Publications:** *Cinema Journal* (quarterly); bibliographies.

**Information Services:** Provides advisory services; conducts seminars, workshops, and an annual conference; provides speakers; distributes publications in the United States and abroad; makes referrals to other sources of information. Services are available free to members.

**Approval Date:** 2/84

**Latest Information Date:** 1/86

**Index Terms:** Media arts; Visual arts; Cinematography; Television arts; Graduate study; Undergraduate study; Lecturers; Motion pictures; International arts activities; Arts resources.

**293**

## Society of Motion Picture and Television Engineers (SMPTE)

862 Scarsdale Ave.
Scarsdale, NY 10583
  Tel.: (914) 472-6606       PUB69-1201

SMPTE is a nonprofit professional association for the exchange and dissemination of technical information on motion picture and television engineering, the preparation of American and international standards, and the conduct of technical conferences and seminars.

**Areas of Interest:** Science and technology of motion pictures, television, photo instrumentation, and high-speed photography, including color film, lighting, and sound recording.

**Holdings:** Complete back issues of the *Journal of the SMPTE* (since 1950) and its predecessors, *Journal of the SMPE* (1930–1949) and *Transactions of the SMPE* (1916–1929).

**Publications:** *SMPTE Journal* (monthly); books, manuals, reports, proceedings, reprints, bibliographies, indexes, directories, glossaries, standards and recommended practices, test films. A publications list is available.

**Information Services:** Answers inquiries; conducts conferences and seminars; provides reference and reproduction services; distributes publications; permits on-site use of collections. Services are primarily for members, but others will be assisted. Fees are charged for some services, such as publications and registration for conferences and seminars.

**Approval Date:** 5/84

**Latest Information Date:** 1/86

**Index Terms:** Photographic equipment; High speed photography; Standardization; Motion pictures; Television systems; Cinematography; Engineering; Education; Color photography; Sound recordings; Illuminating.

**294**

**University of California, Berkeley**
**University Art Museum**
**Pacific Film Archive**
**Film/Media Community Service Project**

2625 Durant Ave.
Berkeley, CA 94720
  Tel.: (415) 642-1437       PUB69-14023

**Areas of Interest:** Films, with special emphasis on experimental films, Japanese films, Russian films, women's films, and children's films; contemporary animation.

**Holdings:** 5,000 films; film research library with 2,000 books, 50 current periodical runs, 50 noncurrent periodical runs, and clipping files on film titles, people, festivals, and subjects (all noncirculating materials).

**Information Services:** Answers inquiries; provides information on film rentals, distribution, equipment, and research resources; provides advisory services; makes referrals to other sources of information; permits on-site use of collection. Information services are free and available to anyone (calls are accepted from 1-5 p.m. P.S.T. only). Screening services are available for a minimal fee to researchers.

**Approval Date:** 2/84

**Latest Information Date:** 1/86

**Index Terms:** Motion pictures; Children's films;

Women in motion pictures; Experimental films; Foreign motion pictures; Motion picture cartoons; Motion picture film collections.

## 295

### University of Illinois
### Film Center

1325 South Oak St.
Champaign, IL 61820
  Tel.: (217) 333-1360         PUB69-12937

**Areas of Interest:** Motion pictures and video recordings for use in physical, biological, engineering, and social sciences education; classic features.

**Holdings:** Over fifteen thousand film titles and fifty-two thousand prints. Scheduling and reporting is by in-house computerized system.

**Publications:** *Lens and Speaker* (semiannual); twenty topical catalogs; *Illinois Film* (745-page general catalog).

**Information Services:** Answers inquiries free; rents films and video programs. Services are available to anyone.

**Approval Date:** 3/84

**Latest Information Date:** 1/86

**Index Terms:** Visual aids; Motion pictures; Video tapes; Video programs; Educational films; Machine readable data bases.

## 296

### University of Texas at Austin
### General Libraries
### Film Library

Drawer W, University Station
Austin, TX 78713-7448
  Tel.: (512) 471-3572         PUB69-16568

**Location:** Education Annex, G-12 San Jacinto and 20th Sts.

The Library is a member of the Consortium of University Film Centers and a contributor to the data base for Bowker and CUFS's union film catalog *Educational Film Locator*.

**Areas of Interest:** Educational films on a wide variety of subjects, chiefly at the college and university level.

**Holdings:** About three thousand titles of 16mm films.

**Publications:** Lists of films available for rent. The Library also publishes a series of media handbooks that explain proper utilization and production of simple audiovisual aids (a brochure describing the handbooks is available).

**Information Services:** Rents films (free previewing is available in the Library); provides free reference and referral services; provides consulting services; answers inquiries; sells handbooks; provides local projectionist and equipment rental service; provides 16mm film cleaning and repair service.

**Approval Date:** 9/85

**Latest Information Date:** 9/85

**Index Terms:** Educational films; Audiovisual aids; Educational materials; Teaching models; Teaching methods; Instructional technology; Continuing education.

## 297

### Women's Independent Film Exchange

50 West 96th St.
New York, NY 10025
  Tel.: (212) 749-1250         PUB69-21107

The Exchange conducts the American Pioneer Women Filmmakers Research Project, which collects information about women filmmakers and directors in the United States from 1910, when Alice Guy-Blache opened her film studio in New York City, to 1970, when the feminist movement opened the field to women.

**Areas of Interest:** Women filmmakers and directors who worked in the United States between 1910 and 1970, including American women who made films abroad and foreign women who made films in the United States.

**Holdings:** Books, articles, and other materials in vertical files; taped interviews of women filmmakers.

**Publications:** Reprints of journal and newspaper articles.

**Information Services:** Answers inquiries; provides advisory, reference, and reproduction services; conducts seminars and workshops; organizes and presents programs; locates films and distribution sources; makes referrals to other sources of information; permits on-site use of collections. Services are free, although contributions are welcomed, and are available to anyone.

**Contact:** Cecile Starr, Codirector

**Approval Date:** 11/84

**Latest Information Date:** 1/86

**Index Terms:** Women in motion pictures; Motion pictures history; Arts resources.

## 298

**Young Filmmakers/Video Arts (YF/VA) (former)**
**Film/Video Arts (F/VA) (current)**

817 Broadway
New York, NY 10003
  Tel.: (212) 673-9361                    PUB69-17389

Partially funded by the National Endowment for the Arts, the New York State Council on the Arts, and private foundations and corporations, F/VA is a major media arts resource center for New York State, providing the region's film and video communities with a variety of services and training programs. It operates an equipment loan program and provides access to in-house postproduction facilities.

**Areas of Interest:** Film-video-sound-radio equipment systems and engineering; cinematography; media education programs.

**Publications:** *Young Filmmakers* and *Young Animators* (both books); directory of film/video works by YF/VA-assisted artists and organizations (annual); *Equip-ment Loan Handbook* (guidebook to the equipment loan services of YF/VA); *A Decade of Cuban Documentary Film: 1972-1982* (48-page catalog); Selected Issues in Media Law.

**Information Services:** Conducts seminars and workshops for a fee; makes referrals to other sources of information; lends film, video, and sound equipment to artists and arts organizations for a small fee; provides film/video postproduction facilities at low cost; offers financial assistance for film rentals and speakers' fees to nonprofit community organizations in New York State; provides production services on a contract basis. Services are generally available to media arts and education groups as well as individual artists. Equipment loans are available only to those who are technically capable of using the equipment.

**Approval Date:** 9/85

**Latest Information Date:** 9/85

**Index Terms:** New York (State); Cinematography; Vocational education; Educational programs; Motion picture production; Motion pictures; Television films; Photographic equipment; Audiovisual equipment; Equipment loan services; Arts resources.

# Television, Video, Radio, Broadcasting, and Cable Organizations

## 299

**Access Innovations, Inc.**
**National Information Center for Educational Media (NICEM)**

P.O. Box 40130
Albuquerque, NM 87196
Tel.: (505) 265-3591
(800) 421-8711          PUB69-9051

NICEM has served as a national information retrieval system for audiovisual educational materials for many years and, since 1977, for special education materials, the latter pursuant to a contract with the U.S. Department of Education's Bureau of Education for the Handicapped.

**Areas of Interest:** Educational media (nonbook) such as films, filmstrips, phonograph records, transparencies, video and audio tapes, cartridges, and slides; special education materials.

**Holdings:** A computer-based data bank of 500,000 nonbook media listings with annotations (the NICEM data base, available online via DIALOG) and a specialized National Information Center for Special Education Materials data bank of about forty thousand items (the NICSEM data base, available online via BRS).

**Publications:** Custom catalogs of media holdings and computer printouts of nonbook subject areas; *Index to 16mm Education Films, Index to 8mm Motion Cartridges, Index to 35mm Filmstrips, Index to Educational Audio Tapes, Index to Educational Video Tapes, Index to Educational Records, Index to Educational Overhead Transparencies, Index to Educational Slides, Index to Producers & Distributors, Index to Psychology, Index to Vocational & Technical Education, Index to Health & Safety Education, Index to Environmental Studies, Index to Nonprint Special Educational Materials—Multimedia* (learner volume and professional volume), *Special Education Thesaurus, Special Education Index to Parent Materials, Master Index to Special Education Materials, Special Education Index to Learner Materials, Special Education Index to Assessment Materials, Special Education Index to In-Service Training Materials, Family Life and Sex Education, Functional Communication Skills, High Interest, Controlled Vocabulary Supplementary Reading Materials for Adolescents and Young Adults, Independent Living Skills for Moderately and Severely Handicapped Students, Personal and Social Development for Moderately and Severely Handicapped Students,* and *NICSEM Source Directory.* A publications pricelist is available.

**Information Services:** Answers inquiries; provides consulting, reference, and literature-searching services; provides custom cataloging, indexing, and retrieval services by subject area. Services are provided at cost.

**Approval Date:** 6/84

**Latest Information Date:** 1/86

**Index Terms:** Educational materials; Audiovisual aids; Educational films; Filmstrips; Phonograph records; Teaching aids; Video tapes; Slides (photography); Special education; Machine readable data bases; Nonbibliographic data bases; NICEM; NICSEM.

## 300

**Agency for Instructional Technology (AIT)**

P.O. Box A
Bloomington, IN 47402-0120
Tel.: (812) 339-2203
(800) 457-4509          PUB69-10065

**Location:** 1111 West 17th St.

AIT is a nonprofit American-Canadian organization established in 1973 to strengthen education through technology. In cooperation with state and provincial agencies, AIT develops instructional materials using television and computers and acquires and distributes a wide variety of television and related printed materials for use as major learning resources. It makes many of these materials available in audiovisual formats.

**Areas of Interest:** All aspects of instructional-educational television; research in and development, production, distribution, and utilization of instructional television; application of technology to education; classroom video materials; classroom computer materials.

**Holdings:** An archive of film, kinescope, and videotape from instructional television from 1956 to the present; raw data and questionnaires from several nationwide studies of educational-instructional television and closed-circuit television; small collection of books, periodicals, and reports.

**Publications:** *AIT Newsletter* (four times a year); annual catalog and guide for users of AIT materials; reports. A publications list is available.

**Information Services:** Answers inquiries; provides consulting and reference services; makes referrals to other sources of information; lends materials; permits on-site use of collections. The collection of

119

video/film materials is available for use by all educational agencies. Extensive services are provided for a fee. Film and videotape clearances for transmission are also provided for a fee.

**Approval Date:** 8/84

**Latest Information Date:** 186

**Index Terms:** Audiovisual education; Educational television; Educational technology; Audiovisual aids; Television films; Video tapes; Research and development; Educational computers; Computer science education.

---

### 301

**American Federation of Television and Radio Artists (AFTRA)**

1350 Avenue of the Americas
New York, NY 10019
Tel.: (212) 265-7700                    PUB69-4330

AFTRA is affiliated with the AFL-CIO.

**Areas of Interest:** Labor in the entertainment industry (radio, television, slide films, nonbroadcast, phonographs, cassettes, cable), including labor-management relations, wages, contracts, and welfare.

**Holdings:** Collection of labor agreements.

**Information Services:** Answers brief inquiries; provides consulting services; makes referrals.

**Approval Date:** 8/84

**Latest Information Date:** 1/86

**Index Terms:** Radio arts; Television arts; Entertainers; Labor contracts; Entertainment industry; Labor relations; Welfare; Wages.

---

### 302

**Association of Independent Video and Filmmakers (AIVF)**

625 Broadway, 9th Floor
New York, NY 10012
Tel.: (212) 473-3400                    PUB69-18804

**Areas of Interest:** Film; video; television; public television; cable television; film and video production, including financing, insurance, legal and accounting problems, and taxes; film and video copyrighting; film and video employment data.

**Holdings:** Files on grants, media arts centers, public television, cable television, film and video festivals,

distributors, and legislation; small collection of magazines; skills file on members.

**Publications:** *The Independent* (monthly magazine); several books related to independent media.

**Information Services:** Answers inquiries; provides reference services; conducts seminars and workshops; distributes publications; makes referrals to other sources of information; permits on-site use of collections. Services are free, except for publications, and available to film and video makers and to others interested in the production and promotion of independent video and film. Memberships are available.

**Approval Date:** 8/85

**Latest Information Date:** 8/85

**Index Terms:** Trade associations; Motion pictures; Video tapes; Television; Public television; Cable television systems; Television films; Financing; Insurance; Legislation; Taxes; Copyrights; Employment; Motion picture production.

---

### 303

**Broadcast Education Association (BEA)**

1771 N St. NW.
Washington, DC 20036
Tel.: (202) 429-5355                    PUB69-13990

BEA is an association of colleges and universities with programs in broadcasting. It encourages high standards in broadcasting education, administers four national scholarships presented annually by the National Association of Broadcasters (NAB), assists in the selection of recipients of NAB research grants, and works to facilitate the recruiting, training, and placement of minorities in broadcasting.

**Areas of Interest:** Education for careers in broadcasting.

**Publications:** *Journal of Broadcasting and Electronic Media* (quarterly); *Feedback* (quarterly newsletter).

**Information Services:** Answers inquiries; distributes publications; makes referrals to other sources of information; conducts seminars. Some services are provided free to members and some at cost to members and others. Services are limited to communications-oriented groups.

**Approval Date:** 8/85

**Latest Information Date:** 8/85

**Index Terms:** Radio broadcasting; Television broadcasting; Broadcasting; Education.

## 304

### Broadcast Information Bureau, Inc.

100 Lafayette Dr.
Syracuse, NY 11791
Tel.: (516) 496-3355          PUB69-17764

Broadcast Information Bureau is a commercial publisher of research source books pertaining to everything available on film and tape for television.

**Areas of Interest:** Theatrical feature films and feature films made for television; projected audiences for individual feature films; films of television series and serials, their running times, story lines, featured performers, number of episodes, and year of production; travel, sports, ecology, and religious films for television; new programs; salaries of television executives.

**Holdings:** Back date references in subject area from 1951. A complete data base of information is available on a limited license for computer studies.

**Publications:** *Facts, Figures & Film: News for Television Executives* (monthly magazine); *TV Feature Film Source Book* (with two supplements); *Series, Serials and Packages* (includes supplement).

**Information Services:** Sells publications. The film and series source books are available to anyone; the newsletter is only available to television executives.

**Approval Date:** 8/85

**Latest Information Date:** 8/85

**Index Terms:** Television films; Video tapes; Television programs; Television scripts; Television production; Travel; Sports; Religious films; Publishing; Feature films; Executive salaries.

## 305

### Broadcasting Foundation of America

Box 1805, Murray Hill Station
New York, NY 10156
Tel.: (212) 679-3388          PUB69-12502

**Areas of Interest:** The Foundation is an educational nonprofit association that produces and distributes international audiotape material and radio programs on contemporary and historical subjects in science, education, public affairs, the arts (including festival concerts and other musical events), travel, health, literature, consumer affairs, and folk music.

**Holdings:** Collection of over fifty thousand audiotapes on the areas above from the United States and over one hundred foreign countries.

**Information Services:** Provides audiotapes on the areas above for a small fee to cover tape cost.

**Approval Date:** 2/84

**Latest Information Date:** 1/86

**Index Terms:** Broadcasting; Tape recordings; Science; Education; History; Public affairs; Performing arts; Travel; Literature (fine arts); Consumer protection; Folk music.

## 306

### Corporation for Public Broadcasting (CPB) Office of Science and Technology

1111 16th St. NW.
Washington, DC 20036
Tel.: (202) 293-6160          PUB69-14318

A private nonprofit corporation funded primarily by the federal government, CPB's mission is to advance public broadcasting and provide increased services to the public.

**Areas of Interest:** Public radio and television broadcasting, including satellites, cable television, UHF/VHF technology, video cassettes, audio technology, teletext, and videotext.

**Holdings:** FM/TV station file and statistics on public radio and television stations. All files are computer based.

**Publications:** *CPB Report* (weekly); technical research reports; annual report; various books and monographs.

**Information Services:** Answers inquiries; conducts seminars and workshops; distributes publications. Services are available to anyone; a charge is made for some services.

**Approval Date:** 4/85

**Latest Information Date:** 4/85

**Index Terms:** Telecommunication; Television broadcasting; Radio broadcasting; Communication satellites; Radio stations; Statistics; Machine readable data bases; Nonbibliographic data bases; FM Stations File; Public Radio and Television Stations Statistics; Videodiscs; Videotex; Teletext.

## 307

### Indiana University
### Audio-Visual Center

Bloomington, IN 47405
  Tel.: (812) 335-8087 (Materials for purchase)
       (812) 335-2103 (Materials for rent)
       (812) 335-8065 (Reference)        PUB69-9338

**Areas of Interest:** Motion pictures and video tapes on all aspects of the physical, biological, and social sciences and arts and humanities.

**Holdings:** Over ten thousand 16mm educational motion pictures and video tapes for rental use; over one thousand titles available for purchase; a computerized data base of the holdings.

**Publications:** Motion picture and video tape descriptions; catalogs.

**Information Services:** Answers inquiries; provides consulting and reference services. Motion pictures and some video tapes may be rented or purchased.

**Approval Date:** 8/84

**Latest Information Date:** 1/86

**Index Terms:** Audiovisual centers; Educational films; Video tapes; Physical sciences; Biology; Social sciences; Engineering; Arts; Commerce; Humanities; Educational resources; Life sciences; Literature (fine arts); Psychology; Education; Motion pictures.

## 308

### Modern Talking Picture Service

5000 Park St. North
St. Petersburg, FL 33709
  Tel.: (813) 541-7571        PUB69-13679

**Areas of Interest:** Distribution of free-loan 16mm films, 35mm films, and videocassette programs to schools, community groups, TV stations, and theaters on such topics as social sciences, physical sciences, biology, engineering, physical education, driver education, public health, business education, vocational guidance, community education, agribusiness education, homemaking, consumer education, and sports.

**Publications:** Free catalogs and brochures describing films.

**Information Services:** Films are available to anyone on free-loan; the only cost to the user is return postage. The free-loan service is made possible by prominent companies, organizations, and government agencies as part of their public information programs.

**Approval Date:** 9/84

**Latest Information Date:** 1/86

**Index Terms:** Educational films; Video tapes; Social sciences; Physical sciences; Biology; Engineering; Teaching aids; Educational programs; Physical education; Driver education; Public health; Business education; Vocational guidance; Community education.

## 309

### The Museum of Broadcasting

1 East 53d St.
New York, NY 10022
  Tel.: (212) 752-4690        PUB69-17264

Granted an absolute museum charter by the New York Board of Regents, the Museum is a publicly supported, charitable organization that preserves and makes available for study selected radio and television programs from the 1920s to the present. Financial support comes from William S. Paley and charitable trusts established by him, contributions from the networks and local stations, related corporations, the National Endowment for the Humanities, the National Endowment for the Arts, the Institute of Museum Services of the U.S. Department of Education, the New York State Council on the Arts, membership dues, voluntary contributions from the public, and gifts from private philanthropies.

**Areas of Interest:** Radio and television broadcasting, including public affairs programs, historical and political documentaries, and drama, comedy, children's, and sports programming; art and architecture.

**Holdings:** 20,000 radio and television broadcasts, including 97 speeches by Churchill, 150 broadcasts by Edward R. Murrow, and an extensive collection of presidential speeches; 2,400 scripts; library of periodicals and books related to broadcasting; growing historical collection of broadcast technology, including receivers, cameras, and microphones; a theater and two videotheques where exhibitions and retrospectives are presented.

**Publications:** Quarterly newsletter; exhibition catalogs and program guide; subject guide to the collections.

**Information Services:** Answers members' inquiries during Museum hours (12-5 p.m., Tues.-Sat.); provides advisory and reference services; makes publications available in the library; makes referrals to other sources of information; permits on-site monitoring of collection. Contributions are requested from nonmembers for use of the theater and the broadcast study centers; special arrangements are made for school groups and scholars. Seminars and a lecture series are held on various aspects of broadcasting.

**Approval Date:** 5/84

**Latest Information Date:** 1/86

**Index Terms:** Museums (institutions); Radio programs; Television programs; Broadcasting; Public affairs; Drama; Educational programs; Sports; Arts; Architecture.

---

### 310

#### National Association of Broadcasters (NAB)

1771 N St. NW.
Washington, DC 20036
Tel.: (202) 293-3500 (General)
(202) 293-3579 (Library)
(202) 293-3529
(Publications Manager)          PUB69-13204

**Areas of Interest:** Broadcast industry.

**Holdings:** The library of 6,700 volumes, 240 periodical subscriptions, and a vertical file collection supports the activities of the NAB staff and membership. Emphasis is on the broadcast industry. It also has access to the DIALOG, Newsnet, and Dow Jones computerized data bases.

**Publications:** *Highlights* (weekly member newsletter); *Radioactive* (monthly); *Engineering Handbook* (6th ed.); pamphlets, brochures, monographs pertaining to broadcast engineering; station management, programming, promotion, and legal matters. A publications list is available.

**Information Services:** Limited reference service is available without charge according to time and effort required. The library is open to the public by appointment; materials do not circulate and no public photocopying facilities are available.

**Approval Date:** 2/84

**Latest Information Date:** 1/86

**Index Terms:** Broadcasting; Mass communication; Radio broadcasting; Television broadcasting; Online information retrieval systems; Legal aspects.

---

### 311

#### National Video Clearinghouse (NVC)

100 Lafayette Dr.
Syosset, NY 11791
Tel.: (516) 364-3686          PUB69-18637

NVC is a commercial information company special-

izing in all facets of video program information.

**Areas of Interest:** Information on video programs and discs, available to home, institution, cable, closed circuit, and broadcast markets.

**Holdings:** Reference library of about two hundred volumes and three thousand magazines. Software information about 40,000 video program titles is stored on and retrieved from a computerized data bank.

**Publications:** *The Video Source Book* (annual reference to educational, informational, and entertainment programs listing subject areas, titles, content descriptions, and format availability); *The Video Tape/and Disc Guide to Home Entertainment* (annual); *The Video Source Book–U.K.* (annual).

**Information Services:** Answers inquiries; provides advisory, reference, and literature-searching services; analyzes data; provides information on research in progress; distributes publications; makes referrals to other sources of information. Services are available at a fee to anyone.

**Approval Date:** 8/85

**Latest Information Date:** 8/85

**Index Terms:** Information brokers; Video programs; Video tapes; Videodiscs.

---

### 312

#### Time-Life Video

Rockefeller Center
New York, NY 10020
Tel.: (212) 484-5940          PUB69-13666

**Areas of Interest:** Films, video cassettes, and filmstrips related primarily to management development and training, but also covering a variety of other subjects, including biology, chemistry, environment, physics, anthropology, psychology, sociology, business and industry, arts and drama, history, philosophy, and political science.

**Holdings:** 16mm films, video cassettes, and 35mm filmstrips for education, library, and business and industry markets.

**Publications:** Catalogs of all programs available.

**Information Services:** Licenses television programs; rents and sells films, video cassettes, and filmstrips; answers inquiries; conducts seminars; makes referrals to other sources of information.

**Approval Date:** 4/85

**Latest Information Date:** 4/85

**Index Terms:** Educational films; Video tapes; Social sciences; Biology; Physical sciences; Educational films; Chemistry; Physics; Anthropology; Psychology; Commerce; History; Philosophy; Political science; Video programs; Management training; Arts resources; Arts; Drama.

## 313

**Vanderbilt University**
**Heard Library**
**Vanderbilt Television News Archive**

Nashville, TN 37240-0007
Tel.: (615) 322-2927          PUB69-18707

**Areas of Interest:** Television network news programs.

**Holdings:** 13,000 hours of videotapes of network evening news broadcasts, August 5, 1968 to date, and related special broadcasts.

**Publications:** *Television News Index and Abstracts: A Guide to the Videotape Collection of the Network Evening News Programs in the Vanderbilt Television News Archive.*

**Information Services:** Answers inquiries; provides advisory, reference, literature-searching, reproduction, microform, and magnetic tape services; lends materials; distributes publication; makes referrals to other sources of information; permits on-site use of collections. Services are available for a fee to anyone.

**Approval Date:** 8/85

**Latest Information Date:** 8/85

**Index Terms:** Libraries; Archives; Television broadcasting; Television news; Broadcast journalism; Television programs; Video tapes.

# International Arts Organizations and Others

## 314

### Academy of American Poets

177 East 87th St.
New York, NY 10028
Tel.: (212) 427-5665                    PUB69-19925

A nonprofit organization of about thirty-five hundred individual members and about fifty affiliated societies, the Academy encourages, stimulates, and fosters the production of American poetry by providing fellowships for poets of proven merit and by granting awards and prizes for poetic achievement. Membership is open to all persons with a genuine interest in American poetry.

**Areas of Interest:** American poets and poetry.

**Holdings:** The Academy's extensive tape archive of poets and writers reading their works is housed at Harvard University.

**Publications:** *Poetry Pilot* (monthly newsletter); *Envoy* (biannual newsletter for affiliated societies); *Booklist* (biannual).

**Information Services:** Answers inquiries; conducts classes, workshops, poetry readings, and historical and literary walking tours; provides speakers and suggests poets for readings; distributes publications; makes referrals to other sources of information. General information, the walking tours, and most readings are available free to the public. Other services are available to the membership.

**Contact:** Mr. Henri Cole, Executive Director

**Approval Date:** 1/84

**Latest Information Date:** 1/86

**Index Terms:** Literature (fine arts); Poetry; American poets; Fellowships; Awards; Scholarships; Arts resources.

## 315

### American Academy and Institute of Arts and Letters Library

633 West 155th St.
New York, NY 10032
Tel.: (212) 368-5900                    PUB69-12812

**Areas of Interest:** Literature; arts and humanities; music art and writing.

**Holdings:** Collection of records, manuscripts, letters, and books of past and present members; Childe Hassam paintings.

**Publications:** Proceedings and exhibition catalogs.

**Information Services:** Permits on-site use of collections by bona fide researchers with prior arrangement.

**Approval Date:** 2/84

**Latest Information Date:** 1/86

**Index Terms:** Literature (fine arts); Arts; Humanities; Music.

## 316

### American Council on Germany

680 Fifth Ave.
New York, NY 10019
Tel.: (212) 541-7878                    PUB69-20208

A membership organization of 200 persons selected by its Board of Directors, the Council conducts fellowship programs, sponsors and participates in international conferences, sponsors German artists and performers in the United States, conducts cooperative projects with American and foreign groups interested in German-American relations, has cooperative arrangements with German organizations, and, in keeping with its interest in foreign affairs, is planning future international projects.

**Areas of Interest:** Political, economic, and cultural relations between the United States and Germany; a variety of exchange programs between the United States and Germany; fund raising; special education; multidisciplinary programs.

**Publications:** Books, journal articles, critical reviews, directories, bibliographies, reprints.

**Information Services:** Answers inquiries; provides current-awareness services; conducts conferences, seminars, and workshops; distributes publications and data compilations in the United States and abroad; provides speakers; makes referrals to other sources of information. Services are available to members and others with a sincere interest in German-American relations.

**Contact:** David Klein, Executive Director

**Approval Date:** 1/84

**Latest Information Date:** 1/86

**Index Terms:** Arts resources; Cultural relations; Cultural exchange; Exchange programs; Germany; United States; Theater; Performance art; Special education; Fund raising; Lecturers.

## 317

### Art Council Aids (ACA)

P.O. Box 641
Beverly Hills, CA 90213                    PUB69-16454

ACA is a commercial organization.

**Areas of Interest:** History of textiles; Japanese masks and folk toys; Asian shadow theater puppets; French eighteenth-century decorative arts; design elements and stimuli; primitive arts of Alaskan Eskimos, Northwest Coast Indians, pre-Columbian Latin America, Africa, Australia, Melanesia, and Polynesia; paintings by children; American painters, 1815–1865.

**Holdings:** Thirty-five color slide sets with commentaries.

**Publications:** *Catalogs* (irregular, available free).

**Information Services:** ACA sells slide series with commentaries as complete teaching aids to universities, colleges, school systems, libraries, and other educational organizations in the United States and abroad. Owners of much of the art used stipulate that the photographs be for classroom use only.

**Approval Date:** 3/85

**Latest Information Date:** 3/85

**Index Terms:** Visual aids; Teaching aids; Arts; Art education; Art history; Anthropology; Folk art; Primitive art; Performing arts; Color slides; Textiles history; French decorative art; Japanese art; Eighteenth century; American painters; Youth oriented.

## 318

### Asia Society
### Information and Reference Service

725 Park Ave.
New York, NY 10021
Tel.: (212) 288-6400                    PUB69-5217

Washington Center of The Asia Society, 1785 Massachusetts Ave. NW., Washington, DC 20036, (202) 387-6500

The Asia Society seeks to educate Americans about Asian affairs and cultures, and to promote effective trans-Pacific dialogue.

**Areas of Interest:** Asian public affairs problems and Asia's arts and civilizations, as revealed through social science research and lectures, seminars, and conferences, as well as exhibitions of traditional Asian arts and performing arts presentations; services to educators and the use of mass media to further the Society's educational goals.

**Holdings:** Small collection of reference works (for members only); staff-use collections in Asian visual and performing arts; current Asian periodicals.

**Publications:** *Asia* (bimonthly); materials for teachers; monthly program guide for members (Sept. through June); Asia Society Gallery catalogs; *Asia in Washington* (monthly calendar of Asia-related events in Washington, D.C.).

**Information Services:** Provides public affairs briefings; conducts intensive lecture and seminar programs in New York, Washington, Houston, Los Angeles, and elsewhere on public affairs and cultural backgrounds.

**Approval Date:** 8/84

**Latest Information Date:** 1/86

**Index Terms:** Asia; Asian studies; Area studies; Cross cultural studies; Social science research; Arts; Performing arts; Lecturers; Public affairs; Cultural background; Cultural exhibitions.

## 319

### Asian Cultural Council

280 Madison Ave.
New York, NY 10016
Tel.: (212) 684-5450                    PUB69-20244

Funded by a number of private corporations, foundations, and individual sponsors, the Council supports cultural exchange in the visual and performing arts between the United States and the countries of Asia. Activities include provision of fellowship opportunities for individual artists, students, scholars, and specialists from Asia to study, conduct research, observe, or pursue creative activities in the United States and opportunities for Americans pursuing similar interests in Asia. The Council participates in international conferences.

**Areas of Interest:** Cultural exchange between the United States and the countries of Asia in dance, music, theater, opera and music theater, indigenous and folk arts, performance art, visual arts, architecture, crafts, and design arts; museum programs; historic preservation.

**Publications:** Information brochure.

**Information Services:** Answers inquiries; makes referrals to other sources of information. Services are free and available to anyone.

**Contact:** Mr. Richard S. Lanier, Director

**Approval Date:** 1/84

**Latest Information Date:** 1/86

**Index Terms:** Arts resources; Cultural exchange; United States; Asia; Dance; Music; Theater; Operas; Music theater; Folk art; Historic preservation; Performance art; Visual arts; Architecture; Handicrafts; Design; Museum programs; International arts activities.

## 320

**Association for Computers and the Humanities (ACH)**

c/o Dr. Donald Ross, Executive Secretary
209 Lind Hall
207 Church St. SE.
Minneapolis, MN 55455
Tel.: (612) 625-2888          PUB69-18735

**Areas of Interest:** Computer applications in linguistics, literature, history, musicology, archaeology, cultural anthropology, and the social sciences.

**Publications:** *ACH Newsletter* (quarterly); bibliographies.

**Information Services:** Answers inquiries; provides advisory services and information on R&D in progress; distributes publications; makes referrals to other sources of information. Services may involve payment of a fee and are available to anyone.

**Approval Date:** 8/84

**Latest Information Date:** 1/86

**Index Terms:** Computer applications; Linguistics; Literature (fine arts); History; Musicology; Archaeology; Ethnology; Social sciences.

## 321

**Atlanta University Center, Inc.
Robert W. Woodruff Library**

111 James P. Brawley Dr. SW.
Atlanta, GA 30314
Tel.: (404) 522-8980          PUB69-20471

The Library provides bibliographical, physical, and intellectual access to recorded knowledge and information in support of learning, teaching, and cultural and research needs of students, staff, faculties, administrators, and researchers of the Atlanta University Center consortium institutions as well as their alumni and the outside scholarly community.

**Areas of Interest:** Race relations; socioeconomic conditions in the Southeast (1944–1968); slavery; religion; theology and philosophy pertaining to the Black church; Black experience; Black graphic and performing arts; Black history; government documents.

**Holdings:** Special collections include 20,000 volumes on the Black Experience, the Southern Regional Council (SRC) Archival Collection, and the Southern Educational Fund (SEF) Archival Collection; 180,000 microfilm and microfiche of government documents and periodicals; access to the DIALOG computerized data bases.

**Publications:** *The Diversified Hexagon* (irregular newsletter); *Government Documents* (periodic list of acquisitions).

**Information Services:** Answers inquiries; provides reference, literature-searching, microform, and reproduction services; makes interlibrary loans, distributes publications; permits on-site use of collections. Services are primarily for students, faculty, and staff of consortium member institutions, but others will be assisted within limits of time and staff. Fees may be charged.

**Contact:** Dr. Guy C. Craft, Director

**Approval Date:** 11/84

**Latest Information Date:** 1/86

**Index Terms:** Race relations; Socioeconomic factors; Slavery; Religion; Theology; Philosophy; Afro-American church; Afro-American history; Afro-American art; Performing arts; Graphic arts; Online information retrieval systems; Government documents; Arts resources.

## 322

**Belgian American Educational Foundation (BAEF)**

195 Church St.
New Haven, CT 06510
Tel.: (203) 777-5765          PUB69-20204

Membership in BAEF is restricted to 250 in the United States and Belgium and is by invitation only. BAEF activities include sponsorship of U.S. and Belgian artists and performers in each other's countries and of fellowships for U.S. students wishing to study in Belgium; membership in international organizations; participation in international conferences and cooperative projects with foreign groups; and maintenance of foreign affiliates. In keeping with its interest in more foreign involvement, BAEF is planning future international projects.

**Areas of Interest:** Educational exchange in all disciplines between the United States and Belgium, including such arts areas as dance, music, theater, media arts, opera and music theater, indigenous and folk arts, literature, performance art, visual arts, architecture, crafts, and design arts; dance and music therapy; art therapy; historic preservation; comprehensive arts education; special education; curriculum design; museum programs; arts management; multidisciplinary programs.

**Holdings:** Collections relevant to the above areas.

**Publications:** Project reports.

**Information Services:** Answers inquiries; conducts seminars and workshops; distributes project reports in the United States and abroad; makes referrals to other sources of information in both the United States and abroad; permits on-site use of collections. Services are free and available to anyone.

**Contact:** Dr. Emile L. Boulpaep, President

**Approval Date:** 1/84

**Latest Information Date:** 1/86

**Index Terms:** Arts resources; Dance; Music; Theater; Curriculum design; Operas; Music theater; Folk art; Literature (fine arts); Historic preservation; Special education; Musicotherapy; Landscaping; Performance art; Visual arts; Comprehensive art education; Handicrafts; Design; Museum programs; Dance therapy; Art therapy; Art management; International arts activities; Exchange programs.

## 323

### Bowling Green State University
### Center for the Study of Popular Culture

Bowling Green, OH 43403
Tel.: (419) 372-2981          PUB69-17041

**Areas of Interest:** Popular culture of all kinds, including popular music and writers.

**Holdings:** Large collection of popular music albums, sheet music, and books pertaining to popular music; archives of popular writers and tapes of their voices in interviews; collection of popular novels, dime novels, and "big-little" books; numerous artifacts in popular culture; large collection of movie posters.

**Publications:** *Journal of Popular Culture, Journal of American Culture, Journal of Regional Cultures, Journal of Cultural Geography,* and *Clues: A Journal of Detection;* books, journal articles, critical reviews, bibliographies.

**Information Services:** Answers inquiries; provides

reference, abstracting, indexing, magnetic tape, and reproduction services; conducts seminars and workshops; distributes publications; makes referrals to other sources of information; permits on-site use of collections. Services are provided at cost, except for on-site use of collections, and are available to anyone.

**Approval Date:** 5/85

**Latest Information Date:** 5/85

**Index Terms:** Popular culture; Popular music; Best sellers; Writers voice recording; Novels; Motion pictures.

## 324

### Brazil–United States Institute (IBEU)

P.O. Box 12154-CEP22050
Rio de Janeiro, BRAZIL
Tel.: (021) 255-8332          PUB69-16746

**Location:** Avenida N.S. de Copacabana, 690, 11th Floor

A nonprofit institution, IBEU seeks to strengthen and widen cultural relations between Brazil and the United States through academic, cultural, and scholarship programs.

**Areas of Interest:** Cultural relations between Brazil and the United States; English language; Portuguese language; Brazilian and North American artists resident in Brazil; U.S. scholarships available to Brazilians.

**Holdings:** Library of over thirty-two thousand volumes, eighty-six periodical titles, and over four thousand recordings; art gallery featuring changing exhibits of works of Brazilian and U.S. artists.

**Publications:** *Bulletin* (semimonthly).

**Information Services:** Provides advisory and literature-searching services; conducts seminars, workshops, and courses in English and Portuguese; distributes publications; counsels students on educational opportunities and scholarships available in the United States. Services are available free to its students and its membership, which is open to everyone.

**Approval Date:** 12/85

**Latest Information Date:** 12/85

**Index Terms:** Cultural exchange; Intercultural programs; Academic guidance; Scholarships; English (second language); Language education; Portuguese language; Music; Arts; Cultural relations; Brazil; United States; Educational opportunities.

**325**

## Brazilian-American Cultural Institute, Inc. (BACI)

4103 Connecticut Ave. NW.
Washington, DC 20008
Tel.: (202) 362-8334                    PUB69-19902

Sponsored by the Brazilian Government and local membership, BACI is an organization of over four hundred members that offers exhibits, concerts, movies, language instruction, seminars, informal meetings, and cultural exchanges between the United States and Brazil.

**Areas of Interest:** Brazilian culture and life; Portuguese language instruction; cultural relations between the United States and Brazil.

**Holdings:** Over four thousand volumes on the arts, history, and literature of Brazil.

**Publications:** Books on Portuguese language and Brazilian studies; language tapes. A publications list is available.

**Information Services:** Answers inquiries; provides reference, literature-searching, and magnetic tape services; conducts seminars and language classes; distributes publications and audiovisual materials. Fees are charged for language courses, publications, and tapes; other services are free. All are available to anyone.

**Contact:** Dr. Jose M. Neistein, Executive Director

**Approval Date:** 3/85

**Latest Information Date:** 3/85

**Index Terms:** Brazil; Culture (social sciences); Music; Theater; Literature (fine arts); Visual arts; Cultural exhibitions; Concerts; Poetry; Lecturers; Touring exhibitions; Language education; Cultural exchange; Arts resources; Motion pictures; International arts activities.

**326–327**

## British American Arts Association (BAAA)

49 Wellington St.
London, WCZE 7BN, ENGLAND
Tel.: 01-379-7755                    PUB69-19980

Partially funded by grants from private foundations and corporations, BAAA is a private, nonprofit organization composed of two related organizations, one in Washington and one in London. It is dedicated to deepening the understanding and affinity between the American and British people through the arts and provides assistance and information about opportunities for transatlantic exchange and collaboration to artists, organizations, and sponsors working in all disciplines throughout both countries.

**Areas of Interest:** British and American cooperation in the arts, including dance, music, theater, media arts, opera and music theater, indigenous and folk arts, performance art, visual arts, architecture, crafts, design arts, and literature; cultural policy in the United States and Great Britain; British cultural organizations; tax policy and governmental and private support for the arts in the United States, Canada, and Great Britain, including tax laws, their effects on the arts, and options in direct subsidy, tax incentives, and marketing transactions as ways to increase the amount and effectiveness of money going to the arts in each country; arts management; fund raising; multidisciplinary studies.

**Publications:** *Tax Policy and Private Support for the Arts in the United States, Canada and Great Britain* (available from the Publishing Center for Cultural Resources, 625 Broadway, New York, NY 10012).

**Information Services:** Answers inquiries; provides advisory, consulting, technical assistance, and reference services and information on research in progress; evaluates and analyzes data; conducts seminars and workshops; provides speakers; makes referrals to other sources of information in Britain and the United States. Information and referral services are available free. All services are available to anyone, although they are intended primarily for professional artists, administrators, and other arts professionals and those interested in providing sponsorship and in the determination of cultural policy.

**Contact:** Ms. Jennifer Williams, Executive Director

**Approval Date:** 2/84

**Latest Information Date:** 2/84

**Index Terms:** British American cultural cooperation; Dance; Music; Theater; Media arts; Operas; Music theater; Folk art; Literature (fine arts); Arts resources; Visual arts; Architecture; Handicrafts; Design; Museum programs; Art management; Fund raising; Cultural policy; Cultural organizations; Cultural exchange; International arts activities; Technical assistance; Tax incentives; Art marketing.

## 328

**Center for Inter-American Relations**

680 Park Ave.
New York, NY 10021
Tel.: (212) 249-8950      PUB69-13524

The Center is a nonprofit, membership corporation financed by foundation grants, membership dues, and corporate and individual gifts. Its aims are to (1) provide a forum for those concerned with political, social, and economic activity in the Americas and (2) deepen the appreciation within the United States of the cultural achievements of its neighbors by promoting the translation and publication of Latin American and Caribbean fiction, poetry, and drama in the United States and by sponsoring exhibitions of Latin American, Caribbean, and Canadian art and performances of Latin American musicians in the United States.

**Areas of Interest:** Political, social, and economic problems of Latin America, the Caribbean, and Canada; music, literature, theater, and visual arts of those areas.

**Holdings:** Art gallery.

**Publications:** *Review* (two times a year); reports and papers resulting from seminars and conferences arranged by the Center; various books on the visual arts (a list is available); a listing of recent publications relating to Latin America; annual report; brochure.

**Information Services:** Answers inquiries or refers inquirers to other sources of information; provides reference and literature-searching services; permits on-site use of collection. The Center's conference and reception rooms may be used by other organizations working in fields related to the Center's activities.

**Approval Date:** 2/84

**Latest Information Date:** 1/86

**Index Terms:** Latin America; Cultural relations; Public affairs; Fine arts; Music; Literature (fine arts); Political science; Social problems; Theater; Canada; Caribbean Area.

## 329

**Center for Southern Folklore**

P.O. Box 40105
Memphis, TN 38104
Tel.: (901) 726-4205      PUB69-16913

**Location:** 1216 Peabody Ave.

Partially sponsored by the National Endowment for the Arts, the National Endowment for the Humanities, the Skaggs Foundation, the Rockefeller Foundation, the Tennessee Arts Commission, and the Memphis Arts Council, the Center is a nonprofit corporation that seeks to document the rapidly disappearing folk and ethnic traditions in the South through films, records, and books.

**Areas of Interest:** Southern folk traditions; folk arts, crafts, music, tales, and religion; social sciences; anthropology; enthnography; folklore; ethnomusicology; oral history; ethnic studies (Jewish, Chinese, Lebanese, and Greek in the South); regional/area studies; cultural history and geography; comparative religion.

**Holdings:** Center for Southern Folklore field tapes; L. O. Taylor Photography, Film, and Disc Collection; Stepp Walker Photo Collection; Victor Bobb Letters and Photographs; Pecolia Warner Quilts; Memphis history; Jewish culture in Memphis; black culture in Memphis.

**Publications:** 16mm films, slide-tape programs, records, books, abstracts, indexes, exhibits, directories, brochure, videotapes, multimedia shows. A publications list is available.

**Information Services:** Answers inquiries; provides advisory, consulting, and reference services; conducts seminars and workshops; provides information on research in progress; distributes data compilations and publications; makes referrals to other sources of information; permits limited on-site use of collections. Services are primarily for elementary, secondary, and college libraries, museums, and individual groups interested in related fields, but others will be assisted. The Center also works with film crews, television personnel, journalists, etc. A fee is charged for research, duplication, and the use of materials such as photographs.

**Approval Date:** 8/85

**Latest Information Date:** 8/85

**Index Terms:** Folklore; Southern United States; Anthropology; Ethnography; Sociology; Folk music; Oral history; Ethnic studies; Area studies; Arts; Crafts; Human geography; Cultural history; Religion; Ethnomusicology; Afro-American studies; Psychology; Ethnicity; Local history; Jews in America; Immigrants; Chinese in America; Arts resources; Urban renewal.

## 330

### Center for United States–China Arts Exchange

423 West 118th St., 1E
New York, NY 10027
Tel.: (212) 280-4648      PUB69-19885

Located at Columbia University, which supplies office space and miscellaneous services, and funded by foundations, corporations, and individual donors, the Center promotes and facilitates exchanges of specialists and materials in the visual, literary, and performing arts between the United States and the People's Republic of China for the purposes of stimulating public interest in and mutual understanding of the arts of both countries. Activities include arrangement of professional contacts and activities for visiting artists of both countries and cooperative projects with foreign groups.

**Areas of Interest:** Dance; music; theater; opera and music theater; indigenous and folk arts; literature; performance art; visual arts; architecture; crafts; design arts.

**Holdings:** Chinese music scores and Chinese-language periodicals on the arts; publications of Chinese professional arts organizations.

**Publications:** *US–China Arts Exhange Newsletter* (annual).

**Information Services:** Answers inquiries; provides advisory and consulting services; distributes newsletter; makes referrals to other sources of information in the United States and China. Services are available at cost to anyone.

**Contact:** Prof. Chou Wen-chung, Director

**Approval Date:** 11/84

**Latest Information Date:** 1/86

**Index Terms:** Arts; International arts activities; International cultural exchange; United States relations with China; Dance; Music; Theater; Operas; Folk arts; Literature (fine arts); Performing arts; Visual arts; Architecture; Handicrafts; Design; Arts resources.

## 331

### The Children's Museum (Indianapolis)

P.O. Box 3000
Indianapolis, IN 46206
Tel.: (317) 924-5431      PUB69-15802

**Location:** 3000 North Meridian St.

The world's largest children's museum, the Museum houses exhibits of general interest and sponsors educational programs and activities for adults as well as youngsters. Included in the Museum is a 350-seat theater where professional performing arts presentations are scheduled throughout the year.

**Areas of Interest:** Computers; railroading; natural history; prehistory; emergence of man; ancient Egypt; American history; toy trains; carousel; science and technology; performing arts; education; American Indian, Eskimo, and African cultures.

**Holdings:** Exhibits; 130,000 artifacts; 5,000-volume library.

**Publications:** Newsletters, brochures, pamphlets, gallery guides.

**Information Services:** Conducts educational workshops and programs; distributes publications; answers inquiries; provides advisory and reference services; permits on-site use of collections and library by persons in museum-related fields and qualified researchers with advance appointments. Museum admission to exhibits is free; programs and activities sometimes have a registration fee. Other specific services are provided free as time permits.

**Contact:** Ms. Margaret Maxwell

**Approval Date:** 2/85

**Latest Information Date:** 2/85

**Index Terms:** Museums (institutions); Youth oriented; Fire fighting; Railroads; Natural history; Science and technology; Anthropology; Performing arts; Education; American history; Egyptology; American Indians; Eskimos; African culture.

## 332

### Copyright Society of the U.S.A.

c/o New York University Law Center
40 Washington Square South
New York, NY 10012
Tel.: (212) 598-2280      PUB69-18010

**Areas of Interest:** Copyright law and rights in literature, music, art, the theater, motion pictures, and other forms of intellectual property.

**Holdings:** Unique collection of copyright materials housed in the Walter J. Derenberg Library

**Publications:** *Journal of the Copyright Society of the U.S.A.* (bimonthly; formerly the *Bulletin*).

**Information Services:** Answers inquiries; provides reference and reproduction services; conducts seminars; distributes publication; makes referrals to other sources of information; permits on-site use of collection. Nonmembers are assessed a fee for services.

**Approval Date:** 2/84

**Latest Information Date:** 1/86

**Index Terms:** Copyrights; Literature (fine arts); Music; Arts; Theater; Motion pictures; Information dissemination; Information exchange.

## 333

**Education Commission of the States (ECS)**
**ECS Clearinghouse**

Lincoln Tower, Room 300
1860 Lincoln St.
Denver, CO 80295
  Tel.: (303) 830-3600        PUB69-10607

**Areas of Interest:** State education policy.

**Publications:** *State Education Leader* (quarterly); *ECS State Leaders Directory* (annual); issuegrams on key issues; major reports on key issues (eight to ten per year).

**Information Services:** Answers inquiries; provides consulting, reference, and duplication services; makes referrals to other sources of information. Services are free and available to anyone.

**Approval Date:** 8/85

**Latest Information Date:** 8/85

**Index Terms:** Educational research; Education; Educational development; Educational evaluation; Science; Writing; Citizenship; Reading; Literature (fine arts); Music; Social studies; Mathematics; Arts; Career education; Machine readable data bases; Nonbibliographic data bases; NAEP Data Files.

## 334

**Faculty Exchange Center**

952 Virginia Ave.
Lancaster, PA 17603
  Tel.: (717) 393-1130        PUB69-20219

The Center has an international membership of about five hundred college and university faculty members working in all academic and arts disciplines and an institutional membership of about one hundred fifty colleges and universities.

**Areas of Interest:** Teaching exchanges on the college and university level; faculty housing exchanges.

**Publications:** Semiannual directory with house exchange supplements.

**Information Services:** Distributes publications and data compilations in the United States and abroad. Services are provided free to faculty whose institutions are members and for a membership fee to other members of the teaching profession.

**Contact:** John Joseph, Executive Secretary

**Approval Date:** 1/84

**Latest Information Date:** 1/86

**Index Terms:** Arts resources; Faculty exchange; Faculty housing exchange; Colleges and universities; International educational exchange.

## 335

**Fulbright Association of Alumni of International Educational and Cultural Exchange**

P.O. Box 1042
Bryn Mawr, PA 19010
  Tel.: (215) 645-5038 or 645-6206     PUB69-18581

**Areas of Interest:** International educational and cultural exchange; the nature of Fulbright grantee experiences.

**Holdings:** Statistically analyzed data on questionnaires distributed to former Fulbright grantees (over three thousand responses); computerized membership list of over 17,000 former Fulbrighters with current address, country of Fulbright grant, and discipline.

**Publications:** *The Fulbrighters' Newsletter* (three times a year); journal articles, directories, research summaries, data compilations.

**Information Services:** Answers inquiries; provides advisory services, mailing list, and information on research in progress; evaluates and analyzes data; conducts seminars and workshops; distributes publications; makes referrals to other sources of information. Services may be subject to a fee and are available to all members of the Association and to groups and individuals interested in promotion of international educational and cultural exchange.

**Approval Date:** 4/85

**Latest Information Date:** 4/85

**Index Terms:** International education; Cultural exchange; International exchange of scientists; International exchange of students.

**336**

## Harvard University
## Dumbarton Oaks

1703 32d St. NW.
Washington, DC 20007
Tel.: (202) 342-3200          PUB69-7275

Since 1940 the property of the Trustees of Harvard University, Dumbarton Oaks is a research institution made up of three separate research programs in Byzantine and medieval studies, Pre-Columbian studies, and the history of landscape architecture.

**Areas of Interest:** (1) Byzantine and medieval art, archaeology, history, literature, theology, music, and law. (2) Pre-Columbian art, archaeology, ethnohistory, and linguistics. (3) History of landscape architecture, garden design, and horticulture.

**Holdings:** (1) The Center for Byzantine Studies includes a research library and a collection of late Antique and Byzantine decorative and minor arts. Studies at the Center embrace the late classical, early Christian, and medieval periods and focus on the history and culture of the Byzantine Empire and its influence in the Slavic and Near Eastern countries and in the Latin West through the fifteenth century. The 95,000 volumes in the library include most of the important collections and editions of sources in Greek and Latin as well as in the pertinent Near Eastern languages. There is a card index listing every title in the bibliographies of the *Byzantinische Zeitschrift* and of Krumbacher's *Geschichte der Byzantinischen Litteratur*. A photographic copy of the Princeton Index of Christian Art is kept up to date. The Center also has a visual research archive of 80,000 mounted black and white photographs of the architecture, art, and archaeology of the early Christian and Byzantine era, as well as 40,000 original negatives and 25,000 color transparencies, and 11,000 mounted photographs which comprise the Census of Objects of Early Christian and Byzantine Art in North American Collections. (2) The Robert Woods Bliss Collection of Pre-Columbian Art consists of objects from Mexico, Guatemala, Honduras, Costa Rica, Panama, Colombia, and Peru. In addition, there is a research library of 15,000 volumes on Latin American art and archaeology, and an archive of 20,000 photographs of Maya pottery and Peruvian textiles. (3) The Garden Library includes a collection of rare and secondary materials in three subject areas: the theory and practice of garden design and horticultural methods, including views and plans of gardens, garden structures, and ornament; architectural treatises and views; and illustrated botanical books from early herbals to nineteenth-century floras. Total holdings are a book and pamphlet collection numbering 13,000 volumes, 900 prints and drawings, 6,200 slides, 700 microfiches, and 3,000 photographs.

**Publications:** *Dumbarton Oaks Papers* (issued annually in one volume); *Dumbarton Oaks Studies* (series of monographs); *Dumbarton Oaks Texts* (critical editions of Byzantine texts with translations and commentary); *Dumbarton Oaks Bibliographies* (subject series); catalogs of objects in the Byzantine collection; *Studies in Pre-Columbian Art and Archaeology* (series of monographs); conference proceedings (including papers from the annual Pre-Columbian conference); *Colloquia on the History of Landscape Architecture* (papers from the annual symposium); miscellaneous catalogs and monographs; exhibition catalogs. A publications list is available.

**Information Services:** The research facilities of the Center for Byzantine Studies are available to advanced scholars. The Pre-Columbian Library is open to advanced scholars with serious research interest, subject to time and space limitations. The Garden Library is open to a limited number of outside readers doing advanced academic and professional research. The art collections are open to the public.

**Approval Date:** 4/85

**Latest Information Date:** 4/85

**Index Terms:** Medieval art; Archaeology; Art history; Byzantine art; Literature (fine arts); Theology; Music; Law (jurisprudence); Pre-Columbian art; Ethnography; Linguistics; Landscape architecture; Gardens; Horticulture; Arts resources.

**337**

## Hispanic Society of America
## Library

613 West 155th St.
New York, NY 10032
Tel.: (212) 926-2234          PUB69-19983

Visitors' entrance: Broadway, between 155th and 156th Sts.

A nonprofit organization of 300 corresponding members and 100 full members elected from among Hispanic authors, artists, composers, and scholars from all countries, the Society maintains a free public museum and reference library. It holds memberships in international organizations and participates in international conferences.

**Areas of Interest:** Art, language, literature, history, archaeology, architecture, music, decorative arts, and culture of Spain and Portugal.

**Holdings:** 20,000 books printed before 1701, including 250 incunabula; 200,000 manuscripts; 200,000 modern books; vertical files. The collections of paintings, sculpture, and decorative arts are maintained in the Museum Department and prints and photographs in the Iconography Department.

**Publications:** Books, bibliographies, reprints. Publication lists are available.

**Information Services:** Answers inquiries; provides reproduction and microfilming services; distributes publications in the United States and abroad; permits on-site use of collections. With the exception of reproduction and microfilming services, which are subject to certain restrictions, and access to rare books and manuscripts, which is restricted to persons with special identification, services are free and available to anyone.

**Contact:** Martha M. de Narvaez, Curator of Manuscripts and Rare Books

**Approval Date:** 12/84

**Latest Information Date:** 1/86

**Index Terms:** Spanish culture; Portuguese culture; Libraries; Museums (institutions); Arts; Languages; Literature (fine arts); Dance; Music; Theater; Operas; Music theater; Folk art; Visual arts; Architecture; Handicrafts; History; Sculpture; Decorative art; Paintings; International arts activities; Arts resources.

## 338

### Howard University
### Moorland-Spingarn Research Center

Founders Library, Room 109
500 Howard Pl. NW.
Washington, DC 20059
Tel.: (202) 636-7239          PUB69-15614

**Areas of Interest:** Reference, bibliography, and research related to Afro-American history and culture, African history and culture, and Afro-Latin and Caribbean history and culture.

**Holdings:** 92,232 books and pamphlets, 9,564 bound periodicals, and theses and dissertations of Howard students, including the Howardiana collection and a large collection of Afro-American authors; major resource of periodicals and newspapers; vertical file of historic and contemporary information; photographs (thousands); 700 oral history transcripts; sheet music of black composers (over 3,400 pieces); over 400 manuscript and archival collections; over 1,500 records, tapes, cassettes, and artifacts.

**Publications:** Bibliographic guides and registers to collections.

**Information Services:** Answers inquiries; provides advisory, reference, literature-searching, current-awareness, photographic, microform, and reproduction services; conducts seminars and workshops; distributes data compilations and publications; makes referrals to other sources of information; permits on-site use of collections. Services are free, except for reproduction, photographic, and special research services, and generally available to anyone.

**Approval Date:** 8/84

**Latest Information Date:** 1/86

**Index Terms:** Afro-American studies; Afro-Latin American studies; Afro-American history; Afro-American culture; African culture; Caribbean Area; Oral history; Photographs; Manuscripts; Music.

## 339

### Information Center on Children's Cultures

331 East 38th St.
New York, NY 10016
Tel.: (212) 686-5522
Ext. 402 or 403          PUB69-12040

The Center is a service of the U.S. Committee for UNICEF.

**Areas of Interest:** Intercultural education; children's literature; developing countries; children in Asia, Latin America, the Near East, Africa, the Caribbean region, and the Pacific Islands.

**Holdings:** Library of about 17,000 books and pamphlets, 4,800 slides, 474 flat pictures, 445 filmstrips, 440 recordings, 3,505 items of children's art, 110 films, 14,260 photographs, and 510 objects (toys, musical instruments, and clothing used by children).

**Publications:** Periodicals, books, journal articles, critical reviews, bibliographies. A publications list is available, as well as a catalog of UNICEF publications.

**Information Services:** Answers inquiries; provides advisory, reference, and reproduction services; conducts seminars and workshops; distributes Center and UNICEF publications; makes referrals to other sources of information; permits on-site use of collection. Bibliographies are distributed free in single copies with a stamped, self-addressed envelope; some materials are available free in quantity for distribution at conferences related to international education; other UNICEF publications are available at cost. Services are available to anyone.

**Approval Date:** 1/84

**Latest Information Date:** 1/86

**Index Terms:** Children; Children's books; Developing countries; Asia; Africa; Middle East; Latin America; Cultural exchange; Intercultural programs; Educational films; Teaching aids; Caribbean Area; Pacific Islands.

## 340

### Information Coordinators, Inc.

1435-37 Randolph St.
Detroit, MI 48226
Tel.: (313) 962-9720          PUB69-16340

Information Coordinators, Inc. is a commercial publishing organization.

**Areas of Interest:** (1) Psychology and sociology of work, including: human relations and personnel concepts; labor-management relations; personnel practices; employee representation; negotiation process and dispute settlement; current negotiations; wages, salaries, income, and fringe benefits; safety and health; education and training; human, industrial, and systems engineering; economics; labor force and manpower; occupations; government and labor-management; laws and legislation; organization concepts and management; labor movement organization; and union and employee organizations. (2) Musicology; ethnomusicology; organology; church music; hymnology; sociology of music; composing; classical and popular music; popular music performers; jazz.

**Publications:** *Work Related Abstracts* and *The Music Index* (both monthly).

**Information Services:** Sells publications.

**Approval Date:** 8/84

**Latest Information Date:** 1/86

**Index Terms:** Bibliographies; Publishing; Wages; Salaries; Labor law; Manpower training programs; Human relations; Labor relations; Personnel management; Safety; Health; Education; Systems engineering; Manpower; Policy sciences; Economics; Government; Legislation; Management; Labor unions; Negotiations; Arbitration; Income; Fringe benefits; Musicology; Ethnomusicology; Performing arts.

## 341

### Irish American Cultural Institute

683 Osceola Ave.
St. Paul, MN 55105
Tel.: (612) 647-5678          PUB69-19896

**Location:** College of Saint Thomas, 2115 Summit Ave.

An organization of over seventy-two thousand members in the United States and twenty-four foreign countries, the Institute grants awards to the arts in Ireland, conducts summer programs in Ireland for American youth, sponsors Irish lecturers and cultural events in the United States, and conducts cooperative projects with Irish groups.

**Areas of Interest:** Irish civilization and culture, including literature, music, theater, and indigenous and folk arts.

**Publications:** *Eire-Ireland* (quarterly journal of Irish studies); *Duchas* (bimonthly newsletter); books.

**Information Services:** Answers inquiries; provides reference services; provides speakers; distributes publications in the United States and abroad; makes referrals to sources of information in the United States and Ireland. With the exception of speakers, information services are free and available to anyone.

**Contact:** Dr. Eoin McKiernan, President

**Approval Date:** 4/85

**Latest Information Date:** 4/85

**Index Terms:** Ireland; Civilization; Culture (social sciences); Literature (fine arts); Music; Theater; Folk art; International arts activities; Lecturers; Awards; Cultural events; Summer programs; Arts resources.

## 342

### Japan Information and Culture Center

Embassy of Japan
917 19th St. NW.
Washington, DC 20006
Tel.: (202) 234-2266 Ext. 412 or 775-0847 (Director)
(202) 234-2266 Ext. 414 (Programs)
(202) 234-2266 Ext. 413 (Films)
(202) 234-2266 Ext. 416 or 417 (Inquiries)
(202) 234-2266 Ext. 413 (Reception)
PUB69-20223

The Center is an activity of the Information and Culture Section of the Embassy of Japan.

**Areas of Interest:** Cultural subjects relating to Japan, including dance, music, theater, music theater, indigenous and folk arts, landscape design, architecture, performance art, visual arts, crafts, and design arts; political and economic aspects of Japanese-U.S. relations.

**Holdings:** 16mm films on various aspects of Japanese life. The Embassy library has about three thousand books in Japanese and English.

**Publications:** Monthly newsletter announcing events at the Center.

**Information Services:** Answers inquiries; lends audiovisual materials; conducts conferences, seminars, lectures, film shows, exhibits, musical performances, and other activities related to Japan; distributes its newsletter; provides speakers; makes referrals to other sources of information. The Embassy library provides reference services and permits on-site use of its collection. All services are free and available to anyone. The Center's facilities are accessible to the handicapped.

**Contact:** Mr. Yasuji Odoko, Deputy Director

**Approval Date:** 1/84

**Latest Information Date:** 1/86

**Index Terms:** Arts resources; Japan; Cultural centers; Dance; Music; Theater; Music theater; Folk art; Landscaping; Architecture; Performance art; Visual arts; Japanese American relations; Motion pictures; Handicapped arts services.

### 343

### Japan-United States Concert Society, Inc.

160 West 71st St., Suite 18G
New York, NY 10023
Tel.: (212) 787-6983                    PUB69-20222

Sponsored by private U.S. corporations, the Society establishes educational aid for young Eastern and Western artists to enhance creative talent in the fine arts in both traditional and modern modes of expression and creates settings in which these artists may perform or exhibit for live audiences and, through critique and study, grow and develop their talents. It sponsors performances and exhibits abroad, sponsors foreign artists and performers in the United States, and is planning future international projects.

**Areas of Interest:** Scholarly and fine arts exchanges, on a people-to-people basis, between East and West, with special emphasis on the acculturation of artists in dance and music of Japan and the United States.

**Information Services:** Answers inquiries; provides reference services. Services are free and available to anyone.

**Contact:** Toshiko Takahara, Executive Director

**Approval Date:** 1/84

**Latest Information Date:** 1/86

**Index Terms:** Japanese American relations; Arts resources; Cultural relations; Dance; Music; Concerts; Exchange programs; Acculturation; Cultural exchange; International arts activities; Handicapped arts services.

### 344

### Japanese American Cultural and Community Center (JACCC)

244 South San Pedro St., Suite 505
Los Angeles, CA 90012
Tel.: (213) 628-2725                    PUB69-20214

Opened in 1980 and located in the Little Tokyo area of Los Angeles, JACCC comprises a community center building, Japanese gardens, the Japan America Theatre, and JACCC Plaza (Isamu Noguchi, designer). It promotes activities that serve to preserve and encourage appreciation of Japanese culture and the Japanese-American heritage.

**Areas of Interest:** Japanese and Japanese-American activities in dance, music, theater, media arts, opera and music theater, indigenous and folk arts, literature, landscape design, performance art, visual arts, architecture, crafts, design arts, and historic preservation; multidisciplinary studies.

**Holdings:** The Center's Franklin D. Murphy Library has about three thousand books in Japanese, another three hundred books in English relating to Japanese Americans, and four hundred references and periodicals in Japanese.

**Publications:** *Newsletter* (three times a year); calendar of events (six times a year).

**Information Services:** Answers inquiries; provides advisory, reference, literature-searching, current-awareness, reproduction, and translation services; conducts seminars and workshops; makes direct and interlibrary loans; makes referrals to other sources of information in the United States and abroad; permits on-site use of collections. Services are available to the public on payment of a membership fee. The Center's facilities are accessible to the handicapped.

**Contact:** Kats Kunitsugu, Library Director Pro Tem

**Approval Date:** 1/84

**Latest Information Date:** 1/86

**Index Terms:** Arts resources; Japanese-American relations; Japanese Americans; Cultural activities; Dance; Music; Theater; Operas; Music theater; Folk art; Literature (fine arts); Historic preservation; Landscaping; Performance art; Visual arts; Architecture; Handicrafts; International arts activities; Handicapped arts services.

---

### 345

**Jewish Community Center of Greater Washington
Cultural Arts Division**

6125 Montrose Rd.
Rockville, MD 20852
  Tel.: (301) 881-0100       PUB69-17977

Sponsored in part by the United Way and the United Jewish Appeal Federation, the Division sponsors performing groups, concerts, theater presentations, lectures, films, workshops, dance programs, and art exhibits, and includes the School for Performing Arts and the Judaic Museum.

**Areas of Interest:** Music, theater, dance, art, and literature, with special emphasis on Jewish culture.

**Information Services:** Answers inquiries; provides advisory and consulting services; conducts seminars and workshops; makes referrals to other sources of information. Services are available to anyone, some on a fee basis.

**Contact:** Ms. Shirley Udelson

**Approval Date:** 2/85

**Latest Information Date:** 2/85

**Index Terms:** Jewish community centers; Cultural activities; Cultural programs; Music; Theater; Dance; Arts; Literature (fine arts).

---

### 346

**Lakeview Museum of Arts and Sciences**

1125 West Lake Ave.
Peoria, IL 61614
  Tel.: (309) 686-7000       PUB69-13483

The Museum is a not-for-profit organization.

**Areas of Interest:** Arts; sciences; Illinois history.

**Holdings:** Artistic and scientific exhibits and collections.

**Publications:** Bimonthly bulletin; exhibition catalogs.

**Information Services:** Answers inquiries; provides advisory and reference services; permits on-site use of

collections. Services are provided at cost to all users. Facilities include a planetarium.

**Approval Date:** 4/85

**Latest Information Date:** 4/85

**Index Terms:** Performing arts; Fine arts; Local history; Science.

---

### 347

**Michigan State University
College of International Studies and Programs
Asian Studies Center**

101 International Center
East Lansing, MI 48824
  Tel.: (517) 353-1680       PUB69-19119

**Areas of Interest:** Asian studies, particularly problems of rural development, theater, East Asian history, and American-East Asian relations.

**Holdings:** Materials on the areas above.

**Publications:** *Offshoots* (biweekly newsletter during the school year); *Journal of South Asian Literature* (semiannual); *East Asia Series Occasional Papers* and *South Asia Series Occasional Papers* (both irregular).

**Information Services:** Answers inquiries; provides advisory and reference services; evaluates data; conducts seminars and workshops; distributes publications; makes referrals to other sources of information; permits on-site use of collection. Services are free and available to anyone.

**Contact:** Dr. Warren Cohen, Director

**Approval Date:** 2/85

**Latest Information Date:** 2/85

**Index Terms:** Colleges and universities; International studies; International programs; Asian studies; Rural development; Theater; History; United States relations with East Asia.

---

### 348

**Museum Computer Network, Inc. (MCN)**

P.O. Box 434
Stony Brook, NY 11790
  Tel.: (516) 246-6077       PUB69-12069

MCN is an international membership organization of museums and other nonprofit institutions maintaining museumlike collections or inventories. Its objective is to assist museums and institutions with similar interests in converting all systematic information in their files and archives from written to machine-readable form, using common standards in the conversion so that each museum's files can, in principle, be merged with those of other museums.

**Areas of Interest:** Computerization of systematic information relating to museum collections, including archaeological specimens and sites, motion pictures, works of art, and documents.

**Publications:** *Manual for Museum Computer Network Data Preparation* (1975); *Spectra* (quarterly newsletter); *GRIPHOS* (1977); *GRIPHOS Users' Guide* (1979).

**Information Services:** Provides consulting services and support and documentation for museum inventory and annual conference. Services are available only to members and are provided at or below cost. Voting membership is open to all nonprofit, record-keeping institutions on an annual fee basis; non-voting membership is unrestricted.

**Approval Date:** 8/85

**Latest Information Date:** 8/85

**Index Terms:** Museums (institutions); Inventory control; Machine readable data bases; Nonbibliographic data bases; GRIPHOS; Computer networks; Computer programs; Antiquities; Archaeological sites; Motion pictures; Art objects; Documents.

---

**349**

---

**National Association for Poetry Therapy (NAPT)**

1029 Henhawk Rd.
Baldwin, NY 11510
  Tel.: (516) 546-2295       PUB69-20354

An organization of 250 certified therapists in the United States and other countries and an associate membership of persons supportive of the Association and students, NAPT provides an information network to all persons interested in poetry therapy, establishes ethics and standards for the training of poetry therapists, and encourages research, education, and publication in the field.

**Areas of Interest:** Poetry therapy; certification and training of psychologists, psychiatrists, social workers, activity directors and personnel, teachers, and occupational therapists as poetry therapists.

**Publications:** Books, poetry collections, journal articles, bibliographies, teaching materials, reprints.

**Information Services:** Answers inquiries; provides advisory and reference services; conducts seminars and workshops; provides speakers; distributes pub-

lications in the United States and abroad; makes referrals to foreign and domestic sources of information. Services are provided free to members and for a negotiated fee to special groups.

**Contact:** Ms. Beverly Bussolati, Secretary

**Approval Date:** 11/84

**Latest Information Date:** 1/86

**Index Terms:** Arts resources; Poetry; Poetry therapy; Teacher training; Literature (fine arts); Psychologists; Psychiatrists; Certification.

---

**350**

---

**National Council on Art in Jewish Life, Inc.**

15 East 84th St.
New York, NY 10028
  Tel.: (212) 879-4500       PUB69-18182

**Areas of Interest:** Information and resources on Jewish life in graphic and plastic art, film, television, and visual arts.

**Holdings:** Resource materials in media and art.

**Publications:** *Jewish Media Round-up* (quarterly); *What's Doing* (quarterly); books, journal articles, state-of-the-art reviews, critical reviews, abstracts, indexes, bibliographies, reprints.

**Information Services:** Answers inquiries; provides advisory and reference services; provides information on research in progress; conducts seminars and workshops; initiates, supports, and participates in exhibits; distributes publications; makes referrals to other sources of information; refers commissions to established artists; permits on-site use of collections. Services are generally free and available to anyone.

**Approval Date:** 11/85

**Latest Information Date:** 11/85

**Index Terms:** Jewish way of life; Jewish art; Jewish culture; Motion pictures; Video tapes; Visual arts.

---

**351**

---

**National Library of Canada/Bibliotheque nationale du Canada**

395 Wellington St.
Ottawa, Ontario, CANADA K1A ON4
  Tel.: (613) 995-9481 (general reference)
       (613) 996-3566 (interlibrary loan and locations)
       (TELEX) 053-4311 or 053-4312
       (ENVOY) OONL. REF (electronic mail);

Compose OONL. REFERENCE (reference request);
Compose ILL.NLC
(interlibrary loan script)                PUB69-13702

**Areas of Interest:** Canadiana; social sciences; humanities; economics; education; geography; history; international relations; law; political science; psychology; sociology; architecture; language and languages; literature; music; performing arts; philosophy; religion; library science; history of the book and printing; bibliography.

**Holdings:** Over one million monograph volumes; more than two million official publications; over 2.2 million items in microform. The Library has been receiving Canadian publications on legal deposit since 1953, and Canadian imprints before that date are collected intensively. The collection of official publications includes those of the Canadian federal and provincial governments, foreign governments, and international organizations. There are special collections on music, Canadian children's books, rare books and manuscripts, Judaica, Canadian textbooks, Canadian native rights, and the performing arts. Using the DOBIS system, the Library maintains a bibliographic data base which includes records for its own holdings of Canadian and foreign publications, the records of a growing network of federal government libraries, and records of other Canadian libraries. Access to the DOBIS data base on a search-only basis is now available to libraries across Canada.

**Publications:** *National Library News* (monthly); *Canadiana 1867–1900: Monographs* (microfiche; quarterly); *BiblioTech* (bimonthly); *Canadian Network Papers* (irregular); *Canadiana* (hard copy and fiche editions); *Canadiana Authorities* (microfiche); *Canadian Theses* (microfiche); *Annual Report of the National Librarian; CONSER Microfiche*; bibliographies, classification schedules, *Union Lists of Serials in the Social Sciences and Humanities Held by Canadian Libraries* (semiannual, microfiche;) Canadian MARC communication formats; *Canadian ISBN Publishers' Directory* (annual); *Symbols of Canadian Libraries* (biennial); *Canadian Union Catalogue of Library Materials for the Handicapped* (quarterly, microfiche). A publications catalog is available.

**Information Services:** Answers inquiries; provides CAN/SDI current-awareness service in the social and behavioral sciences and humanities and automated retrospective searching using such data base services as DIALOG, QL Systems, MINISIS, Bookline, CAN/OLE, BRS, InfoGlobe, Wilsonline, VU/TEXT, TEXTLINE, Dunserve II, CSG Insight, and Informatech; provides documentation and reference service in Canadian studies, including library and information science, children's literature, music, and

library services for handicapped persons, and a Multilingual Biblioservice (i.e., national loan collection of books in languages other than English and French); provides advisory, referral, and copying services; provides a national and international loan and location service to other libraries; permits on-site use of collections; experiments with the library applications of new technologies and provides documentation and advice in this area. Basic services are free; certain specialized services are not.

**Approval Date:** 9/85

**Latest Information Date:** 9/85

**Index Terms:** Libraries; Union catalogs; Library automation; Humanities; Social sciences; Library science; Machine readable data bases; Bibliographic data bases; Referral centers; Children's literature; Canadiana; Economics; Library information networks; Education; Geography; History; International relations; Law (jurisprudence); Political science; Languages; Literature (fine arts); Music; Performing arts; Philosophy; Religion; Printing history; Bibliographies; Online information retrieval systems; Canadian newspapers; Canadian government publications.

---

**352**

---

**National Museums of Canada**
**National Museum of Man**
**Canadian Ethnology Service**

Ottawa, Ontario, CANADA K1A OM8
Tel.: (613) 996-4540                PUB69-17313

The Service undertakes research (by staff and by contract) in, collects artifacts reflecting, and disseminates information on the traditional cultures and languages of Canadian Indians, Inuit, and Metis.

**Areas of Interest:** Canadian ethnology and museology of Indians, Inuit, and Metis, including ethnography, linguistics, music, ethnohistory, material culture, and conservation.

**Holdings:** About 55,000 artifacts, 90 percent of which are Canadian Inuit and Indian materials (including contemporary native art), with emphasis on Inuit (11,000) and Pacific Coast Indian (9,000) traditional material culture; audiovisual and manuscript collections of Canadian anthropology. The Service participates in the National Inventory Programme (CDC, Paris).

**Publications:** Research reports, scholarly papers, monographs, brochures, catalogs of exhibits, reprints, popular publications.

**Information Services:** Answers scientific and museological inquiries; provides advisory and reference services; arranges traveling exhibits; lends artifacts and exchanges publications with museums and scholarly institutions subject to restrictions imposed regarding the condition of the material. Access to the collections is by appointment only and is restricted to researchers. Some archival material is confidential. Provision may be made for Xeroxing (limit 100 pages), photographing, and tape reproduction. Research contracts on Canadian urgent ethnology are awarded each year (deadline for submission is December 1, directed to Chief Ethnologist, address as above).

**Approval Date:** 2/84

**Latest Information Date:** 2/84

**Index Terms:** Museums (institutions); Canada; Ethnology; Ethnography; Linguistics; Material culture; Canadian Indians; Eskimos; Museum techniques; Anthropology; Conservation; Music; Audiovisual aids; Manuscripts; Touring exhibitions; Arts.

## 353

**NewsBank, Inc.**

58 Pine St.
New Canaan, CT 06840
Tel.: (203) 966-1100          PUB69-16513

NewsBank, Inc. is a publishing company specializing in providing indexes to current information materials, particularly newspapers and broadcasts from hundreds of sources. Articles are clipped and reproduced on microfiche; organized for browsing; indexed by subject, name of person, institution, or organization; and liberally cross-referenced.

**Areas of Interest:** All aspects of current information on life in the United States organized into two main areas: urban affairs, especially social and economic, and culture, with emphasis on the arts; personalities organized by subject, name, and sometimes by occupation; political and social developments around the world, organized by region, subject, and name.

**Holdings:** Microfiche files include reproductions from U.S. newspapers in over one hundred cities. Cumulative indexes cover these files, plus translations from hundreds of news sources (magazines, newspapers, government press releases, television and radio broadcasts).

**Publications:** *The NewsBank Library:* Business and Economic Development, Consumer Affairs, Education, Employment, Environment, Government Structure, Health, Housing and Building, International Affairs and Defense, Law and Legal Systems, Political Development, Social Relations, Transportation, Welfare and Social Problems (monthly, quarterly, annually); *NewsBank Review of the Arts:* Film and Television, Fine Arts and Architecture, Literature, and Performing Arts (monthly, four-monthly, annually); *Names in the News* (monthly, quarterly, annually); *U.S. Foreign Broadcast Information Service Daily Reports Indexes:* People's Republic of China, Soviet Union, Eastern Europe, Latin America, Middle East & Africa, South Asia, Western Europe, Asia and Pacific (monthly, annually).

**Information Services:** Answers inquiries; provides advisory, reference, literature-searching, reproduction, and microfilm services; provides information on R&D in progress. Publications are available by subscription.

**Approval Date:** 4/85

**Latest Information Date:** 4/85

**Index Terms:** Urban affairs; Bibliographic data bases; Current events; Commerce; Economic development; Consumers; Education; Employment; Environmental sciences; Public health; Housing; Urban renewal; Law (jurisprudence); Political science; Social relations; Transportation; Welfare; Poverty; Motion pictures; Television arts; Fine arts; Performing arts; News reporting; International affairs; National defense; Indexing; Biographies.

## 354

**Old Cienega Village Museum at El Rancho de las Golondrinas**

Route 2, Box 214
Santa Fe, NM 87505
Tel.: (505) 471-2261          PUB69-19031

**Areas of Interest:** Spanish colonial history, arts, crafts, customs, dances, drama, farming methods, use of irrigation, and building methods.

**Holdings:** The Museum consists of five dwellings furnished with Spanish colonial artifacts, three grist mills, a large mill, a wheelwright shop, a blacksmith shop, a morada, a family chapel, barns, corrals, a molasses mill, outdoor ovens, a school house, a dyeing and wool processing shed, and a platform for performing folk dances, folk music, and drama.

**Information Services:** Answers inquiries; conducts seminars, workshops, and Museum tours; conducts a spring festival (first weekend of May) and a harvest festival (first weekend of October) at which time household and farming tasks are performed as they were in eighteenth- and nineteenth-century New Mexico (includes folk dances, music, and drama performances); makes referrals to other sources of information. Information on tour times, etc. is available. Except for admission to the Museum, services are free. All are available to anyone.

**Contact:** Mr. George Paloheimo, Curator

**Approval Date:** 2/85

**Latest Information Date:** 2/85

**Index Terms:** Spanish colonial history; New Mexico; Arts; Handicrafts; Folk dance; Drama; Farming methods; Irrigation; Construction; Museums (institutions); Historic preservation.

## 355

**Poets & Writers, Inc.**

201 West 54th St.
New York, NY 10019
Tel.: (212) 757-1766                    PUB69-19966

Funded by the National Endowment for the Arts, New York State Council on the Arts, New York City Department of Cultural Affairs, foundations, corporations, and individuals, Poets & Writers, Inc. provides information to writers, editors, publishers, sponsors of literary events, and others interested in contemporary literature.

**Areas of Interest:** Information on poets and fiction writers who have published their work in the United States; manuscript submission; information on writers' organizations, colonies, workshops, and readings; the law as it affects writers, including copyright and tax law; literary agents; literary bookshops; funding sources for writers.

**Holdings:** Computerized data base on U.S. poets and fiction writers, including names, addresses, publications, work preferences, minority affiliations, and other data submitted by the writers themselves; computerized list of sponsors of literary events.

**Publications:** *Coda: Poets & Writers Newsletter* (five issues a year); *A Directory of American Poets and Fiction Writers; A Writer's Guide to Copyright; Literary Agent: A Writer's Guide; Literary Bookstores: A List in Progress; Sponsors List* (of organizations sponsoring readings and workshops for poets and writers); reprints.

**Information Services:** Answers inquiries; provides advisory services; distributes publications, computer printouts, and computer-generated mailing labels on writers; makes referrals to other sources of information. Except for publications, printouts, and mailing

labels, services are free and all are available to anyone. Poets and fiction writers wishing to be included in the data base and subsequent editions of the directory must meet Poets & Writers, Inc.'s criteria and pay a one-time fee.

**Contact:** Ms. Dorothy Allison, Director of Information Services

**Approval Date:** 2/84

**Latest Information Date:** 1/86

**Index Terms:** Poets; Writers; Information centers; Information exchange; Information services; Education; Employment opportunities; Legal aspects; Copyrights; Taxes; Machine readable data bases; Bibliographic data bases; U.S. Poets and Fiction Writers; Computerized list of sponsors of literary events; Arts resources.

## 356

**Royal Oak Foundation, Inc.**

41 East 72d St.
New York, NY 10021
Tel.: (212) 861-0529                    PUB69-19946

Affiliated with the National Trust of England, Wales, and Northern Ireland, the Foundation is a nonprofit organization of 5,000 members promoting the preservation of the Anglo-American architectural heritage through sponsorship of cultural exchanges between the United States and the United Kingdom and through fund raising in the United States in aid of National Trust properties.

**Areas of Interest:** British architecture; British collections of paintings, sculpture, porcelains, and other art objects; landscape design, design arts, and decorative arts in Britain; historic preservation, maintenance, and restoration of architectural monuments, historic sites, and places of natural beauty in the United Kingdom.

**Holdings:** Slides, films, and literature of 250 National Trust properties in the United Kingdom.

**Publications:** Semiannual newsletter; *Heritage of England: Silver Through Ten Reigns; Painting as a Pastime: The Paintings of Winston Churchill;* Painting as a Pastime (poster); Christmas gift catalog; lists of National Trust properties open to view.

**Information Services:** Answers inquiries; provides advisory and reference services; conducts seminars, workshops, exhibits, lectures, and tours to Great Britain; provides speakers; distributes its own publications, audiovisual materials, and publications of the National Trust; makes referrals to other sources of information; permits on-site use of collections. Some services are free to nonmembers; others are subject to a fee. Special arrangements are available for handicapped visitors to National Trust properties on request.

**Contact:** Mr. Arthur Prager, Executive Director

**Approval Date:** 1/84

**Latest Information Date:** 1/86

**Index Terms:** Anglo-American cultural heritage; Art objects; Paintings; Sculpture; Porcelain; Landscaping; Design; Decorative art; Historic preservation; Maintenance; Restoration; Historic buildings; Historic sites; Visual arts; Architecture; International arts activities; Handicapped arts services; Fund raising; Arts resources.

## 357

### Smithsonian Institution
### Office of Folklife Programs

2600 L'Enfant Plaza
Washington, DC 20560
Tel.: (202) 287-3424          PUB69-17195

The Office works to create a national cultural milieu in which authentic folk expression can thrive and develop. Since its inception, the Folklife Program has directed its attention to the identification and study of folk traditions and to the development of methods for presenting them in a national setting to general audiences. As an academically oriented program, it also pursues university teaching, research into foreign folklife traditions that shed light on cultures that have taken root in American soil, and the publishing of studies.

**Areas of Interest:** Research, documentation, and presentation of American folklife traditions; Festival of American Folklife.

**Publications:** Analytic and documentary studies.

**Information Services:** Answers inquiries; coordinates research and performance activities; makes referrals to other sources of information.

**Approval Date:** 4/85

**Latest Information Date:** 4/85

**Index Terms:** United States; Folklore; Folk music; Material culture; American ethnic art; Graduate study.

## 358

### Society for the Anthropology of Visual Communication (SAVICOM)

c/o Dr. Carroll Williams, President
Anthropological Film Center
P.O. Box 493
Santa Fe, NM 87501
Tel.: (505) 983-4127          PUB69-16427

SAVICOM brings together and supports researchers, scholars, and practitioners who are studying human behavior in context through visual means and who are interested in: (1) the study, use, and production of anthropological films and photography for research and teaching; (2) the analysis of visual symbolic forms from a cultural-historical framework; (3) visual theories, technologies, and methodologies for recording and analyzing behavior and the relationships among the different modes of communication; (4) the analysis of the structuring of reality as evidenced by visual productions and artifacts; (5) the cross-cultural study of art and artifacts from a social, cultural, and visual perception; (6) the study of the forms of social organization surrounding the planning, production, and use of visual symbolic forms; (7) the support of urgent ethnographic filming; and (8) the use of the media in cultural feedback.

**Areas of Interest:** Communication and culture; anthropology of visual communication; films; photography; television; art; dance; body movement; mass media.

**Publications:** *Studies in Visual Communication* (quarterly journal); *SAVICOM Newsletter* (three times a year); *Handbook for Proxemic Research*; occasional papers.

**Information Services:** Answers inquiries; provides advisory and consulting services; conducts seminars and workshops; makes referrals to other sources of information. Services are primarily for members, but others will be assisted. Consulting services are provided for a fee. Publications are available from SAVICOM, P.O. Box 13358, Philadelphia, PA. 19101.

**Approval Date:** 12/85

**Latest Information Date:** 12/85

**Index Terms:** Visual communication; Anthropology; Behavioral science research; Motion pictures; Photography; Television films; Arts; Dance; Mass media; Cross cultural studies; Ethnography; Social organization; Educational programs; Visual anthropology; Movement (acting); Body language.

## 359

### Society of Arts and Crafts (SAC)

175 Newbury St.
Boston, MA 02116
Tel.: (617) 266-1810        PUB69-20457

A nonprofit organization founded in 1897, SAC promotes the best in contemporary American crafts, the development of higher standards of design and execution in the crafts, and seeks to educate the public to appreciate fine craftsmanship.

**Areas of Interest:** American contemporary crafts in all media, including ceramics, glass, wood, jewelry, and fiber, with special emphasis on contemporary furniture.

**Holdings:** Library-Resource Center that includes a collection of rare books, periodicals, art newsletters, photos, slides, and artists' biographies; lists of available apprentices and apprenticeships; changing exhibits of arts and crafts.

**Publications:** Brochure, craftspeople's policy.

**Information Services:** Answers inquiries; provides advisory and consulting services, including career advice to artists; makes referrals to other sources of information; permits on-site use of collections. The above services are free and available to anyone. SAC also sponsors and arranges lectures, workshops, and special exhibits for individuals, special groups, cultural institutions, and schools for a fee.

**Approval Date:** 7/84

**Latest Information Date:** 1/86

**Index Terms:** Arts resources; American crafts; Handicrafts.

## 360

### State Historical Society of Missouri

1020 Lowry St.
Columbia, MO 65202
Tel.: (314) 882-7083        PUB69-2961

**Areas of Interest:** History, government, culture, folklore, literature, art, music, biography, genealogy, religious and fraternal organizations, educational institutions, patriotic societies, politics, commerce, and economics of Missouri from 1790 to the present; history of Western America.

**Holdings:** 430,000 volumes of books, pamphlets, magazines, newspapers, and official publications; over 500,000 pages of original manuscripts; 150,000 State archival records; 19,500 newspaper articles. The Society's newspaper collections extend from 1808 to the present and contain 2,400 bound volumes and 27.2 million pages on microfilm.

**Publications:** *Missouri Historical Review* (quarterly). Nonperiodic publications include *Missouri Historic Sites Catalog*, a guide to historic sites in each county, and *Missouri Newspapers: When and Where, 1808-1963*, an index of Missouri newspaper holdings throughout the United States.

**Information Services:** Literature searches are performed, unless extensive research is required, and technical questions are answered. Evaluations of the historical authenticity, abundance, and general scope of material in the collection will be given on request. In addition, documents may be duplicated, and referrals to additional resource materials are provided. Both the library collection and services are available to the general public.

**Approval Date:** 12/85

**Latest Information Date:** 12/85

**Index Terms:** Professional associations; Folklore; Literature (fine arts); Biographies; Genealogy; Music; Political systems; Missouri; Archives; History; Clemens, Samuel Langhorne; Field, Eugene; Fine arts; State government; Economics; Commerce; Historic sites.

## 361

### Swedish Information Service (SIS)

825 Third Ave., 37th Floor
New York, NY 10022
Tel.: (212) 751-5900        PUB69-17935

A unit of the Swedish Ministry for Foreign Affairs responsible to the embassy in Washington and working in close cooperation with the embassy in Ottawa and the consulates general in the United States and Canada, SIS provides a central source of information to persons and organizations in North America.

**Areas of Interest:** Information about Sweden, including education, labor, environment, energy, literature, art, politics, social programming, folklore, music, crafts, communications, geography, economy, and practically all subjects except tourism and detailed information on industry and trade.

**Holdings:** A library of current Swedish newspapers, periodicals, and reference works, English-language pamphlets, pocket books, fact sheets, and brochures; a collection of photographs, color transparencies, motion pictures, slide talks, and filmstrips, for which a catalog is available.

**Publications:** *Social Change in Sweden; Working Life in Sweden; Human Environment in Sweden; Political Life in Sweden; Cultural Life in Sweden.*

**Information Services:** Answers inquiries; provides advisory, reference, and literature-searching services; provides information on R&D in progress; conducts seminars and workshops; distributes publications; makes referrals to other sources of information; permits on-site use of collections. Services are free and primarily for researchers, scholars, other professionals, and the media, but are also available to the general public.

**Approval Date:** 9/84

**Latest Information Date:** 1/86

**Index Terms:** Information services; Documentation; Education; Labor; Environments; Energy; Literature (fine arts); Crafts; Communication; Geography; Economics; Social change; Cultural exchange; Music; Folklore; Political systems; Sweden.

## 362

**Texas Tech University**
**University Library**
**Archive of Turkish Oral Narrative**

Texas Tech University Library, 3d Floor
Lubbock, TX 79409
   Tel.: (806) 742-1922            PUB69-19520

**Areas of Interest:** Turkish folk tales, folk music, folk art, folk architecture, folk customs, folk costumes, folk drama, story-telling techniques, folk legends, folk epics, folk minstrelsy, geography, archaeology, culinary arts, folk crafts, tourist attractions, children's games, riddles, and proverbs; Kemalistic reforms.

**Holdings:** Over three thousand field-recorded oral narratives in Turkish, collected in rural and urban Turkey from 1961 to date; 702 typewritten tales translated into English, bound, annotated, and indexed by title and classification, name of narrator, precise location of narration, province of narration, subject, and key word; 1,100 tales translated into English and ready for further processing; 136 tales transcribed from dialect into standard Turkish and translated into English but otherwise unprocessed; all reference tools and background works necessary to support folk narrative and sociological research related to Turkey; bound runs of related scholarly journals; Turkish, French, and English volumes of published Turkish tales; Turkish periodicals, art albums, and volumes on Turkish handicrafts; slides, records, films, filmstrips; Xerox copies of Turkey-related materials from the William Hugh Jansen Collection (1951–53; originals are in the University of Kentucky

Libraries); Archive Exhibits Collection of Turkish artifacts; Wolfram Eberhard collection of Turkish minstral tales (1951–53).

**Publications:** Bibliography of all U.S. published materials on Turkish folklore and ethnology; catalogs. Twenty tape-recorded three-minute Turkish folk tales are available for use on radio broadcasts.

**Information Services:** Answers inquiries; provides advisory and reference services; analyzes data; conducts lectures on-site and provides lecturers and story-tellers; distributes publications and data compilations; makes referrals to other sources of information; permits on-site use of collections. Typewriters with Turkish characters are supplied by the Archive staff for on-site use only. On-site users are not permitted to make taped or mechanical copies of Archive holdings for removal from the premises. Some duplication samples will be provided by the Archive on request without a fee. Except for the provision of lecturers and story tellers, services are free and all are available to anyone. Translators are occasionally available for hire. Two tours of Turkey are led by Archive staff each year as an extension of the Archive services.

**Contact:** Prof. Warren S. Walker, Director

**Approval Date:** 11/84

**Latest Information Date:** 1/86

**Index Terms:** Turkey; Folklore; Folk music; Folk art; Story telling; Handicrafts; Oral history; Proverbs; Arts resources; Sociological research.

## 363

**University of Chicago**
**Oriental Institute**

1155 East 58th St.
Chicago, IL 60637
   Tel.: (312) 962-9514         PUB69-20242

Partially funded by the National Endowment for the Humanities, the U.S. Department of Education's Institute of Museum Services, and the Illinois Arts Council, the Institute conducts research projects on the ancient Near East and carries out archaeological excavations in the countries of the region. International activities include participation in international conferences and sponsorship of foreign scholars. Membership in the Institute, currently numbering about twenty-five hundred individuals in the United States and abroad, is open to both laymen and scholars.

**Areas of Interest:** The ancient Near East, including

archaeology, history, languages, literature, art, architecture, religion, political organization, and culture.

**Holdings:** Extensive collection of artifacts from Egypt, Jordan, Turkey, Syria, Israel, Iraq, Saudi Arabia, Yemen, Nubia, Cyprus, and Iran. The Institute's library, focusing on the ancient Near East, Northwest Semitic languages, Egyptology, and archaeology, contains 10,000 books, 5,500 volumes of journals, and 7,800 pamphlets and reprints.

**Publications:** *Journal of Near Eastern Studies* (quarterly); *Oriental Institute Publications, Oriental Institute Communications,* and *Studies in Ancient Oriental Civilizations* (all monograph series); *Chicago Assyrian Dictionary;* project reports, teaching materials.

**Information Services:** Answers inquiries; provides advisory, consulting, reference, and reproduction services; provides audiovisual materials for students and teachers; evaluates and analyzes data; conducts seminars and workshops; provides speakers; distributes publications in the United States and abroad; makes referrals to other sources of information. All users are charged for reproductions, audiovisual materials, publications, and speakers. Other services are provided free to members and at a fee to others. On-site use of the collections is restricted to members and scholars in the field. The Institute's facilities are accessible to the handicapped and a special "hands on" exhibit for the blind is maintained.

**Contact:** Mr. David Baird, Assistant to the Director

**Approval Date:** 1/84

**Latest Information Date:** 1/86

**Index Terms:** Arts resources; Near East; Archaeology; Ancient history; Languages; Literature (fine arts); Architecture; Religion; Political parties; Culture (social sciences); Teacher training; Historic preservation; Handicrafts; Museum programs; International arts activities; Handicapped arts services.

---

### 364

**University of South Dakota**
**Institute of Indian Studies**

Box 133
Vermillion, SD 57069
Tel.: (605) 677-5209          PUB69-13643

The Institute is a nonacademic department of the University which serves as the focal point for the planning, advice, and coordination of University resources within the University, tribal groups, community colleges, federal and state agencies, and those concerned with the welfare and education of the Native American people. The University has the capacity and the commitment to maintain comprehensive, academic, research, and service programs to the Indian people on a permanent basis.

**Areas of Interest:** Contemporary affairs and history of Northern Plains Indians, including the Sioux, Chippewa, Cree, Salish, Crow, and other tribes; Indian languages, religion, and music; alcoholism among Indians.

**Holdings:** A library of over four thousand volumes, twenty-one journal and other serial subscriptions, news article clippings, tribal constitutions, conference reports, photographs, music recordings, and oral history tapes and transcripts.

**Publications:** *Newsletter* (quarterly). The newsletter is also available on microfilm through the Microfilm Corporation of America.

**Information Services:** Answers inquiries; provides advisory, reference, literature-searching, translation, and reproduction services; makes direct and interlibrary loans; makes referrals to other sources of information; permits on-site use of collections. Services are free and primarily for Indian tribes and individuals, but others will be assisted.

**Approval Date:** 4/85

**Latest Information Date:** 4/85

**Index Terms:** American Indians; Ethnology; Alcoholism; American Indian languages; Religion; Music; Oral history; Native American studies; Colleges and universities.

---

### 365

**University of Wisconsin-Madison**
**African Studies Program**

1454 Van Hise Hall
1220 Linden Dr.
Madison, WI 53706
Tel.: (608) 262-2380          PUB69-15534

Sponsored by the U.S. Department of Education, the Program acts as a center for knowledge of African languages, culture, society, economy, law, and agriculture and as a specialized center for information on introducing African studies in kindergarten through twelfth grade, colleges, and universities.

**Areas of Interest:** African studies; African language and linguistics, including Arabic, Swahili, Hausa, Xhosa, Bambara, Bemba, Luhya, Kamba, Meru, Pedi, Nyanja, Fula, Kikuyu, Lingala, Mende, Shona, Sotho, Tswana, Wolof, and Zulu; African history; African education and education policy; African art, music, and literature; African sociology, anthropology, government, politics, and law; African society, culture, folklore, customs, migration, and ethnicity; African economics, development, cities, and urban areas; African agriculture, land tenure, and agricultural policy; African health and welfare; mass communication in Africa; education on Africa in U.S. schools.

**Holdings:** Collection of over one hundred thousand items (books, bound serials, microfilms, etc.) on Africa; special map library with African holdings; various specialized data sources on Africa in the Data and Program Library; special holdings on African journalism and mass communications and on African agriculture and land tenure; special collection of materials for teaching about Africa in American schools.

**Publications:** *African Economic History; Ba Shiru* (journal of African languages and literature); *Occasional Papers in African Studies* (series); various African-languages courses and materials; *Wisconsin African Studies News and Notes; Films About Africa: A Directory; African Series in the University of Wisconsin Press;* books, technical reports, state-of-the-art reviews, bibliographies, journal articles, data compilations, reprints.

**Information Services:** Answers inquiries; provides advisory, reference, translation, magnetic tape, and reproduction services; conducts seminars and workshops; evaluates data; distributes publications; makes direct and interlibrary loans; makes referrals to other sources of information; permits on-site use of collections. Services to schools and colleges in the immediate six-state area are free, as are most quick-answer services to others. Users using information for profit will be charged by the individual project.

**Approval Date:** 4/85

**Latest Information Date:** 4/85

**Index Terms:** African studies; Africa; Culture (social sciences); Linguistics; Maps; Journalism; Mass communication; African languages; History; Political systems; Education; Educational policy; Music; Economics; Urban areas; Agriculture; Land titles; Public health; Welfare.

---

### 366

**Visual Artists and Galleries Association (VAGA)**

141 5th Ave.
New York, NY 10010
Tel.: (212) 505-2280               PUB69-19934

A membership organization of 200 individual artists

and commercial galleries, VAGA acts as a clearinghouse for licensing the reproduction rights to members' works and policies against unauthorized reproduction. Protection is available abroad as well as in the United States through its association with the Societe de la Propriete Artistique et des Dessins et Modeles (SPADEM) and reciprocal arrangements with similar national organizations in Western Europe and the Soviet Union. Membership is open to all visual artists and commercial galleries.

**Areas of Interest:** Copyrights in all areas of the visual arts, including painting, sculpture, photography, poster art, art prints, crafts, and design arts.

**Publications:** *VAGA News Bulletin* (semiannual); membership directories.

**Information Services:** Answers inquiries; provides advisory, consulting, and reference services; provides speakers; distributes publications; makes referrals to other sources of information. Information on members and their works available for reproduction is provided to publishers, manufacturers, and other arts users. Other services are available to members. Facilities are accessible to the handicapped.

**Contact:** Ms. Mary C. Foster, Executive Director

**Approval Date:** 4/84

**Latest Information Date:** 1/86

**Index Terms:** Media arts; Visual arts; Arts resources; Copyrights; Intellectual property; Paintings; Sculpture; Photography; Prints; Lecturers; Legal aspects; International arts activities.

---

### 367

**West Virginia University
University Library
West Virginia and Regional History Collection**

Colson Hall, Downtown Campus
Morgantown, WV 26506
Tel.: (304) 293-3536               PUB69-7314

**Areas of Interest:** History, sociology, economics, literature, art, and music of the southern Appalachians, especially West Virginia; family history (of WV only), i.e., genealogy.

**Holdings:** 30,000 books and government documents; 4,000 theses and dissertations; 2,500 maps and charts; 100,000 photographs; 20,000 reels of microfilm, including 13,000 reels of West Virginia newspapers; 1,800 sound tapes; 9,000 linear feet of archives and manuscripts.

**Publications:** *Appalachian Bibliography: Appalachian*

*Outlook* (quarterly bibliography of books and articles on Appalachia); *The Coal Industry in America: A Bibliography and Guide to Studies; Guide to Coal Mining Collections in the United States; Guide to Manuscripts and Archives in the West Virginia Collection; West Virginia History: A Bibliography and Guide to Research;* numerous other bibliographies and indexes on particular topics.

**Information Services:** The staff will answer inquiries and make literature searches without charge; extensive searches are not made. Loan, referral, and duplication services are also available. The collection is open to the public.

**Approval Date:** 4/85

**Latest Information Date:** 4/85

**Index Terms:** West Virginia; History; Commerce; Social structure; Literature (fine arts); Arts; Folk music.

# Geographic Index

# Organizations Index

# Subject Index